COUNTERBUDGET

THE NATIONAL URBAN COALITION

COUNTERBUDGET

A Blueprint for Changing National Priorities
1971–1976

Robert S. Benson *and* Harold Wolman, *editors*

Foreword by
SOL M. LINOWITZ

PRAEGER PUBLISHERS
New York • Washington • London

PRAEGER PUBLISHERS
111 Fourth Avenue, New York, N.Y. 10003, U.S.A.
5, Cromwell Place, London S.W. 7, England

Published in the United States of America in 1971
by Praeger Publishers, Inc.

© 1971 by the National Urban Coalition

Library of Congress Catalog Card Number : 73-154605

Printed in the United States of America

DEDICATION

To the memory of Walter Reuther, whose entire life was devoted to achieving a more desirable ordering of priorities for America.

Foreword

by Sol M. Linowitz
Chairman, the National Urban Coalition

From its inception in the riot-torn summer of 1967, the National Urban Coalition has emphasized the need to formulate goals and priorities to determine our future course as a nation. Indeed, the Coalition's original statement of purpose expressed the conviction that a new set of national priorities was a prerequisite to the achievement of the Coalition's principal objectives: the restoration of America's deteriorating cities and the reunification of our divided society.

I believe that the publication of this alternative budget represents a milestone in the growing national debate over what our priorities should be.

The book consists of two separate but related documents: the "Statement on National Priorities," issued by the National Urban Coalition's Steering Committee, and the twenty-five chapters that comprise the Coalition staff report setting forth a proposed federal budget for each of the next five years.

The "Statement on National Priorities" constitutes compelling evidence that Americans can rise above their differences in the pursuit of solutions to common problems. The six national goals framed by the Statement are the product of a consensus that emerged from the broad diversity of interests and perspectives represented on the Steering Committee. It is true that not every member agreed with every recommendation in the Statement. Yet, after hours of deliberation and revision, the members of the Coalition's governing body unanimously approved the document. Our success in reaching a consensus on national priorities within this microcosm of American leadership has convinced me that the country as a whole is capable of building a similar consensus on goals and priorities.

The staff report that follows the Steering Committee Statement contains the first effort by a major nongovernmental group to set forth a complete and comprehensive plan for revising national priorities. As the instrument through which public resources are allocated, the federal budget is the medium for setting national priorities. Accordingly, a blueprint for changing America's priorities is presented in the form of a proposed federal budget for each of the next five years.

Unlike the "Statement on National Priorities," these yearly budgets were neither formally reviewed nor approved by the members of our Steering Committee. But the budgets are completely consistent with the goals and broad proposals advanced in the approved Statement and represent one possible strategy for achieving those goals.

The alternative five-year budget is not offered in opposition or reaction to the current federal budget. Rather, we offer it as a thoughtful alternative to simply extending present priorities into the future. Our purpose in publishing our set of priorities is to stimulate a more informed public debate over how resources ought to be allocated to attain the goals most Americans share.

The National Urban Coalition is indebted to Robert S. Benson for his vision in conceiving this project, and to him, Harold Wolman, and their associates for the high caliber of analysis and other professional talents they brought to this work.

Washington, D.C.
February 11, 1971

STATEMENT ON
NATIONAL PRIORITIES

by the
Steering Committee of the National Urban Coalition

An Imperative for Americans

Almost a year ago, the National Urban Coalition embarked upon a project that no other private organization had ever attempted. We decided to explore in some detail the reordering of national priorities that is so widely felt to be an imperative for Americans. We decided to do this for two main reasons: first, because we shared the conviction that a shift in priorities is needed; and second, because the National Urban Coalition encompasses, perhaps uniquely, many of the disparate and often competing elements of American leadership that must ultimately be drawn together if an altered agenda is ever to be achieved. If a consensus on national priorities could be reached within this microcosm, it was thought, then perhaps a real reordering would be possible in the larger world outside.

The past two years have witnessed a tremendous amount of talk about reordering national priorities, most of it vague and undisciplined. Nevertheless, the message from all of that talk cannot be denied: The American people want to change emphases. It is now time to take a careful look at how that could be done, for without precise analysis there is little chance of really achieving a desirable reordering of priorities.

The idea is not new. Both the Johnson and Nixon Administrations have emphasized the need for explicit consideration of where we wish to go as a nation. On July 20, 1970, President Richard M. Nixon's Committee on National Goals called for "constructive public discussion of alternative goals, priorities, and policies, with all groups of people participating." The fruits of such discussion, the committee said, "should be incorporated into policies aimed at alleviating the problems or enhancing the opportunities." Three years earlier, President Lyndon B. Johnson's Commission on Budget Concepts (whose chairman was David Kennedy, President Nixon's first Secretary of the Treasury) recommended that a private organization attempt to project national needs over a five-year period, basing its revenue assumptions on a high-employment economy.

Both of these recommendations are consistent with the approach taken here. When the staff of the Coalition's National Priorities Project first addressed this task, they decided to use the federal budget for their analytical framework in devising a five-year projection of program and dollar requirements to meet national needs. Unread as it may be, the federal budget is the single most important instrument for the setting of national priorities.

The budget's importance cannot be overstated. Federal outlays will probably exceed $210 billion in this fiscal year. The choices made within it reflect our national values. In addition, the budget helps to determine national economic policy.

But there are deficiencies in the way that the budget is shaped— deficiencies that, in the absence of reform, reduce the prospects for achieving significant change in our arrangement of priorities. One of the flaws is that budget allocations are too often determined through what might be called the let's-see-what-we-gave-them-last-year-and-give-them-a-little-more-this-year approach. This practice militates against new ideas and tends to preserve programs that may no longer serve their original purposes.

Another flaw is the lack of openness from beginning to end of the budget process. Secrecy reigns. There is little public participation. The annual federal budget is issued each January after months of internal debate and negotiation at every level of government. At no time along the path is the budget open to public scrutiny. It continues in Congress, where the substantive committees and the appropriations committees examine individual segments of the budget, often behind closed doors. At no time does any one body in the Congress consciously and deliberately scrutinize the budget as a whole, with an eye toward setting over-all priorities.

We suggest that the budget process be opened to broad public participation and that the executive and legislative branches of government create mechanisms through which the choices facing Americans can be consciously and regularly examined.

In using the federal budget as a framework, the National Priorities Project staff evolved a draft National Priorities paper. It took the form of an alternative budget covering the fiscal years 1972 through 1976. It circulated widely. The staff convened meeting after meeting to review and revise it. They discussed it at length with leaders representing business, labor, local government, blacks, Mexican-Americans, American Indians, white ethnic groups, religion, education, youth, women, local Urban Coalition memberships, and social-welfare organizations.

The statement that follows—developed from that draft paper— has the general support of the members of the National Urban Coalition's Executive Committee. Like other Americans, each of us has his own ideas of what is right and what is wrong with the nation's current set of priorities. On a subject as complex as this, not all members will agree with every statement made. The choices are difficult.

We do not pretend that we have solved the country's problems or even designed the final blueprint for doing so. But it is our hope that this modest beginning will generate discussion and debate throughout the country and lead to precise and disciplined thinking about what "more of this" and "less of that" really implies.

Goals and Recommendations

The American malaise, which all of us feel in one way or another, has its roots in the distance between national ideal and national reality.

The national ideal is a country where every American gets an equal chance to perform, where a job exists for everyone who wants one, where health care and personal safety are assured, where we live in harmony with each other, and where each of us has a decent place to live.

The national reality needs no full recital here. We know that cities are in trouble, that poverty continues in the midst of wealth, that unemployment is high, that malnutrition is widespread, that injustice exists, that tensions endure. In sum, we know that our society is not functioning the way it is supposed to.

But if we solve the greatest of our ills—our paralysis of spirit and will—we can narrow the distance between what we have and what we want. Indeed, we *must* marshal our good sense and our good will. There is no sensible alternative.

In our view, the United States must pursue *six major goals* between now and 1976. It must try to:

1. Achieve full employment with a high level of economic growth and reasonable price stability—all of our other policy goals depend upon it.

2. Provide all citizens with an equal opportunity to participate in American society and in the shaping of governmental decisions affecting their lives.

3. Guarantee that no American will go without the basic necessities: food, shelter, health care, a healthy environment, personal safety, and an adequate income.

4. Rectify the imbalance in revenues between the federal government and state and local governments.

5. Assure adequate national security against military threats from abroad.

6. Meet our obligations to assist in the economic development of the world's less-developed nations.

These are the goals. We can move a long way toward them by 1976. We recognize that they cannot be reached without meeting three basic requirements: a reordering of budget priorities, an increase in revenues through a more equitable system of taxation, and a reshaping of government to assure a more responsive and effective delivery of programs and services. But they can and must be achieved.

Let us briefly examine the validity of each of our goals and explore how they can be met.

Goal One: Full Employment

The budget should direct the nation back to full employment and a healthy rate of growth and economic activity. The immediate goal should be to reduce unemployment from its present level of approximately 6 per cent. Ultimately, the rate of unemployment

AN IMPERATIVE FOR AMERICANS

should be reduced steadily and carefully until work opportunities exist for all who desire them. A real growth rate exceeding 4 per cent annually will be needed to accomplish this goal.

With the economy once again operating at full capacity, resources will become available to meet crucial public needs that are not now being met. A strongly growing economy will automatically produce a fiscal dividend in the form of greater revenues, which, in turn, will enable the federal government to provide a reasonable level of performance in essential programs and services now pinched for funds. The additional state and local revenues generated by such an economy will help save some of our cities and states from the bankruptcy that they are fast approaching. Moreover, the single most effective program to eliminate poverty is an economy growing fast enough to provide jobs for the unemployed and for new recruits to the work force.

Full employment should be accomplished through the application of stimulative fiscal policy directed by the Administration and supported by Congress. This effort should be accompanied by a monetary policy that will assure sufficient liquidity to support the expansion. To control inflation, the Administration should take effective action to prevent excessive price and wage increases and to remove employment barriers that are both inflationary and unfair.

Even with full employment, improved manpower training programs will be necessary, particularly to upgrade the skills of workers now on the bottom of the job ladder.

Goal Two: Equal Opportunity

We believe that the *sine qua non* of full participation in American life is the opportunity for a quality education. For many Americans, our educational system falls far short of providing that opportunity.

A part of the reason for this is that education begins—or fails to begin—before children reach school age. Research studies have concluded that about 50 per cent of one's intellectual development occurs between birth and the age of five and that such development is heavily influenced by environment. More recently, television's "Sesame Street" has impressively demonstrated the degree to which preschool children can learn when new knowledge is imaginatively and entertainingly presented.

For these and other reasons, the need for new programs in pre-school education is clear. But since state and local governments lack the funds for such programs, the federal government must provide subsidies in this area so that the opportunity for preschool education will be available to all children.

At the elementary and secondary education levels, we believe that the federal government should be more zealous in seeing to it that the results of federally funded education programs reflect a minimum standard of performance. For example, "compensatory education" programs under Title I of the Elementary and Secondary Education Act should be focused on reading and mathematics because Americans who cannot read and calculate live perpetually on the margin of society. So it is, too, with those who cannot speak English; bilingual education should also be expanded and improved.

As for higher education, the federal government must expand the availability of financial aid for students so that no American is denied the opportunity to continue his studies because of insufficient funds.

Other aspects of equal opportunity do not require legislation. They require enforcement. Although the last decade produced progressive laws against discrimination in public facilities, employment, housing, and voting, the achievement was too largely a legislative triumph. The triumph will be empty so long as we lack effective implementation of those landmark laws. To be sure, enforcement agencies need more funds and more staff. But these alone will not suffice. What is needed, above all, is a commitment to enforcement by the national leadership. Without it, these laws will lose much of their meaning.

Finally, if equal opportunity is to be fully achieved, citizens of all races, classes, and income groups must have the chance to help shape the governmental programs and services that affect them. Government, moreover, must be held accountable to the citizens it serves. Here, too, it is a matter of will.

Goal Three: The Basic Necessities

The United States has the richest, most productive economy in the world. But many Americans nonetheless lack the basic necessities for a tolerable life: food, shelter, health care, a healthy environment, personal safety, and an adequate income. This need not be so. We can see to it that no Americans are deprived of these necessities.

It almost goes without saying that the most vital of these is an adequate income. A reasonable income allows individuals to purchase most of the other basic necessities with dignity and free choice.

The majority of the income of most Americans comes from productive employment. As mentioned earlier, the federal government must shape its policies so that the economy will provide maximum opportunities for jobs at a living wage. We favor the following measures to accomplish this:

1. *The use of fiscal and monetary policy to achieve sustained economic growth and high employment.* Although effective action should be taken to keep wage and price increases within reasonable limits, we may have to be prepared to accept a somewhat higher degree of inflation than we have been willing to accept in the past.

2. *Increasing the minimum wage to an adequate level, and broadening the law to include coverage of more workers.*

3. *Creation of a program for public-service employment that would generate jobs at all levels of government as well as in nonprofit, public-service organizations.* These jobs would fill a clear need that cannot now be met because of insufficient revenues. Among them would be such positions as health aide, police aide, preschool teacher, and pollution-control worker. All of these jobs should have the opportunity for career advancement built in. The federal government should provide subsidies to cover training costs, as well as a large portion of the workers' salaries. *One million of these jobs should be created by 1976.*

For some Americans, wages and jobs will not suffice. Employment income must be supplemented by broader and better social insurance and income-support programs. Both social security and unemployment compensation programs should be changed to provide greater benefits and wider coverage. Unemployment compensation programs should be federally administered, like the present Old Age, Survivors, and Disability Insurance (OASDI) program, and should have uniform standards. In addition, the present public-assistance program, acknowledged to be a failure by virtually every element of American society, should give way to the new initiative for a cash-assistance program.

To be more specific, the federal government should scrap the present Aid to Families with Dependent Children (AFDC) welfare program. In its place it should establish a program that, by 1976, would assure every household an adequate income, whether or not the head of the household is employed. The amount of the allowance would vary according to the number of people in the household. Work incentives would be built into the program; families would be allowed to keep a significant share of each dollar earned. Equally important, the program should be financed and administered entirely by the federal government. This would serve two purposes: (1) it would relieve the financial pressure on states and localities, and (2) it would assure greater equity for the recipients.

Assuring an adequate income would equip all households with the ability to meet the expenses of food, clothing, and transportation. But this income would not necessarily be enough to enable all households to purchase adequate health care and housing—two categories that require further discussion.

Many Americans now lack decent health care because of two major deficiencies: (1) inadequate supply and poor distribution of medical manpower and health facilities, with inner-city and rural areas particularly short-changed; and (2) an incentive system that tends to produce a far greater emphasis on high-cost curative care administered in expensive settings (hospitals) than on low-cost preventive care. As a consequence of these two deficiencies, the cost of health care is very high for *all* elements of the population. To those in the low and lower-middle income groups, it is often prohibitive.

We feel that any workable remedy must be composed of two essential parts. The federal government must institute a national health insurance program—paid for partly out of new taxes—to assure every American that there is at least no economic barrier to adequate health care. And, to make sure that adequate care is really available, the federal government must increase the supply of medical manpower—especially nurses and paramedical personnel—through expanded federal education and manpower training grants. At the same time, the distribution of health facilities should be widened through a significant expansion of community health centers—staffed in part by members of a domestic health service corps. As in other fields, community residents should be given a major voice in determining the nature of local health programs.

Housing, like health, also suffers from inadequate supply. Thus, even an "adequate" income is no guarantee that a family will be able to find decent shelter at a reasonable price.

In 1968, Congress set a ten-year national goal of 26 million new and rehabilitated dwelling units—enough to bring substantial assistance to families now living in substandard housing—6 million to be low- and moderate-income units, subsidized by the federal government. After two years, we had hardly begun. Public and private housing starts in 1969 and 1970 fell 650,000 units short of the original 3,675,000-unit goal for those years, as high interest rates pulled money out of the mortgage market. Housing available to low- and moderate-income families ultimately depends upon the condition of the economy. Thus, if private housing starts continue to lag, more federally subsidized units will be the only way to ensure all Americans adequate shelter.

In 1949, Congress and the President declared the goal of a decent home and a suitable living environment for every American. If that goal is to be met, the federal government must:

1. *Ensure that substantially increased funds will be channeled into the mortgage market, thereby increasing the total supply of housing.*

2. *Appropriate enough funds with sufficient "lead time" to finance effectively the federally subsidized portion of the ten-year goal, as well as additional units if private starts continue to fall short.*

3. *Reshape the federal housing programs to meet the social needs of their beneficiaries.* This change involves increased tenant

services, greater provisions for home ownership, preservation of functioning neighborhoods, and assurance that federally subsidized housing will be of high quality.

4. *Broaden the eligibility criteria for participation in federally subsidized programs.* Currently, the *most* needy families are not eligible. Neither do families with incomes just above the poverty line qualify for all these programs, even though housing on the private market is unavailable to them at reasonable cost. At the same time, the government should ensure that families residing in federally subsidized rental housing represent a wider spectrum of income classes.

5. *Simplify (and reduce the number of) housing regulations now strangling federal housing programs.*

A third requirement for national and individual well-being is adequate personal safety. Large numbers of Americans at all income levels do not now feel safe. The number of serious crimes reported has increased 148 per cent since 1960. Most of the increase has threatened city dwellers—particularly residents of low-income areas.

Illusory demands for "law and order" have not provided solutions. What we need, instead, is reconstruction of our system of criminal justice—action that will reduce crime without jeopardizing civil liberties. The most effective way to reduce crime is to treat its social, psychological, and economic causes; indeed, many of the programs and approaches discussed elsewhere in this statement will help to accomplish that end. In addition, however, the federal government should take the following actions in the field of law enforcement and criminal justice:

1. *Improve the woefully underfunded corrections system.* The percentage of jail "repeaters" is remarkably high; if substantial numbers of offenders were rehabilitated, the crime rate could be cut significantly. Facilities for rehabilitation of drug addicts and alcoholics convicted of crimes should be vastly increased. So should research into better methods of treating these problems. The social costs of our past failure to provide such remedial programs is immense.

2. *Provide funds for modernization of the court system at all levels.*

3. *Expand federal aid to local police, but require that the emphasis be on police recruitment, training, research, and salaries, rather than on equipment.*

4. *Undertake a concerted effort to diminish organized crime—particularly to cope with the dealers in hard drugs.*

Goal Four: Rectifying the Revenue Imbalance

State and local governments face a steadily worsening financial crisis. Their revenues are falling farther and farther behind their expenditures, and an increase in state and local tax rates is usually political suicide. By 1976, the gap between revenues and expenditures necessary to achieve high quality services at the local and state levels is expected to be in the area of $90 billion.

The federal government must respond to this crisis. A revenue-sharing program alone is unlikely to close the gap, since the program most widely discussed thus far would provide states and localities with only $5 billion per year by 1976. The most important single contribution the federal government can make is to ensure a growing economy that will automatically enhance state and local tax revenues. (Economic growth alone accounted for more than 55 per cent of increased state revenue between 1966 and 1968.)

In addition, the federal government should assume the state and local costs of certain functions having to do with national problems. We have already recommended a cash-assistance scheme and national health insurance, which would replace the current public-assistance and Medicaid programs respectively. When our recommended proposals become fully effective, the cost now imposed by these latter programs—$5.6 billion to states and localities in fiscal year (FY) 1970—would be borne entirely by the federal government.*

Beyond that, state and local governments must place greater reliance on their own tax bases and on more equitable tax systems. To encourage such self-reliance, federal programs should be designed to stimulate greater tax effort, tax reform, and structural

* Years are federal fiscal years unless otherwise indicated. The federal fiscal year of 1971, for example, extends from July 1, 1971, through June 30, 1972.

change at the state and local levels. With the prospect of additional funds, these governments will be more likely to undertake politically difficult reforms than they would be in the absence of such incentives.

To achieve these goals, we urge:

1. A revenue-sharing program for states and localities. The program's payment formula should (a) take into account need as well as population, (b) ensure that a substantial portion of the funds will be passed through to the cities, and (c) reward those states which make a relatively greater tax effort and raise a relatively higher proportion of their revenues through a progressive income tax.

2. A program of general aid to elementary and secondary education, available only to states that assume at least 55 per cent of the costs of such education. In the average state today, the state pays 44 per cent of these costs; local government pays the rest. States paying a higher percentage of these costs would receive relatively more federal money. By providing an incentive for states to assume a greater portion of the costs of public education, this program would greatly relieve the pressure on overburdened local property taxes, which now provide the revenues to pay the lion's share of these expenses. The funds should be allocated to eligible states primarily on the basis of need.

3. A revised Model Cities program, adequately funded and changed to focus on entire cities rather than on single neighborhoods. As an incentive for wider metropolitan planning, a single, coordinated application from two or more contiguous communities should, if accepted, be rewarded with funds that would exceed the amount they would have received through separate applications. Also, grants should be awarded only on condition that a specified percentage of the funds would be spent in low-income neighborhoods and that citizen participation in decision-making would be assured.

Goal Five: Providing for Military Security

The United States needs sufficient forces and technology to deter attack from abroad. However, the advent of the nuclear age has rendered every country vulnerable to military attack, regardless of how much or how little it spends for national security. Any level of spending requires accepting risks. In this setting, the following are needed to meet our national security requirements:

1. A credible "second strike" strategic capability that will deter military attack by making it clear to potential attackers that they will themselves suffer unacceptable levels of damage should they initiate an attack on the United States.

2. Adequate general-purpose forces to support our commitments to allied nations whose own security is important to American interests.

3. Sufficient research and development activity to ensure that our military technology does not become outmoded.

Even with prudent reductions from current expenditure levels, these needs will continue to require multibillion-dollar expenditures.

Goal Six: Meeting Foreign Economic Assistance Obligations

Modern industrialized nations, among which the United States stands pre-eminent, cannot abandon their responsibility to the developing countries. In recent years, our financial commitment has slackened while the less-developed nations have grown in their ability to use development assistance funds in a productive way. The first requirement for rapid international development is continued vigorous expansion of world trade. This will be possible only if advanced countries remove many obstacles to the growth of export earnings for less-developed economies and encourage the flow of private capital to these nations.

Foreign economic assistance, when granted to help create self-reliance among nations, can also contribute directly to an expanded world economy and to improved prospects for world peace. To be effective, however, our assistance programs must be restructured and redirected. Most fundamentally, the entire program must be based on a less visible U.S. role, and on far more realistic and modest expectations about what our assistance can accomplish. Three specific changes are needed:

1. The amount of official U.S. development assistance funds should rise from its present level of 0.28 per cent of the Gross National Product (GNP) toward a goal of 0.70 per cent of the GNP by 1975. This is the percentage recommended by the World Bank's Commission on International Development (the Pearson Commission).

2. The proportion of funds channeled through multilateral insti-tutions such as the World Bank should be substantially increased.

3. The form of economic assistance should be shifted to greater utilization of grants and soft loans, less of hard loans.

REQUIREMENTS FOR ACHIEVING THE SIX GOALS

At the beginning of this statement, we mentioned three require-ments for achieving our goals. These requirements—to repeat—are: (1) reordering budget priorities—that is, cutting spending in areas of lower priority and applying those funds to areas of higher priority; (2) increasing tax revenues—first through achieving a more equitable tax system, then through higher tax rates; and (3) reorganizing government structures to bring about more responsive and effective delivery of programs and services.

Perhaps it would be useful to discuss briefly what might be done in each of these areas.

First, our analysis of present budget priorities suggests several categories where cuts can be made:

1. Agricultural subsidy programs could wisely be cut by $1.2 billion between now and 1976. In their place, farm residents should be provided with expanded nonfarm job opportunities, backed up by income assurances through the cash-assistance pro-gram, described under Goal Three.

2. Federal highway subsidies could be reduced by about $1.8 billion by 1976, with these funds applied to the more urgent need for mass transit.

3. Still more could be saved by reducing expenditures for Army Corps of Engineers public works projects (currently $1.4 billion), merchant marine subsidies ($330 million), and the Supersonic Transport plane (SST) ($275 million).

Dwarfing all of the above, however, is a potential reduction in military spending by 1976 of about $20 billion, most of which should occur during the next two years. Such a reduction could be achieved through the following actions:

1. A substantial further reduction of current U.S. military spend-ing in Vietnam, which now accounts for $13 billion of the $74.5 billion defense budget.

2. *Persuading our allies in Europe and Asia to assume a larger share of defense costs in those areas.*

3. *Elimination of wastefully duplicative strategic deterrent forces and a cessation of attempts to build unnecessary strategic defense systems, such as Safeguard.*

4. *Elimination (without replacement) of systems rendered impotent, and therefore obsolete, by changing technology.*

5. *Improved management and operating efficiencies.*

All of these reductions can be accomplished without threatening the goal of providing for adequate national security against military threats.

Reduction in defense expenditures should be accompanied by a planned program of reconversion, which would provide income assistance, relocation allowances, and training and jobs at similar skill levels for workers laid off because of cutbacks in defense spending.

Even assuming that all of these proposed budget cuts can be effected, however, more funds will be needed if we are to move far toward meeting our goals. This brings us to our second requirement—increasing tax revenues. We estimate that a rise of about 10 per cent in individual and corporate income taxes will be needed, *assuming that the expenditure cuts suggested above are made.* For every recommended dollar reduction *not* achieved, taxes will have to be increased correspondingly. These tax increases should not be undertaken immediately because they might interfere with restoration of full employment. But they will be required by the middle of the coming five-year period. Tax increases will become more feasible politically if the public becomes convinced that the tax system is equitable. Thus, reform of the tax structure—to eliminate the inequities—must become a first line of attack.

As for our third requirement—reorganization of governmental structures—let us review some of the major reforms already mentioned in our discussion of goals. They call for the federal government to:

- rationalize the process by which the federal budget is assembled and open that process to broader public scrutiny;
- provide financial incentives (a) for states to rely on graduated

state income taxes, and (b) for individual communities to join
together for area-wide planning;

- place all of the responsibility for administration and financing of
the proposed income-maintenance program in the hands of the
federal government;
- take measures that would help to achieve a better and more
widely available delivery of health services; and
- effect changes that would bring more investment funds into the
mortgage market and streamline the federally subsidized housing
programs.

Other reforms—many of them involving no expenditure at all—
must also be sought if the government is to become more effective.
Among them would be:

1. *A requirement that municipalities provide housing for low-
and moderate-income residents as a condition of municipal receipt
of federal aid.*

2. *Provisions to allow citizens to participate meaningfully in the
design of programs that directly affect them.*

3. *Assignment of a higher priority to consumer affairs in the
federal government, with stronger enforcement of regulations and
laws in this area.*

4. *Stricter federal legislation against environmental pollution,
along with stronger enforcement of existing laws.*

5. *A restructuring of the family-planning-assistance program to
ensure that these services can be obtained by all who desire them.*

The reforms listed here are meant to be suggestive, not comprehensive. They are intended to demonstrate directions that the
federal government should take. Their purpose, in each case, is
to assure that programs and laws serve the ends for which they
were devised.

Without such reforms, we risk simply throwing money away or,
worse, achieving undesirable results. Governmental bureaucracy
must be made as efficient and responsive as possible. Most of the
major new program initiatives we have recommended that will
cost large sums of money—national health insurance, a cash-
assistance program, revenue-sharing, including general aid to education—require very simple administrative mechanisms. The fed-

eral government role in these programs is almost completely that of collecting and dispensing monies.

Perhaps the most important reform, however, is a change in our attitude toward the future. The United States must begin to plan consciously for the future needs of its population; muddling through is no longer good enough. Such an emphasis on looking ahead explains why the Coalition's National Priorities Project adopted a five-year rather than the traditional one-year budget framework.

But even five years is a short time. We must embrace the future with a freshness of imagination, a national consciousness open to new ideas and concepts. We must be willing to readjust preconceived ideas to meet those changes which the remainder of this century will surely bring. Adjusting to these changes, the nature of which can now only dimly be perceived, will require thinking on a new scale—and a greater willingness to commit our vast resources to public purposes.

THE WILL TO ACT

There is little room for doubt about our ability to reach the goals that we have outlined. The American economy can supply the resources, while preserving the freedom of enterprise that has made it the envy of the world. The government, properly reformed, can deliver the services. The programs that we have suggested are not revolutionary or, in most cases, even new. Most have been discussed in this country for years, and many have long been public policy in Western European nations.

A remaining question concerns our national will.

Whenever there has been the prospect of a budget surplus in the United States, Americans have traditionally chosen the fruits of tax reductions in preference to the support of domestic needs with public funds. Will we soon be ready to make the sacrifices—particularly in the form of higher taxes—needed to reach our goals? If not, we may later lament our hesitation. We must forge the national commitment and see it through.

The above statement was unanimously approved by the Steering Committee of the National Urban Coalition on January 11, 1971. Members present at that meeting are listed below:

Arnold Aronson
Secretary, Leadership Conference on Civil Rights
New York, N.Y.

Albert E. Arent
Chairman, National Jewish Community Relations Advisory Council
Washington, D.C.

Mrs. Bruce B. Benson
President, League of Women Voters of the United States
Washington, D.C.

Joseph J. Bernal
State Senator
San Antonio, Texas

His Eminence John Cardinal Dearden
Archbishop of Detroit
Detroit, Michigan, and
President, U.S. Catholic Conference of Bishops
Washington, D.C.

Edwin D. Etherington
Old Lyme, Connecticut, and
Former President, Wesleyan University
Middletown, Connecticut

John W. Gardner
Chairman, Common Cause
Washington, D.C.

Warren Gilmore
President, Youth Organizations United
Washington, D.C.

Ernest Green
Director, Joint Apprenticeship Program
New York, N.Y.

Mrs. Fred R. Harris
President, Americans for Indian Opportunity
Washington, D.C.

Richard Gordon Hatcher
Mayor
Gary, Indiana

Dorothy I. Height
President, National Council of Negro Women, Inc.
Washington, D.C.

Andrew Heiskell
Chairman, Time, Inc.
New York, N.Y.

Mrs. Aileen C. Hernandez
President, National Organization of Women
San Francisco, California

Samuel C. Johnson
Chairman and President, S. C. Johnson & Son, Inc.
Racine, Wisconsin

Vernon E. Jordan, Jr.
Executive Director, United Negro College Fund, Inc.
New York, N.Y.

Stephen F. Keating
President, Honeywell, Inc.
Minneapolis, Minnesota

Joseph D. Keenan
International Secretary, International Brotherhood of Electrical Workers, AFL-CIO
Washington, D.C.

John V. Lindsay
Mayor
New York, N.Y.

J. Irwin Miller
Chairman, Cummins Engine Company
Columbus, Indiana

C. McKim Norton, Esq.
Counsel, Regional Plan Association
New York, N.Y.

Louis Nunez
President, Aspira of America, Inc.
New York, N.Y.

James M. Roche
Chairman, General Motors Corporation
Detroit, Michigan

David Rockefeller
Chairman, Chase Manhattan Bank
New York, N.Y.

H. I. Romnes
Chairman, American Telephone and Telegraph
New York, N.Y.

Henry Santiestevan
Executive Director, Southwest Council of La Raza
Phoenix, Arizona

Mark R. Shedd
Superintendent of Schools
Philadelphia, Pennsylvania

John G. Simon
President, Taconic Foundation, Inc.
New York, N.Y.

Martin Stone
President, Monogram Industries
Los Angeles, California

James H. J. Tate
Mayor
Philadelphia, Pennsylvania, and President, U.S. Conference of Mayors
Washington, D.C.

Mrs. Theodore O. Wedel
President, National Conference of Churches
Washington, D.C.

Leonard Woodcock
President, United Auto Workers
Detroit, Michigan

Whitney M. Young, Jr.
Executive Director, National Urban League
New York, N.Y.

Sol M. Linowitz
Chairman, National Urban Coalition
Washington, D.C.

Staff Acknowledgments

The report that follows is the product of a year's work by a team of National Urban Coalition staff members and consultants, supplemented by contributions from nearly one thousand members of the Coalition's various constituencies. We wish that space limitations did not preclude our acknowledging gratitude to each of those persons. A comprehensive list of participants would convey dramatically the broad cross section of the American public that has had a voice in shaping the report's recommendations.

The preparation and writing of the report itself was performed by the Coalition's National Priorities Project Staff, and responsibility for its contents rests with them. They are:

Robert S. Benson, Director
Harold Wolman, Deputy Director

Timothy J. Adams	Diane Liptack
Beverly Brown	Vernon K. Richey
Savanna L. Davis	Douglas Ross
Carole Horn	David Thomas III
R. D. Ben Laime	Christine Thompson
Judith K. Leva	

Their work was greatly aided by the contributions of Data Resources, Inc., the Inner City Fund, and the Urban Institute, and a number of staff consultants who provided back-up studies or analysis of special problems. These consultants included: Manuel Aragon, Robert Aten, William Colman, Gary Comstock, Thomas Dolembo, Laszlo Ecker-Racz, Otto Eckstein, John H. Gardner, Robert Grosse, Jocelyn Gutchess, Richard Kolm, Lawrence Lewin, Ruby Martin, John Moeller, Jonas Morris, Elliott Morss, Donald Ogilvie, Phillip Patterson, Juergen Schmandt, James Scoville, Arnold Trebach, Charles Warden, and Herbert Winokur. Providing similar helpful assistance were Ann Rosewater and Barney

Sellers of the National Urban Coalition staff. In every case, these individuals made valuable contributions to a particular section or sections of the report. In no case are they responsible for the contents or conclusions of the final report, which often reflects the resolution of difficult choices among numerous worthwhile policy objectives.

In addition, a large number of distinguished experts in various fields gave us the benefit of their counsel and advice. Their recommendations are reflected in the Counterbudget.

A special debt of gratitude is owed to Nat Weinberg, whose fresh ideas and breadth of expertise never ceased to amaze us. Charles L. Schultze and Nancy Teeters of the Brookings Institution were particularly helpful in guiding our development of basic economic assumptions. Richard Elwell's skillful hand smoothed the final text.

Finally, we extend our deepest appreciation to Carl Holman and Peter Libassi, under whose general supervision the work on this project was performed and whose advocacy and support were critical during the project's early stages. Their sound advice unraveled many complex knots; the flaws that may remain in no way reflect upon their contributions.

Washington, D.C.
February 11, 1971

Contents

INTERNATIONAL AFFAIRS

EFFECTS OF THE COUNTERBUDGET

MAKING THE AGENDA POSSIBLE

List of Charts

List of Tables

Tables in **boldface** type show recommended budget outlays

INTRODUCTION

We looked comprehensively and searchingly at how our nation's priorities could be re-ordered within the context of the realities of the federal budget and the American economy. Our report constitutes a broad statement of public needs in America and recommendations for meeting those needs.

1

Reordering Within the Realities

The United States today is a tangle of paradoxes.

Our Gross National Product (GNP) doubles in a decade, yet our cities and states teeter on the edge of bankruptcy.

Our doctors transplant whole organs and heal the most complex disorders of the human body, yet our infant mortality rate exceeds that of many European countries.

Our Congress passes civil-rights laws of sweeping dimensions, yet discrimination still denies jobs and housing to millions of Americans who want and need them.

Our people buy increasing quantities of consumer goods every year to enjoy a higher standard of living, yet we experience a deterioration in the quality of American life as the production and use of these goods destroys the human environment.

It is not that we are making no progress.

We are progressing. However, the realization that progress is occurring sends expectations soaring and widens the gap between what we are as a nation and what we wish to be. Tensions and frustrations build. For despite the fact that we are moving forward in many areas in absolute terms, relative to our rising aspirations we often seem to be standing still.

Our failure to resolve these paradoxes and close the gap between our hopes and reality has driven an increasing number of Americans to ask whether we are using to best advantage the massive human and material resources at our command. As a result, there has been increasing discussion of the need to reorder our national priorities. Congress and the President have participated in, and encouraged, this public debate. The Joint Economic Committee, at hearings on national priorities in 1970, stressed "the need for

Congress to question searchingly the adequacy of the fiscal 1971 budget with respect to the share of the budgetary resources allocated to social problems" and "the need for similar searching inquiry into the adequacy of the proposed cuts in defense spending." Later that year, as the "Statement on National Priorities" at the front of this book points out, President Nixon's Committee on National Goals called for

> constructive public discussion of alternative priorities and policies, with all groups of people participating. The fruits of this public discussion should be incorporated into policies aimed at alleviating the problems or enhancing the opportunities.

Three years previously, President Lyndon B. Johnson's Commission on Budget Concepts had recommended that private organizations devote themselves to a study of priorities by preparing five-year projections of future needs and revenues.

We have accepted the challenge posed by these groups, and others. But we also have attempted to move beyond the easy rhetoric of "reordering priorities" to infuse more precision and clarity into public debate. It is for this reason that we have chosen the federal budget as our vehicle for examining priorities. For, as Kermit Gordon, president of the Brookings Institution and former director of the Bureau of the Budget, observes in the foreword to *Setting National Priorities: The 1971 Budget* (Washington, D.C.: The Brookings Institution, 1970) by Charles L. Schultze, also a former Bureau of the Budget director:

> Even though the spotlight of public attention and concern is today sharply focused on the issue of priorities in American society, the public is neither well informed nor much concerned about the composition—as opposed to the total size—of the budget of the Federal government. This is a singular inconsistency, for the President's annual budget is the vehicle for the most important and comprehensive collection of priority decisions which our society makes in the course of a year.

In order to eliminate this inconsistency, we looked comprehensively and searchingly at how our nation's priorities could be reordered within the context of the realities of the federal budget and the American economy. Our report constitutes a broad statement of public needs in America and recommendations for meeting those needs. But it is not merely a "wish list" of lofty aspirations. Rather, it proposes a detailed federal budget offering careful estimates of the costs of recommended programs and revenues for each of the next five years. In addition, we have included an assessment of the probable consequences of its recommendations on various sectors of the American population and on the national economy.

One need be neither a fiscal expert nor a budget analyst to follow the format of our budget. Indeed, it is our hope that this study will make the annual federal budget comprehensible to those readers who have never examined one before. It is essential that concerned citizens learn to handle this official document. Otherwise, national priorities will continue to be set within the closed ranks of whatever Administration is in power. As long as secrecy prevails, the public's role in charting the nation's future must remain one of reaction—reaction too often characterized by frustration, a sense of impotence, and, worse, ignorance.

Although diverse opinion was sought throughout formulation of our budget, its final contents could not possibly reflect everyone's views and choices. Reasonable men and women will disagree in their reactions to many of the resource-allocation recommendations we have made.

Persuading others to accept our priorities is not our primary purpose. Instead, we wish to stimulate a vastly more informed public debate on what national priorities ought to be. If we succeed in raising "reordering national priorities" from its present status as a near-cliché to a topic marked by meaningful and disciplined discussion, we will consider our efforts a success.

DEVELOPING THE COUNTERBUDGET

The task of constructing an entire federal budget is not an easy one, but it is certainly within the capabilities of a public-interest organization representing concerned citizens.

We began with a vision of the United States as we would like it to be and a belief that public policy must play an important role in translating that vision into reality. We then framed six broad public policy goals for the next five years. These goals, approved by the National Urban Coalition Steering Committee, called upon the federal government to:

- achieve full employment with a high level of economic growth and reasonable price stability;
- provide all citizens with an equal opportunity to participate in American society and in the shaping of governmental decisions affecting their lives;
- guarantee that no American will go without the basic necessities —food, shelter, health care, a healthy environment, personal safety, and an adequate income;
- rectify the imbalance in revenues between the federal government and state and local governments;
- assure adequate national security against military threats from abroad;
- meet our obligations to assist in the economic development of the world's less-developed nations.

Next we considered how the federal government could move toward meeting these six goals during the fiscal years 1972-76. Staff and consultants prepared resource papers in every major area of federal activity (education, crime, housing, and so forth). In these papers we attempted to ascertain the distance between present conditions and our goals by setting forth estimates of quantitative and qualitative needs in each area. Alternative policies and programs to move us closer to our goals then were suggested and their costs projected. Finally, we recommended specific policies and programs from among these alternatives.

However, the total costs of all our preferred alternatives far exceeded preliminary estimates of available revenues, even after including additional revenues from reform designed to make the tax system more equitable. This meant difficult choices would have to be made, choices that are the very essence of setting priorities.

The first choice we confronted was how to divide the nation's resources between public and private sectors. Since the amount of desirable outlays exceeded available revenues, one possible solution was to increase the amount of available revenues through raising taxes. This decision was a difficult one, for it involved choosing between that portion of our public needs which we wished to meet and the level of taxes that we were willing to pay. Almost everyone would like to maximize the former and minimize the latter, but such a combination is not logically possible. We chose to recommend increasing the amount of revenues available in order to meet a higher portion of our public needs than are now being met. But we were not willing to raise taxes to the staggering level necessary to allow us to make all the public outlays we felt were desirable on the scale we would have preferred.

After projecting how much revenue would be available each year under recommended changes in federal tax structures and rates, we were able to calculate a target level for budget outlays for each year. This level was based on the full-employment surplus concept: Outlays were set equal to slightly less than the amount of revenue the federal government could be expected to collect if the economy were operating at full employment.

We then had to make another set of excruciatingly difficult choices. Faced with a scarcity of resources, we had to decide what set of desirable outlays was *most* desirable.

The criteria for our choices should be made quite explicit. We chose that set of budget outlays which, in our judgment, would move the United States farthest in the direction of our vision of what it should be, and, specifically, nearest our six broad policy goals. This choice compelled us to allocate federal dollars to programs based on what they could accomplish. We rejected the tendency to look solely at the amount of money spent on an activity as an indicator of accomplishment. Instead, we focused on comparing the expected gains to American society resulting from spending scarce federal resources for various purposes. We tried to allocate funds for those programs which promised the largest benefits per dollar invested. Comparing the benefits to be gained from spending scarce resources for various purposes, we eventually arrived at our target level of expenditures by eliminating those outlays which we expected would move us the least distance toward our goals.

Hundreds of people—including our own National Urban Coalition Steering Committee members, academic experts, and former governmental officials—participated at various points in this priority-setting process. Our final recommendations reflect consideration of the diversity of views and points of consensus that emerged from uncounted meetings and discussions. Finally, we sent our entire budget to independent consultants who assessed its probable impact on the national economy and on labor markets. Otto Eckstein, former member of the Council of Economic Advisers, analyzed the over-all economic impact of our proposals, and James Scoville of the Institute of Labor and Industrial Relations at the University of Illinois examined manpower-impact issues. (Their conclusions are presented in chapters 21 and 22, respectively.)

Summary of Recommendations

The result of our extended period of discussion and deliberation was a set of priority choices for best utilizing limited national resources to achieve our six major goals. The budget recommendations in dollars* described in the following pages and in Table 1:2 (see pages 12 and 13) reflect these choices.

Program Priorities

Our first priority should be to assure that every American possesses the basic necessities of life. People usually lack these necessities because they lack the income to purchase them. Outlays for programs that put more money directly into people's pockets without first filtering funds through a large bureaucracy will produce immediate benefits and move us well along toward the achievement of one of our basic goals. In some cases, even people with moderate incomes may be unable to purchase necessities because resources are in short supply or are poorly dis-

* All dollar figures are "current"—i.e., they include allowance for probable inflation—rather than "real." Thus, since we project that inflation, as measured by the Bureau of Labor Statistics Consumer Price Index, will be 21 per cent between 1971 and 1976, $121 in 1976 would purchase the same amount of goods and services that $100 can purchase in 1971.

Summary of Recommended Federal Outlays

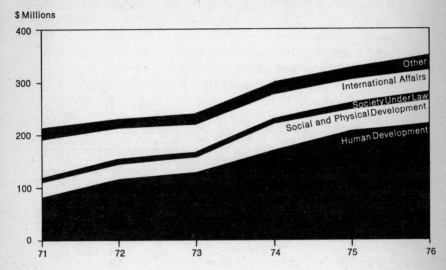

$ Millions

tributed. Housing and health care are areas in which such problems frequently occur. Accordingly, outlays for increases in housing and in the supply of trained health personnel also promise large social returns for each tax dollar invested. Therefore, *it is in these human development programs that we recommend the largest absolute increases in budget outlays.*

We propose that health expenditures rise by $51.6 billion between 1971 and 1976, with most of this increase simply the product of funneling current private payments for health services through a new government national health insurance (NHI) trust fund. Other important programs concerned with the supply and distribution of health resources also are included in the total.

We also recommend that social-insurance expenditures—primarily Old Age, Survivors, and Disability Insurance (OASDI) and unemployment insurance—be increased to $35.6 billion.

Recommended outlays for income support would rise by $28.7 billion and would end poverty, as officially defined, in the United States by 1975. Although income-support programs can provide either cash or in-kind (food stamps, social services, etc.) assistance, we strongly prefer cash assistance, since it allows families the freedom and responsibility to allocate their resources according to their personal priorities. As a result, we favor phasing out the food-stamp program but not until all Americans are assured a nonpoverty income.

Our recommended outlays for these new and revised programs, together with proposed changes in the federal income tax and social-security payroll tax, would have a significant impact on income distribution in the United States. (See Table 1:1.)

TABLE 1:1

COMPARATIVE CHANGES IN 1976 DISPOSABLE INCOME FOR A FAMILY OF FOUR[1]
(In current dollars)

Disposable Income Under Present Laws	Disposable Income Under Recommended Changes	Change in Disposable Income
$ 0	$ 4,708	+ $4,708
3,574	5,907	+ 2,332
4,931	6,871	+ 1,940
6,054	7,522	+ 1,468
7,784	8,454	+ 671
9,909	10,061	+ 152
11,305	11,185	− 120
14,051	13,678	− 373
19,363	18,588	− 774
35,355	32,708	− 2,647

[1] Based on changes in income-maintenance programs and in federal income tax and social security tax rates and on the institution of a special tax on individuals to finance national health insurance. (The table assumes state and local taxes are maintained at present rates and structures.) The table does not reflect value of in-kind income such as health care, food stamps, housing subsidies, or day-care subsidies. Since health care would be provided free under national health insurance, no disposable income would have to be spent for health purposes.

We recommend that education outlays increase by $11.1 billion. We believe that the federal government's principal role in early, elementary, and secondary education must be to assure that every student leaving the public school system possesses the information and skills to participate successfully in the economy. It is both easier and less expensive to provide these skills to students already in school than to older youths and adults who have fallen into the pool of the unskilled jobless. Accordingly, *our recommended outlays for education emphasize the increased availability of pre-*

school training, elementary programs aimed at achieving high-performance levels in reading and mathematics, and career preparation and placement programs in all of the nation's secondary schools.

Traditional manpower programs, which have concentrated on training unskilled youth, have not proved very successful at preparing participants for work; we have chosen to shift our efforts for dealing with this challenge to the education system. *The outlays we do recommend for manpower training programs are primarily for upgrading the skills of presently employed workers, unemployed adults, and women re-entering the labor market. Our total recommended outlays for manpower training programs remain nearly stable.*

Our budget also recommends significant increases in spending for social and physical development. New programs would provide $9.6 billion in direct fiscal relief for states and localities, while metropolitan development outlays would increase by more than $6 billion. States and localities will, and should continue to, provide the essential day-to-day services—police and fire protection, education, sanitation, transportation, and many others. Needs in these areas are, of course, much greater than the assistance we recommend. States and localities properly should be expected to bear the major share of the burden of raising revenues to pay for these services. Our primary reason for recommending increased federal outlays for these purposes is to provide states and localities with a better capacity for providing *quality* services to their residents. At the present time, many states and localities lack that capacity due to poorly trained personnel, inequitable tax systems, and inefficient government organization. We have tried to tie incentives for improving the capabilities of these jurisdictions to our proposals for increased federal assistance. *As a part of a fiscal relief strategy designed to improve the quality of services, we recommend the establishment of a $4.5 billion public-service employment program* to allow states and localities to provide needed services that they are presently unable to pay for. *Altogether, direct federal assistance to states and localities would rise from its 1971 level of $30 billion to $52 billion in 1976.*

TABLE 1:2
SUMMARY OF ADMINISTRATION BUDGET AND COUNTERBUDGET OUTLAYS
(In millions of current dollars)

	Administration[1]		Urban Coalition Recommendations				
	Estimated 1971	Proposed 1972	1972	1973	1974	1975	1976
Human Development							
Employment and Manpower Training	2,806	2,968	4,394	6,293	7,305	7,936	8,381
Conversion to a Peacetime Economy	178	216	1,944	1,906	292	161	127
Income Maintenance: Social Insurance	47,665	50,932	56,527	61,088	66,499	71,754	83,268
Income Maintenance: Income Support	11,300	13,587	19,961	20,357	31,338	39,302	39,962
Health	17,257	19,140	19,745	24,335	61,180	63,990	68,850
Education	9,351	10,075	10,846	12,334	16,776	19,099	20,494
Subtotal	88,557	96,918	113,289	126,313	183,390	202,242	221,082
Social and Physical Development							
Fiscal Relief for States and Localities[2]	—	3,750	5,100	6,995	7,875	8,835	9,600
Metropolitan Development	2,520	3,078	4,216	6,456	7,781	8,726	8,858
Housing	1,678	1,973	2,139	2,473	2,719	3,261	3,753
Transportation	7,763	8,279	7,707	7,645	7,707	8,263	8,735
Environment and Natural Resources	3,374	4,116	3,882	4,352	4,581	4,921	5,183
Family Planning and Population Growth	87	140	287	506	341	270	249
Rural Development and Agriculture	5,871	6,136	5,453	5,816	5,943	5,968	5,945
Research and Development[3]	5,956	5,894	5,955	6,265	6,590	6,980	7,265
Subtotal	27,249	33,366	34,739	40,508	43,537	47,224	49,588
Society Under Law							
Law Enforcement and Criminal Justice	932	1,285	1,799	2,272	2,942	3,338	3,811
Equal Opportunity	111	130	185	228	257	261	263
Consumer Protection	110	128	138	158	180	198	211
Subtotal	1,153	1,543	2,122	2,658	3,379	3,797	4,285

International Affairs						
National Defense and Military Assistance	74,500	76,000	60,240	50,335	48,550	50,025	50,425
Foreign Economic Assistance	2,993	3,240	3,500	4,760	5,410	6,245	7,445
Subtotal	77,493	79,240	63,740	55,095	53,960	56,270	57,870
Other						
Interest	19,433	19,687	19,687	22,220	23,900	25,680	28,670
Maintenance of the Mortgage Market	−977	−230	−230	−170	−130	−100	50
Postal Service[4]	2,353	1,333	327	300	330	360	400
Other Government Activities[5]	6,491	7,092	6,771	7,049	7,429	7,620	7,952
Subtotal	27,300	27,882	26,555	29,399	31,429	33,560	37,072
Less: Duplications	−1,800	−1,946	−1,978	−2,178	−3,711	−3,987	−4,249
Employer Share, Employee Retirement	−2,486	−2,461	−2,461	−2,660	−2,880	−3,120	−3,375
Interest Received by Trust Funds	−4,711	−5,310	−5,310	−6,707	−7,557	−8,159	−8,788
TOTAL	212,755	229,232	230,824	242,428	301,377	327,827	353,485

[1] The Administration figures are those estimated for 1971 and proposed for 1972 in *Budget of the United States Government, Fiscal Year 1972.*

[2] Fiscal relief includes a proposed new program of general aid to elementary and secondary education, with funding beginning at $1 billion in 1972 and building to $4 billion by 1976.

[3] Includes NASA, the AEC, and the basic research activities supported by the National Science Foundation. Other R&D activities are included in the budgets of their appropriate functional areas.

[4] The decline in recommended federal outlays for support of the U.S. Postal Service reflects an assumed implementation of the recommendation of the President's Commission on Postal Organization that postal subsidies (free and reduced-rate mail and other public-service costs) be limited to 3 per cent of total postal revenue requirements.

[5] Other government activities for 1971 were determined as the residual factor after all specifically analyzed programs were accounted for. The residual figure was then used as a base and adjusted for subsequent years by the following index, based on combined forecasts (as a proxy of workload) of price increases and population growth:

1971	1972	1973	1974	1975	1976
100.0	104.3	108.6	112.9	117.4	122.5

Outlays for certain other purposes that constitute a high priority do not increase by large absolute amounts in our budget recommendations, either because present expenditures are low and it takes time to "gear up" or because benefits would be slight from additional outlays above the healthy increases we recommend. For example, *recommended spending for law enforcement and criminal justice increases by 310 per cent—a higher percentage increase than for any other purpose. Yet, the absolute increase in expenditures is less than $3 billion.* Foreign economic assistance is another example. *Assisting in the economic development of the world's less-developed nations is one of our six goals; for this purpose, we recommended increasing outlays by $4.5 billion above the current $3.0 billion level.* Yet, we still fall short of providing the 0.7 per cent of Gross National Product in official aid recommended as a goal by the World Bank's Commission on International Development, because we do not believe that aid-dispensing institutions can productively absorb more.

Setting priorities forces one to decide that spending in some areas is less important than in others. Thus, although the needs in the area of environment protection and restoration are indisputable, we concluded that it was relatively more important to direct resources in the next five years toward ending poverty, reforming education, and improving the capabilities of states and localities to provide quality services. As a result, *we recommend that outlays for environment and natural resource programs increase by only $1.8 billion—53 per cent above present levels.* Even so, *federal support for pollution-control efforts would triple—from $0.7 billion to $2.1 billion—between 1971 and 1976.* With programs funded at this level, we hope to prevent further deterioration of the environment and to set up the structure for eventually dealing comprehensively with pollution.

Our recommended outlays for transportation also remain nearly stable, increasing by only 12 per cent—not enough to cover inflation—between 1971 and 1976. Within transportation, we recommend shifting $1.8 billion from highway programs to mass transit, where these tax dollars would yield much higher public benefits. We already have a superb highway system, while nearly every one of our urban transit systems is in desperate need of expansion and refurbishment.

The amount the United States spends on rural development and agriculture is a reflection of our previous lack of ability to change priorities as circumstances change: A substantial portion of the $6 billion we spend in this area supports obsolete and wasteful programs. American society would benefit if some outlays for these programs were redirected to other purposes. *We suggest that the price-support component of agricultural subsidies be eliminated and replaced by our income-support program. Total spending for agricultural programs should decrease while spending for rural industrial development should rise. The net result would be a small real dollar decrease in total spending for rural development and agriculture.*

Our largest recommended reduction in outlays is for national defense and military assistance—a cut of $24 billion from the present level of $74.5 billion to $50.4 billion in 1976. This recommended cutback is based on a careful assessment of U.S. international interests and the potential military threats posed by other nations to our security. Assuring adequate national security against military threats from abroad is one of our six basic goals, and second to none in terms of importance.

The critical question is what level of expenditures is required to provide *adequate* national security. A close scrutiny of the present Pentagon budget reveals a number of programs that either contribute little to our national strength or actually reduce our safety by fueling a continuation of the arms race. The total strength and security of our society would be increased by reallocating the $24 billion in military funds for such programs to domestic public uses where the American taxpayer will receive more for his money.

Although our budgets in nearly all areas of domestic affairs call for more federal outlays, we do not intend simply to increase funding for existing programs. Throughout the chapters that follow, we recommend new programs, reforms in existing programs, and, in some cases, elimination of existing programs. By 1976, the Counterbudget outlays reflect significant expenditures for new programs. (See Table 1:2.)

Among the new programs we propose are:

National health insurance

Public-service employment

Cash assistance for the poor and near-poor (replacing the present welfare system)

Preschool education

General aid to elementary and secondary education

Elementary and secondary education grants for meeting minimum federal reading and mathematics objectives

A career-preparation program tied to secondary schools

A higher education-loan program with repayment tied to percentage of future income

Grants for upgrading local police-department personnel

A discharge-fee system to curb pollution

A long-term, whole-farm land-retirement program (to replace the present agricultural-subsidy programs)

A series of programs designed to produce reform in the tax systems and structure of states and localities

Our 1976 budget proposals also include expenditures for programs in which we recommend major reforms—and, in many cases, increased expenditures. These include:

- OASDI and unemployment insurance;
- food stamps;
- social services;
- Model Cities;
- manpower training; and
- consumer protection.

The 67 per cent increase in total federal outlays we recommend over a five-year period includes major shifts in the portions of the federal budget spent for various purposes. Health, which in 1971 accounted for only 8.1 per cent of federal outlays, would account for 19.5 per cent in 1976; income support would increase from 5.3 per cent to 11.3 per cent. National defense and military assistance outlays would fall from 35 per cent of total federal outlays to 14.3 per cent in 1976. (See Table 1:3.)

TABLE 1:3
FEDERAL OUTLAYS, BY PER CENT

	Administration Estimate for 1971	Proposed for 1976
Employment and Manpower Training	1.3	2.4
Conversion to a Peacetime Economy	0.1	—
Social Insurance	22.4	23.6
Income Support	5.3	11.3
Health	8.1	19.5
Education	4.4	5.8
Fiscal Relief for States and Localities	—	2.7
Metropolitan Development	1.2	2.5
Housing	0.8	1.1
Transportation	3.6	2.5
Environment and Natural Resources	1.6	1.5
Family Planning and Population Growth	—	0.1
Rural Development and Agriculture	2.8	1.7
Research and Development	2.8	2.1
Law Enforcement and Criminal Justice	0.4	1.1
Equal Opportunity	0.1	0.1
Consumer Protection	0.1	0.1
National Defense and Military Assistance	35.0	14.3
Foreign Economic Assistance	1.4	2.1
Net Interests	6.9	5.6
Other Activities	1.7	—
TOTAL	100.0	100.0

REVENUES AND ECONOMIC POLICY

Our budget proposes that federal outlays rise from their 1971 total of $212.8 billion to $353.5 billion in 1976—an increase of nearly $141 billion. This increase will be possible only if additional revenues are collected by implementing new tax measures and producing a healthy rate of economic growth—both of which will require an active federal role.

Restoration of full employment represents the first step toward putting the national economy back on a sound footing. The federal government can contribute greatly to the attainment of this objective by stimulating economic growth through the enactment of sizable budget deficits in 1972 and 1973.* Creation and support

* Our recommended budget expenditure levels are set at the full-employment surplus level—the level of revenues that would be produced if the economy were at full employment. For 1974–76, when we assume that full employment will be achieved, our proposed budgets show very slight surpluses of revenues over outlays. In 1972 and 1973, actual deficits are recommended because full employment will not have been achieved.

The Federal Budget as a Per Cent of GNP

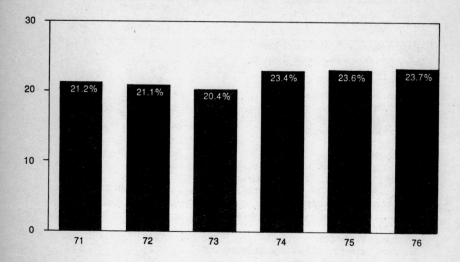

of a large public-service employment program is another federal action that would serve to reduce the jobless rate and increase economic activity. In addition, a monetary policy that will assure the liquidity necessary for such an expansionary fiscal policy is essential. Reducing unemployment from its present 6 per cent level to the full-employment standard of less than 4 per cent will require a real growth rate of more than 5 per cent a year between now and 1974 with a rate of at least 4 per cent in the years thereafter. If such expansionary fiscal and monetary policies are to be pursued without engendering a runaway inflation, the federal government will have to resort to much stronger measures to prevent excessive price and wage increases than those being used today. The first step ought to be the full application of the great moral power of the office of the President on uncooperative corporations and labor unions. If suasion proves inadequate, serious consideration should be given to adoption of formal price-wage guidelines or—as a last resort—price and wage controls.

Rapid economic growth without excessive inflation also will serve as a major source of the additional tax revenues so sorely needed at all levels of government. Financing our recommended programs will take about $159 billion in *new* federal revenues over the next five years—the difference between estimated 1971 federal revenues of $194 billion and required 1976 revenues of $353 billion. We estimate that the rate of economic growth required to restore full employment will produce $90 billion in new federal tax revenues.* This fiscal dividend of $90 billion will account for 55 per cent of the $159 billion in total new federal revenue needed.

These projections suggest then that 1976 federal revenues under existing tax laws will amount to $284 billion. Since our 1976 budget outlays are nearly $70 billion greater than these expected resources, it is clear that additional revenues will be necessary to finance our recommended outlays. (Nearly $115 billion of our proposed outlays in 1976 will be financed from· revenues raised through trust funds. Outlays for trust fund activities would increase $55 billion between 1971 and 1976. As a result, while total budget outlays would increase by $140 billion during that period, outlays funded by general revenues and other federal funds would increase by only $85 billion—from $153.5 billion to $238.5 billion.) The additional revenues will have to be raised through taxation.

We recommend changes in the social-security and unemployment-insurance payroll taxes, a new tax on individual incomes and corporate payrolls that will finance a significant portion of national health insurance, and increased reliance on user charges, particularly for certain transportation purposes. The total additional revenue from these tax changes would amount to slightly more than $44 billion—still $24 billion less than would be needed to pay for the recommended $353.5 billion in outlays we propose.

We also recommend reforms in federal estate and gift taxes and individual and corporate income taxes, primarily to make these taxes more equitable than they now are. These reforms would yield nearly $6 billion more annually in taxes.

* Our revenue projections are based on the following key economic assumptions:

	1971	1972	1973	1974	1975	1976
GNP	1,004	1,094	1,190	1,288	1,388	1,489
GNP Price Deflator	100.0	103.3	106.5	109.7	113.0	116.4
Consumer Price Index	100.0	104.1	108.2	112.3	116.6	121.0
Unemployment Rate	5.6	5.0	4.0	3.5	3.5	3.5

Despite all these increased yields, federal revenues in 1976 would still fall about $18 billion short of total outlays in our budget. Therefore, we urge adoption of a 10 per cent surtax on individual income and corporate profits to make up this deficit. However, we recommend that this surtax be instituted only after the economy has returned to full employment and only after we have achieved tax reform designed to make our tax system more equitable.

These spending and revenue recommendations would produce the budget patterns shown in Table 1:4.

THE SCOPE OF CHANGE

Our proposed budgets hardly portend revolutionary changes. Under our recommendations, the public sector would receive a higher portion of the nation's total economic resources, but still not as high a portion as in most Western European countries. Federal government spending, which has remained a virtually constant 20 per cent of GNP since 1950, would increase under our recommendations to 23.7 per cent of GNP in 1976.

Similarily, the new programs we propose, although innovative, can hardly be considered radical. Most are already seriously and widely discussed as public policy alternatives; many have long been law in Western European democracies.

In fact, we have been criticized by some people with whom we have discussed our proposals for our lack of daring and farsightedness. To such criticism, we can say in defense only that we consciously worked within a five-year framework and that our budgets are for the fiscal years from 1972 through 1976—not for the year 2000. Much of what we hope will be accomplished by the year 2000 simply cannot be accomplished by 1976 because of economic, manpower, and time constraints.

Despite the significant increase we propose in the federal budget, our recommendations do not imply a burgeoning federal bureaucracy or a great increase in federal power at the expense of states and localities.

Most of the higher-cost new programs recommended require little administrative effort other than determination of eligibility,

TABLE 1:4
THE BUDGET AT A GLANCE[1]
(In millions of current dollars)

	Administration			Urban Coalition Recommendations			
	Estimated 1971	Proposed 1972	1972	1973	1974	1975	1976
Receipts	194,193	217,593	213,600	241,900	303,500	328,100	353,500
Outlays	212,755	229,232	230,824	242,428	301,377	327,827	353,485
Surplus or (Deficit)	(18,567)	(11,639)	(17,124)	(528)	2,123	273	15

[1] Budget outlays on the unified budget basis employed here do not include tax expenditures (selective reductions in tax liabilities designed to achieve particular social and economic objectives). Tax expenditures have the same fiscal impact as a direct increase in budget outlays. Examples of tax expenditures include deductions for mortgage interest on owner-occupied homes, for medical expenses, and for charitable contributions, the exemption of interest on state and local debt, and the exclusion of interest on life insurance policies. In 1969, tax expenditures for all purposes totaled $47.2 billion.

which can be accomplished through recourse to existing, highly mechanized Social Security Administration or Internal Revenue Service records. Many of the recommended federal programs providing aid to states and localities are designed to strengthen the capabilities of those jurisdictions to cope with their own problems.

Nor are we laboring under any illusions that more spending, in itself, will allow us to accomplish our goals. More federal spending —viewed as an investment that will provide widespread benefit to the American people—clearly is necessary. The social costs of not making this investment would be far higher than the actual expenditures we recommend. But it is true that money alone cannot assure that we will reach our goals. Reform is needed at all levels of government.

On the federal level, the amount of red tape required of recipients of federal aid must be greatly reduced. The interest of the consumer and of the public must be built into the federal decision-making process to counterbalance the special interests that have too often dominated in the past. Finally, the federal government must develop its capacity to evaluate, with maximum candor, the efficacy of its own programs. All too frequently, federal programs have an impact far removed from original intent. Until we are able to evaluate our efforts, a truly rational formulation of public policy will be impossible, even by men of the best will.

State and local governments must be far more responsive to the needs of their citizens than they have been in the past. More and better planning will be necessary if these jurisdictions are to make effective use of increased federal funds. So will cooperation among adjoining metropolitan jurisdictions, since so many physical and social problems span political subdivisions. In particular, suburban jurisdictions must contribute to the solution of problems in the central cities; they must be prevented from intensifying the city's problems by maintaining segregated schools and housing. All of these developments should be encouraged by incentives and requirements that are tied to receipt of federal funds.

Finally, a word about commitment. No one doubts that the United States possesses the resources and knowledge to reach our goals. What Americans have lacked in the past has been the will to change. William James once defined courage as "the capacity to will effectively." This is the capacity we must summon. If we do, we can find again the reserves of vitality that can lead us to the attainment of our ideals as a nation—whether they be in this set of national priorities or in one that the reader may wish to devise for himself.

HUMAN
DEVELOPMENT

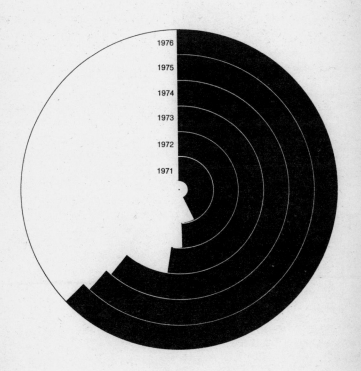

2

Employment and Manpower Training

There is no more sharply meaningful national economic indicator than the rate of unemployment. The production of the American worker and the purchasing power of the paycheck he or she brings home are the energy poles of the American economic dynamo. When a worker is laid off not only is his production lost—his purchases are curtailed, his credit is cut off, and his savings are drained. The dynamo loses a bit of its energy.

Each increase of 0.1 per cent in the rate of unemployment translates to 86,000 men and women made idle. The economic cost of their enforced idleness is enormous. So is the social cost. The effects of unemployment on individuals, families, and communities should carry weight equal to that of other economic factors in the governmental choices that affect the level of employment in the nation.

Recognizing the debilitating impact of unemployment, the United States, twenty-five years ago, pledged itself to full employment. The Employment Act of 1946 declared that the federal government has the responsibility for creating and maintaining

conditions under which there will be afforded useful employment opportunities, including self-employment, for those able, willing, and seeking to work, and to promote maximum employment, production, and purchasing power.

In December, 1970, however, the rate of unemployment exceeded 6 per cent, a figure far beyond any definition of "full employment." The unemployment rate among youth is much higher (more than 9 per cent for those aged twenty to twenty-four), and

27

among black youth, higher still (14 per cent among those of the same age group). The pledge undertaken in 1946 remains a promise rather than a reality. Public policy has been declared, but we have not yet taken the necessary steps to implement it.

Toward Full Employment

The obvious first step toward full employment is to improve the performance of the American economy. If the economy is operating at or near full capacity, unemployment will be low. A high level of aggregate demand (total demand for goods and services) will ensure the availability of jobs. Therefore, maximum utilization of America's prodigious productive capacity along with maintenance of a healthy rate of economic growth (in excess of 4 per cent over the long term) should be primary goals of national economic policy.

But, historically, high levels of demand and unemployment rates below 4 per cent have been accompanied by price instability. This association of events has given rise to the assumption that an unemployment rate near 4 per cent represents "full employment" and that attempts to reduce the unemployment rate further will have an inflationary effect on wages and prices, since all workers who possess useful skills will already be fully employed. However, manpower specialists are aware that the rate of unemployment we call full employment (the President's 1970 *Economic Report* assumes a 3.8 per cent unemployment rate as the "full employment" indicator) is not the best we can achieve. Rather, they claim, it reflects correctable defects in the labor market structure. Acceptance of a 4 per cent rate of unemployment represents a loss to the nation of the productivity and purchasing power of millions of workers. The "structural" deficiencies that underlie acceptance of a 4 per cent unemployment rate include:

- mismatching of skills and jobs;
- inadequate mobility in the labor market, which makes it difficult to match job seekers with available jobs within their skill range; and
- racial, sexual, and religious discrimination.

By successfully attacking these structural problems and by achieving high levels of productivity increase, we should be able to reduce employment, in the long run, far below 3.8 per cent while still retaining stable prices, that is, prices that increase less than 3 per cent a year.

However, in the short run, there will continue to be problems in simultaneously achieving high levels of employment and price stability. There are several alternative policies to cope with this situation:

- Decrease aggregate demand (through monetary and fiscal policies) and accept higher levels of unemployment in order to achieve stable prices.
- Decrease aggregate demand but expand public-service jobs as unemployment increases, paying for the expanded public-service employment out of increased taxes.
- Accept higher price levels to avoid higher unemployment.
- Institute short-term guidelines or controls on credit, wages, and prices to maintain high employment and stable prices.

Traditionally, the United States has opted for the first alternative, while most Western countries facing the same dilemma have opted for one or a combination of the other three. The result has been that, except during wartime, the United States has not been able to move its unemployment rate much below 4 per cent without "unacceptable" price inflation. However, as practices in the European countries have shown, the unemployment rate can be pushed much lower if a revised concept of "acceptable" inflation is adopted.

We strongly recommend that a rate of inflation higher than 3 per cent be accepted for a short term, if it appears necessary to do so to reduce unemployment significantly below 4 per cent. The short-term cost of such a policy is preferable to the irretrievable social and human misery brought on by unemployment. Paul Samuelson, Nobel Prize economics laureate, in a 1971 television interview stated his conviction that, however undesirable it may be, we may have to live with a 4 per cent rate of price increase for the next few years.

If inflation exceeds even the 4 per cent level, we recommend that efforts to decrease aggregate demand be undertaken, but not solely in the area of monetary policy. Higher interest rates, since they increase the cost of consumer and mortgage credit, have an adverse impact on the average American. Raising taxes (particularly after institution of the tax reform we recommend in Chapter 23) would decrease excess demands for goods and services where such demands really are excess—at the higher income levels. Such inflation-combating tax increases should be accompanied by an expanded public-service employment program to offset any resulting unemployment. But, if such fiscal policy is to be effective, it must become more flexible. The President should be given the power to raise or to lower taxes, within specified limits, as economic conditions warrant.

Should moderate fiscal and monetary efforts not be sufficient to balance prices and employment at acceptable levels, serious consideration should be given to short-term selective controls or incentives over credit, wages, and prices as a preferable alternative to massive efforts to cut demand. A variety of possible policies exists: "jawboning," federal guidelines, creation of a wage-price review commission, and direct governmental controls. Any one or a combination of these incentives or controls might prove a greatly desirable alternative to high unemployment and sluggish growth.

The American economy will have to be able to absorb an expected large and rapid increase in the civilian labor force. We estimate that growth in the labor force will easily exceed 10 million people between now and 1976. Such an expansion will occur because:

1. The number of Americans eligible to enter the labor force will increase by 15 million between 1971 and 1976.*

2. The number of military personnel (not counted as part of the civilian labor force) will be reduced. In 1971, there were 3 million Americans in the military. Under our recommendations, only 2 million Americans will be serving in the armed forces in 1976. As a result of the cutback, more Americans will enter the civilian labor force. (Measures to help ex-military and military-related workers to enter peacetime jobs are discussed in Chapter 3.)

3. An increasing percentage of women can be expected to enter the labor force due to changing perceptions of the role of women in our society, greater provisions for child care, and the

* Years are federal fiscal years unless specifically used as dates or otherwise stated in this and succeeding chapters.

gradual breakdown of sexual discrimination in the labor market. In 1969, approximately 43 per cent of American women were in the labor force. In 1949, only 33 per cent were.

4. As opportunity for employment increases, the so-called hidden unemployed will enter or re-enter the labor force. According to 1970 Department of Labor estimates, nearly 700,000 people were not in the labor force or seeking employment because they believed they would not be able to get a job. These people are not, at present, counted as unemployed. If they were, the December, 1970, unemployment rate (seasonally adjusted) would have been 6.8 per cent, rather than 6.2 per cent.

Unemployment Rates and Size of the Civilian Labor Force

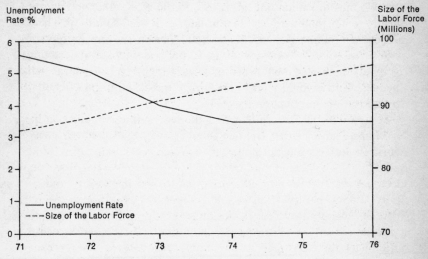

In addition to a substantial increase in its labor force, the United States will be absorbing the uncertain impact of advancing technology and automation. It is clear that we will continue to be able to produce more goods with fewer workers. Some economists have predicted a permanent employment crisis as machines replace men and become the major productive resource. Such a crisis has not proved as imminent as early proponents of the thesis argued. But the possibility is nonetheless real and threatens most of the basic assumptions behind manpower planning—including that fundamental value of American society, the "work ethic."

Work has long been viewed as a normal condition of life for American men (and increasingly for women). Indeed, the lack of employment on the part of an able-bodied male adult has been viewed traditionally as a sure sign of moral unworthiness. At the same time, human labor was, and is, necessary to produce the goods Americans desire. But, if the technology of the future enables us to continue increasing production while employing a relatively smaller portion of the labor force, will work still be considered desirable for moral reasons?

Some economic philosophers, Robert Theobald, for one, suggest that we must abandon our adherence to the work ethic and accept leisure rather than work as the normal and desired condition. There are certain public policies that would hasten movement toward a leisure society. Examples of such policies include the setting of a very high minimum wage or a very high level of guaranteed income. Either would tend to encourage the substitution of capital for labor in the production process.

Many other observers insist that the work ethic continues to be valid and that it neither can nor should be changed. In their view, work should be the normal condition for most Americans, and public policy choices should ensure that widespread unemployment does not result from advancing technology and increasing productivity. Policy choices that would support a work-based society include putting into effect devices that would permit more people to be employed for shorter periods of time (shorter work weeks and longer vacations are two examples) or a conscious acceptance of less productivity and efficiency to keep more Americans employed.

The choices before public policy-makers are fundamental. What is chosen will shape the nation's future. Clearly, however, within the next five years, changes in attitudes are likely to be incremental rather than fundamental. During that time, the work ethic will not disappear, and full employment will remain a primary American value and goal.

Although the impact of technology during the next five years is uncertain, we can say with confidence that the trend toward more jobs in services and in human relations will continue and accelerate. This will occur partly because goods-producing jobs are more easily automated and partly because rising income and education have created an increased demand for services, in both the private and public sectors.

To avoid a serious, long-term unemployment problem, jobs must be created and skills developed in the areas that will grow as a result of the changing demand patterns. In the private sector, jobs will be created as a matter of course in response to consumer demands as long as a healthy growth rate is maintained. In the public sector, however, the response is not so direct. Nevertheless, it is in the public sector that the increased demand for services exists.

PUBLIC-SERVICE EMPLOYMENT

It is difficult to project precisely total need in the public sector. The National Commission on Technology, Automation, and Economic Progress estimated in the latter half of the 1960's that the public sector as a whole could productively absorb several million additional employees, mostly in jobs that are needed but do not now formally exist. These jobs are not there because, unlike those of the private sector, where the cost of labor is paid for by selling products, public employee wages must be paid from extremely scarce tax revenues.

In a 1968 sample survey taken for the National Urban Coalition, mayors of thirty-four cities of over 100,000 population listed the numbers of additional workers they then needed (but could not hire, chiefly due to lack of revenues) to carry out necessary municipal services. Their responses indicated that the nation's 130 cities over 100,000 population had an immediate need for more than 140,000 new employees in thirteen categories of municipal services, ranging from education to police. (See Table 2:1.) The needs of these cities have undoubtedly increased since 1968. Very limited public-service employment programs do exist, but the federal government does not now provide salary support for par-

TABLE 2:1

PROJECTION OF ADDITIONAL NONPROFESSIONAL PUBLIC-SERVICE JOB POSSIBILITIES IN 130 CITIES WITH POPULATIONS OF 100,000 OR MORE, BY POPULATION SIZE[1]

1968

Function or Program	Total (130 cities)	Population size 100,000-250,000 (80 cities)	250,000-750,000 (40 cities)	750,000 or more (10 cities)
Antipollution Enforcement	900	568	232	100
Education	39,134	10,704	15,000	13,430
General Administration	5,313	2,864	1,236	1,213
Health and Hospitals	18,790	6,120	6,596	6,074
Highway and/or Traffic Control	7,179	3,608	2,168	1,403
Housing Codes and Inspection	1,473	440	576	457
Library	3,159	1,176	908	1,075
Police	11,616	2,360	3,916	5,340
Fire	5,390	2,720	1,648	1,022
Recreation and Parks	14,359	5,696	2,900	5,763
Urban Renewal (or Rehabilitation), including Model Cities	7,800	5,304	1,104	1,392
Sanitation	7,534	2,816	1,868	2,850
Welfare	18,497	544	2,428	15,525
TOTAL	141,144	44,920	40,580	55,644

[1] Based on replies of 34 cities. Excludes answers to "other" categories.

SOURCE: Harold Sheppard, *The Nature of the Job Problem and the Role of New Public Service Employment.* The W. E. Upjohn Institute for Employment Research, 1969.

ticipants—a condition that greatly limits the potential usefulness of the programs.

We recommend that the federal government provide state and local governments and nonprofit public-service organizations with a grant of $4,500 yearly for each public-service job created, with the recipient jurisdiction required to match that grant with at least a $1,000 contribution of its own. The grant would be applied primarily to salary and initial training costs, but could also be applied to administrative costs. The employee would receive at least the national minimum wage or the prevailing minimum wage in the area, whichever is higher. The federal government would specify the categories of jobs for which the grants could be used. Eligible categories would include both paraprofessionals and professionals in health, law enforcement, education, environmental control, and similar areas. To qualify for grants, recipient governments or organizations would have to ensure that the created jobs would provide entry-level employees with opportunities for advancement.

We estimate that state and local governments could absorb 250,000 public-service jobs during 1972 and an additional 350,000 the following year. By 1976, a total of 1 million public-service jobs would be created under the recommended program. The number could be further expanded if unemployment rose. Total employment would increase by more than the number of public-service jobs created, since these new jobs would probably be held by individuals who tend to consume a relatively high portion of their incomes, thereby boosting aggregate demand.

The precise impact on the unemployment rate of this recommended public-service employment program is difficult to assess because it is unclear how many of the newly created jobs would go to the unemployed and how many would go to those just entering the labor force. However, we estimate that the unemployment rate would be reduced to 4 per cent in 1973 and to 3.5 per cent or below thereafter. This would mark the best nonwartime national employment performance in forty years. Federal outlays for this public-service employment program would amount to $1.1 billion in 1972 and $4.5 billion in 1976. However, these outlays would be partially offset by increased taxes paid by the workers entering the public-service jobs.

CORRECTING IMBALANCES AND DEFICIENCIES

To achieve high employment with reasonable price stability, better basic education, more effective attacks on racial and sexual discrimination, improved labor market mobility, and effective manpower training programs, in addition to new public-service jobs, will all be necessary.

Manpower training programs are intended to provide jobs for participants and to lower the unemployment rate. Judged by these criteria, the programs have been a disappointment. Without changes, there is no reason to expect improvement.

In theory, manpower training programs can reduce unemployment rates that are already relatively low. By training workers in areas of skill shortages and linking training programs directly to job openings in these areas, the total number of people employed can be increased and the inflationary effects of labor scarcity reduced. Unfortunately, efforts to train for areas in need of skilled workers have not shown success in the past. In addition, manpower training programs during periods of high employment have not led to jobs but have served merely as income-maintenance programs for the participants.

During times of less-than-full employment, manpower training programs cannot be expected, even in theory, to lead directly to a job or to affect the unemployment rate significantly. In a tight job market, unfilled jobs requiring relatively low skills are scarce. In the absence of a job-creation program, and with no change in the national economy's performance, significant numbers of people can become employed directly as a result of manpower training programs only if they replace currently employed workers.

The justification for manpower training programs during times of less-than-full employment is either as a form of income maintenance (since those in training receive living allowances) or as an opportunity for the unemployed to acquire relevant skills so that, when the economy improves, they will be in a position to secure jobs. Particularly as advancing technology renders many present skills outmoded, manpower training programs can play an important role in upgrading the abilities of the labor force.

Present manpower training programs have focused almost totally on the unemployed, and on unemployed youth in particular. These programs have not by themselves been very successful. Enrollees are usually almost totally unskilled when they enter. When they leave, they are often unable to find employment utilizing the modest skills they may have acquired. The recommended public-service employment program (including the training associated with it) would seem a much more appropriate program for unemployed youth. Manpower training programs in the future should concentrate on skill upgrading, particularly for the underemployed poor and lower- and middle-income workers, for labor force re-entrants, and for vocational rehabilitation for the disabled.

In 1970, 1.35 million individuals* were enrolled in manpower training programs. We expect this number to rise to nearly 1.9 million by 1976.

Administration of manpower training must undergo a great deal of improvement if these efforts are to be effective. Currently, there is a bewildering patchwork of programs. There is almost unanimous agreement that the various programs should be consolidated, and that manpower funds should be distributed with greater attention to local needs.

We propose that a portion of federal manpower funds be set aside for consolidated manpower grants to cities with populations over 75,000 to be given to the cities after they have submitted to the federal government manpower plans satisfying clear federal standards; the remaining portion of federal manpower and training funds would be given to states, upon receipt of a state manpower plan, for distribution among their various localities with populations under 75,000. A federal distribution formula based on local unemployment rates, total number of unemployed, and per capita income would determine allocation of the funds among various cities and states. To encourage widespread participation in

---

* The figure is expressed in man-years. Since the average period in a program is less than one year, many more individuals actually participated. Participation data and projections do not include enrollees in the vocational rehabilitation program.

manpower training programs, day-care facilities, which we recommend and describe in Chapter 6, should be made available to all enrollees.

A major barrier to labor mobility is the ineffectiveness of present job placement services. Federal responsibility in this area lies with the federal-state Employment Service system. The ability of this system to respond to the needs of the unemployed has been seriously questioned.

An effective job placement system must be nation-wide in scope. The present, largely state-controlled system is obsolete. Foremost among the changes needed is the federalization of the Employment Service to permit it to pursue national policy and national goals. A second basic change would entail a significant upgrading of Employment Service personnel through training. Establishment of some higher-salaried positions than now exist would attract better-qualified persons. *We therefore recommend intensive research efforts to develop more effective job placement systems, including further development of computerized job banks.* These actions, combined with reforms in unemployment insurance (described in Chapter 4), should make involuntary unemployment both less difficult financially and shorter in duration.

In addition, to meet a pressing short-term need until the benefits of this basic recommendation are broadly felt, we recommend that a relocation allowance be provided as an adjustment benefit for workers displaced from defense-related industries during the next two years. (See Chapter 3.) The impact and cost of this program should be studied to determine if it should be extended to include other unemployed workers.

We also recommend significantly increased funding for all levels of education, and particularly for career preparation and continuing education (see Chapter 6), and for explicitly outlined programs to achieve an end to racial and sexual discrimination in employment (see Chapter 16).

Budget proposals for Employment and Manpower Training are summarized in Table 2:2 on the following page.

TABLE 2:2
EMPLOYMENT AND MANPOWER TRAINING
(Outlays, in millions of current dollars)

	Administration Estimated Proposed		Urban Coalition Recommendations				
	1971	1972	1972	1973	1974	1975	1976
Public-Service Employment[1]	97		1,125	2,700	3,150	3,937	4,500
Number of Jobs (in thousands)			(250)	(600)	(750)	(875)	(1,000)
Manpower Training Grants[2]	1,585	1,809	1,893	2,050	2,463	2,246	2,074
Vocational Rehabilitation[3]	604	620	676	703	730	758	787
U.S. Employment Service Administration	344	363	450	500	550	575	600
Research and Development	176	176	250	340	412	420	420
TOTAL	2,806	2,968	4,394	6,293	7,305	7,936	8,381

[1] The Administration estimate includes the Mainstream and Public Service Careers programs.
[2] Child-care components are included in the education budget.
[3] Vocational Rehabilitation includes Veterans Vocational Rehabilitation.

3

Conversion to a Peacetime Economy

The sharp defense-spending cut expected at the end of the war in Southeast Asia will produce jarring economic hardships for some segments of American society. Such an experience is hardly new in the United States. Government policy changes such as military demobilization, the closing of military bases, or the liberalization of trade agreements all have caused acute adjustment problems for certain workers, companies, and geographical areas. The federal government has in the past done little to alleviate the undesirable side effects of its policy changes. However, the major shift in government spending—from destruction overseas to building at home—that we recommend requires federal action to assure that these side effects do not become insuperable political obstacles.

Already, we are faced with major conversion problems as our military involvement in Southeast Asia—and the defense spending associated with it—winds down. These conversion problems will be intensified by any further reductions in the defense budget.

Defense spending is currently an important component of our economy. At the height of the Vietnam War (1968), more than 10 per cent of our national labor force was employed in defense-related jobs. This percentage has already dropped substantially due to decreased Vietnam spending and is expected to reach 7.4 per cent by the end of 1971.* *We recommend a real decrease in defense spending of approximately $12 billion beyond that which is directly attributable to a decrease of spending in Vietnam.* (See Chapter 18.) Assuming that the additional cuts in the defense

* Years are federal fiscal years unless otherwise indicated.

40

budget we recommend are made, defense-related employment should fall to about 5.5 per cent of the national labor force by 1973 and well below 5 per cent by 1976.

The decrease in defense employment will occur in three areas: armed forces personnel, Department of Defense civilian employees, and employees of defense-related industries (military hardware producers and their primary suppliers). After our recommended cuts, 3.6 million fewer Americans would be employed in defense jobs by 1973 than in 1968. According to Department of Defense estimates, nearly 2.2 million of these jobs will have disappeared by June, 1971. (See Table 3:1.)

TABLE 3:1
DEFENSE-RELATED EMPLOYMENT[1]
(In millions of employees)

	Actual 1968	1971	Projected 1972	1973	1975
Armed Forces	3.5	2.6	2.1	2.0	2.0
Civil Service	1.3	1.1	1.0	0.9	0.9
Defense-related Industry	3.5	2.4	2.2	1.9	1.9
TOTAL	8.3	6.1	5.3	4.8	4.8

[1] Measured at end of fiscal year.

The resulting unemployment will hit certain skills, industries, and geographical areas. Large numbers of highly trained specialists —engineers, physicists, systems analysts—will lose their jobs, as will even larger numbers of skilled workers—craftsmen, foremen, operatives. The aircraft, ordnance, and communications and electronics industries will be particularly hard hit. Since these industries are concentrated in a few geographical areas, the economy of those areas will also suffer. Seattle, Los Angeles, San Diego, Fort Worth, Bridgeport, and the Cambridge-Boston area are already feeling significant stress.

Yet the federal government has no clear policies to relieve these problems of its own making. Although we are now in the midst of a substantial defense cutback, unemployed defense workers receive virtually no assistance in their efforts to find employment in an economy with virtually no growth.

The problem of economic conversion is not without precedent for the U.S. economy. Defense spending fell from 37.5 per cent of the GNP at the end of World War II (1945) to only 6.6 per cent in 1947. In the same period, almost 10 million men and women were demobilized from the armed forces. However, post–World War II conversion was bolstered by a backlog of savings and consumer demand that had been pent up during four years of total mobilization.

Economists agree that maintenance of aggregate demand (total demand for goods and services) is the primary requirement for assurance of a smooth transition period, and that the federal government must assure that other expenditures are substituted for declining defense outlays. Certainly, there will be no difficulty finding alternative uses for federal funds. There are tremendous unmet needs—in metropolitan development, health, housing, income maintenance, fiscal relief to states and localities, education, pollution control, to name only a few. *We recommend increases totaling $54 billion over 1971 levels in federal nondefense spending by 1973.* These spending increases should assure a healthy growth rate in the over-all national economy and prevent any rise in the national unemployment rate. Nonetheless, there will be microeconomic problems concentrated among the occupations, industries, and geographical areas we have already mentioned. Specific policies must be devised to deal with these problems.

UNEMPLOYED WORKERS

Programs suggested elsewhere in this book will do much to ease the conversion of workers from defense-related to other employment. These include improvements in unemployment insurance, a cash-assistance program, and a public-service employment program (see Chapter 4). However, a more specific supplementary program of assistance should be provided immediately for the "conversion-unemployed."

The precedent for such a program already exists for workers displaced as a result of the Trade Expansion Act of 1962. Provisions from that Act could be used as models for an adjustment-assistance program meeting the needs of former defense workers. *The new adjustment-assistance program would guarantee eligible defense workers an income equal to 75 per cent of their previous salary for a year. A former defense worker working at another job at less than 75 per cent of his previous salary would receive adjustment assistance sufficient to bring his total salary to the guaranteed level.* Some lower-paid recipients would become eligible for cash-assistance grants (with the adjustment grants considered earned income). Workers receiving adjustment assistance would, of course, not be eligible for unemployment insurance.

Suitable employment for some workers might only be available in other cities or states. Therefore, *we also recommend that eligible workers be provided with a relocation allowance to give them the necessary mobility for seeking other jobs. The relocation allowance would cover moving expenses plus a "tiding-over" payment equal to two and one-half weeks of the worker's previous salary.* We estimate that total costs of such programs would be $1.6 billion in 1972 and $1.4 billion in 1973.

The defense-related unemployed should also be given preference in the proposed public-service employment program and manpower training programs. The unique component of the conversion-unemployed population will be scientists, engineers, and technicians whose skills are directly related to military needs and are no longer in great demand in the economy. The education and talents of these individuals constitute a valuable national resource. They should be directed toward new needs and problems. We can expect —and our budget would encourage—increased demand for engineering and design skills in mass transit, pollution control, and housing. *We propose that "conversion-fellowships" be made available to enable highly skilled people to return to school for retraining in whatever area they wish. Such a fellowship would pay full tuition for two years and would provide a $6,000 living allowance the second year* (the recipient would be receiving adjustment assistance the first year). *One hundred thousand of these fellowships would be made available over the next three years.*

The Special Problems of Veterans

Military dischargees, many of whom are unskilled, will also need better programs to aid their re-entry into civilian life. The number of dischargees is now about double that of pre-Vietnam years (about 1 million in 1970 compared to 550,000 yearly from 1963 to 1965). Approximately 840,000 and 580,000 servicemen will be discharged in 1972 and 1973 respectively under our recommended defense posture. Discharges would level off at 400,000 through 1974–76.

The unemployment rate of war veterans aged 20–29 was 6.5 per cent in March, 1970, a full percentage point above that of nonveterans of the same age. *Clearly, present programs of predischarge counseling and training for military personnel must be greatly improved and expanded. Counseling should be available to all, and training in civilian employment skills should be offered.* Costs for these programs would be $100 million in 1972, and $65 million in 1973. In 1971, the total cost for these programs was $14 million.

Veterans' education (G.I. Bill) participation rates are far below those experienced with World War II veterans. Approximately 15 per cent of Vietnam veterans are now enrolled in schools. We should attempt to increase participation to 20 per cent by 1974. Less than 10 per cent of military dischargees participate in veterans' on-the-job training programs—a figure that we expect to see increase to 15 per cent immediately and fall back to 10 per cent by 1974.

DISADVANTAGED AREAS

Some states and localities face localized depressions as large defense-related industries or military bases are closed or cut back. The Office of Economic Adjustment in the Department of Defense was set up in 1961 to provide planning and technical assistance for communities suffering the consequences of defense cutbacks of any kind. The Office has worked solely with communities affected by shutdowns of military bases and has assisted more than one hundred. The Economic Development Administration (EDA) also is authorized to assist communities where bases have closed, if unemployment exceeds the national average by 50 per cent. Assistance includes grants and loan guarantees for new or expanding commercial or industrial firms.

We recommend that a new Office of Economic Conversion be created to provide technical and planning assistance to commu-

nities affected by declines in defense-related spending or other government-induced conversion problems. The office would also coordinate (but not run) other governmental programs that can assist such communities. Primary among these would be EDA assistance programs, which should be made available to affected communities.

DISADVANTAGED FIRMS

A number of economic conversion schemes have proposed mechanisms to encourage defense firms to diversify or convert to civilian production. However, there is widespread doubt concerning the ability of major defense contractors to convert effectively. In many cases, top management is unfamiliar with the competitive world of the commercial marketplace; major defense concerns often have low capitalization, limited generalized marketing capacity, and insufficient experience in producing high-volume output at low unit cost. It is not surprising that there is a discouraging history of failure in commercial diversification efforts by defense firms. In this context, *there is no compelling reason to artificially protect defense firms from the healthy competition of the market, and we therefore recommend no special programs.* Those firms which are able to adapt will survive of their own accord.

Budget proposals for Economic Conversion are summarized in Table 3:2 on the following page.

TABLE 3:2
CONVERSION TO A PEACETIME ECONOMY
(Outlays, in millions of current dollars)

	Administration		Urban Coalition Recommendations				
	Estimated 1971	Proposed 1972	1972	1973	1974	1975	1976
Adjustment Assistance			1,347	1,228			
Relocation Assistance			212	199			
Conversion Fellowships			90	267	174	39	
Predischarge Counseling and Manpower Training	14	13	98	71	51	52	54
Veterans' On-the-Job Training[1]	164	203	197	141	67	70	73
TOTAL[2]	178	216	1,944	1,906	292	161	127

[1] Counted here rather than in the budget for employment and manpower training.
[2] Veterans' education outlays subsumed under education budget and not included in totals here.

4

Income Maintenance

The Urban Coalition Counterbudget is a budget for a growing, productive United States. The programs and policies we endorse or propose assume an economy providing a high level of employment and a government goal of a decent job at a decent wage for all Americans. These assumptions include an economic policy that ensures maximum utilization of our productive capacity and, consequently, high levels of growth and employment; a public-service employment program providing 1 million jobs by 1976; a minimum wage increasing to $2.50 by 1976, with coverage for more categories of employees; and short-term wage, price, and credit controls if necessary. Since we expect that most Americans will continue to rely on wages and salaries from employment for a high portion of their income, it is obvious that recommendations made in other chapters probably will affect most Americans more directly than will our specific proposals for social insurance and income support.

Yet all Americans are affected, if only indirectly, by the fact that some Americans do not receive an adequate share of the benefits of the economy even when it is operating at full capacity. For these Americans, wages from employment will not suffice. In 1969, nearly 24 million persons lived on incomes below the subsistence level as calculated by the Census Bureau—$3,743 for a family of four in 1969.* Projections suggest that in 1976, under present

---

* More than 45 million Americans currently have incomes below the Bureau of Labor Statistics poverty level, which represents the lowest standard of living consistent with well-being ($5,948 for a family of four).

income-maintenance programs, 21 million will still be below the poverty line.*

There is no need to justify federal efforts to eliminate poverty. That goal, clearly stated in the Economic Opportunity Act of 1965, has been incorporated to some degree in almost every activity of the federal government. Numerous government programs are designed to assist poor people to become independent wage earners; these range from training of individuals to programs to stimulate the economic growth of regions. From our projections above, it can be seen that we expect these efforts, in a growing economy, to have significant effects in reducing the number and percentage of Americans living in poverty. Nevertheless, there will remain, in 1976, the 21 million people unable to pay for basic needs, and additional millions lacking an acceptable standard of living even though they are able to sustain themselves.

The continued existence of poverty will have widespread consequences. Inadequate income not infrequently means inadequate health, housing, and education. In addition, society as a whole suffers both through loss of economic productivity (resulting in a lowered GNP) and through unrealized human potential.

The causes of inadequate income are many—inadequate employment opportunity in the economy, lack of skills, disability, old age, and family responsibilities. Income-maintenance programs to supplement income from productive employment must be designed to help people in widely divergent circumstances.

PRESENT SOCIAL INSURANCE AND INCOME SUPPORT

Present government programs for income maintenance provide both *in-kind assistance* (food stamps, housing subsidies, Medicare) and *cash assistance*. There are two basic ways the government supplies cash: through *social insurance,* such as Old Age, Survivors, and Disability Insurance (OASDI), commonly called "Social Security," and unemployment compensation, and through *income support,* such as Aid to Families with Dependent Children (AFDC)

---

* These estimates as well as cost estimates for most of the income-maintenance programs discussed in this chapter are derived from the "income-maintenance simulation model" of the Urban Institute.

and Old Age Assistance (OAA). *In general, we favor cash rather than in-kind assistance, since the recipient is provided with a greater degree of personal freedom and dignity in determining how to allocate his personal resources. However, in those cases where supply (particularly in housing and health care) does not readily expand to meet increased demand from low-income families, in-kind assistance must be continued, at least until the imbalance is corrected.*

Present social insurance programs are deficient in both the extent of coverage and benefit levels. The federal social security program, probably the soundest of all current income-maintenance programs, nonetheless does not provide adequate benefits for many recipients. Large numbers of workers are not covered by unemployment insurance; those who are covered receive an average of only 34 per cent of their previous weekly wage.

Present income-support programs, particularly Aid to Families with Dependent Children, have been widely criticized by nearly all elements of American society. The AFDC defects include the following:

- Benefit levels vary widely from state to state and are insufficient almost everywhere.
- The program is structured in many states to encourage family break-ups.
- The program affords recipients little incentive to work.

Both kinds of programs must be expanded to provide every household an adequate income. Greatly improved social insurance programs must be devised for Americans who, through age, disability, or involuntary unemployment, no longer earn income. In addition, new and effective programs of income support are needed for those whose income is inadequate. As a consequence of our recommendations for these programs, poverty, as officially defined, will be eliminated in the United States by 1975.

Social insurance and income-support programs are intricately joined pieces of a national income maintenance policy. The objective is to design programs that will fit the needs of people in a variety of situations and can be administered efficiently. The most

50   HUMAN DEVELOPMENT

dramatic changes we suggest from present programs for most families are in the area of income support.

INCOME-SUPPORT ALTERNATIVES*

Alternative income-support plans that have been suggested to replace present public assistance to households include: (1) reforms in the current AFDC system; (2) institution of a child allowance; (3) a wage-subsidy approach; and (4) institution of a cash-assistance program similar to President Nixon's proposed family-assistance plan (FAP).

The first alternative cannot even be considered since the present AFDC program is demeaning in fact and concept. Piecemeal reforms will not suffice. The President's Commission on Income Maintenance (the Heineman Commission) in 1969 termed the system "untenable."

Child allowances would provide monthly payments of an equal amount per child to *all* families with children. Since every family would receive an equal amount per child, it is argued that there would be no stigma attached to receiving the assistance. However, since allowances would not vary with family income, such a program would tend to redistribute income from single people to families and from small to large families but not between income groups. As a result, allowances would be paid to many families not in need. Although a part of these payments could be recouped through income taxation, the cost of even a moderate allowance would be high and still leave many families in poverty. The Social Security Administration has calculated that a plan providing $600 yearly per child would have a gross cost of $43 billion and a net cost of $28 billion after taxes (assuming present income tax exemptions for children were eliminated).

Wage-subsidy proposals would provide a government subsidy to make up the difference between an employee's wage and a standard set by the federal government. Such an approach seems to be based on the false assumption that most present recipients of public assistance are employable and can be "moved off welfare" into private employment. Unfortunately, the vast majority of present public-assistance recipients are aged, blind, disabled, or women with

---

* Other than support to the elderly and disabled, discussed on pp. 60 ff.

young children. Wage-subsidy proposals also suffer from two significant difficulties. First, they act as a subsidy to the employer, who can keep wages low while knowing that the government will contribute up to the standard level. Secondly, since wages are not tied to family size, a wage-subsidy program would not be a very effective income-support device for large families.

We therefore recommend that the present welfare system be replaced by a cash-assistance grant (CAG) program similar in mechanism to the Nixon Administration's family-assistance program (FAP), providing for a cash allowance based on family size, but reduced by an established percentage (for example, 50 per cent, or 50 cents) for each one dollar earned. To elucidate:

- suppose the annual *cash-assistance level* for a family of four is set at $3,500;
- suppose a particular family earns $2,000;
- then, 50 per cent of each dollar earned, or $1,000, would be subtracted from the total of the cash-assistance grant ($3,500);
- leaving a cash-assistance grant of $2,500; and
- making a total family income of $2,000 earned + $2,500 cash assistance, or $4,500.

Cash-Assistance Grants: Variables and Advantages

The major policy variables involved in devising a workable CAG program are:

- *coverage*—that is, number and kinds of households eligible for receiving the cash grants;
- *the size of the basic cash allowance*—that is, the amount of cash assistance a household with no other income would receive (the basic cash allowance varies with family size);
- the percentage, called the *offset tax rate,* applied to each dollar of earned income in order to reduce the size of the basic cash allowance.

Let us look closely at each of these critical policy choices.

1. *Coverage:* The Nixon Administration proposal would cover only families with children, thereby excluding single individuals and childless couples, including most of the aged. Single individuals and the aged have particularly high rates of poverty. The President's Commission on Income Maintenance has suggested univer-

sal coverage. However, the wider the coverage, the greater the total program costs will be.

We recommend that households with children and households with heads under 65 be covered by the cash-assistance grant program; childless households headed by the elderly should be dealt with separately because of their special needs.

2. *The size of the cash allowance.* The Nixon Administration's original proposal would have given $500 each for the first two family members and $300 for each additional member—$1,600 for a family of four. The President's Commission on Income Maintenance proposed an allowance of $2,400. Some groups have called for a goal of an allowance equal to the poverty line, while the National Welfare Rights Organization wants an allowance of $5,500, loosely pegged to the Bureau of Labor Statistics (BLS) low-income standard-of-living budget. The higher the level of the cash allowance, the higher the total program costs will be.

What is an adequate level for a cash allowance? As a goal, it is completely inconsistent to advocate a level below "the poverty level." The official Census Bureau poverty level ($3,743 for a family of four in calendar year 1969) was established as the income level below which a family becomes dependent upon a variety of social programs to survive. It is just such a condition of dependency that income maintenance is designed to eliminate.

Repeatedly, moreover, the official poverty level has been criticized as inadequate. It is constructed from a Department of Agriculture economy food plan designed for "emergency or temporary use when funds are low." For households of three or more, the poverty line is three times the cost of the 1963 economy food plan, adjusted for cost-of-living increases. Mollie Orshansky, of the Social Security Administration, who devised the line, terms it, "The lowest amount of income which would make possible a level of living conforming to minimally acceptable American consumption standards."

Is the poverty line inadequate? In an interview, Miss Orshansky commented that "Whatever the rationale for the poverty line, it should be relative over time. The line should be adjusted periodically to take into account the rising *real* standard of living enjoyed by the majority of Americans. However, the official poverty line

Cash-Assistance Grants in 1976
For Families of Four With Different Levels of Income

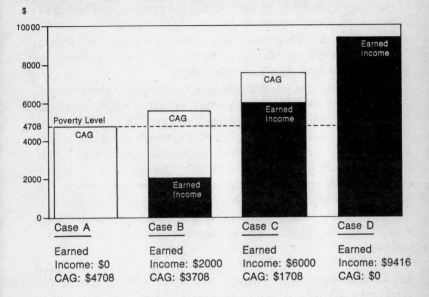

$

	Case A	Case B	Case C	Case D
Earned Income:	$0	$2000	$6000	$9416
CAG:	$4708	$3708	$1708	$0

($3,743 in 1969) has not been so adjusted." She suggested that by 1976 the poverty level should be adjusted upward 25 per cent (from $4,708 to $5,898 for a family of four in 1976). Concurring with her reasoning, we will use a figure 25 per cent above the present poverty line to represent the *target* poverty-level basic cash allowance for our cash-assistance grant program.

Unfortunately, a basic cash allowance equaling such a target poverty level by 1976* would involve an inordinate cost—$51.6 billion, assuming we used a 50 per cent offset rate. Instead, *we recommend a basic cash allowance that approaches the target poverty level by increments.* By 1976, the allowance would reach the Census Bureau poverty level as now defined (for that year, $4,708 for a family of four); by 1980, it would, we hope, have reached the full target poverty level for that year. Total costs for the CAG program in 1976 would be $28 billion.

* Years are federal fiscal years unless otherwise indicated.

3. *The Offset Rate.* The third policy consideration, the offset rate, is of importance because it helps determine both the total cost of the program and the degree to which the program will impair the incentive to work. Lower offset rates strengthen the incentive to work but, at the same time, raise the total cost of the program because the lower the offset rate, the more income a recipient can earn before his cash allowance disappears.

Work incentives—as distinguished from work requirements—are a relevant consideration in every nonslave society. Rational human beings will work only when they perceive that it is worth their while to do so. Thus, many people would not work if they knew that for each dollar they made, the government would immediately tax away 75 per cent of it. This is particularly true if they are guaranteed a minimum level of income sufficient to meet basic needs whether they work or not. Alternatives to providing work incentives are either instituting a restrictive work requirement or leaving many necessary jobs in the economy unfilled.

If the offset rate is high, the work incentive is weakened. Using our CAG program as an example, in 1976 a family of four would receive $4,708. If the offset tax were as high as 75 per cent, a family head working full time and earning $5,000 would lose all but $1,000 of his cash assistance; his total income (before taxes) would be about $5,900, an increase of only $1,200 for a year's full-time work.

An infinite number of choices exist for setting the CAG offset rate. The most attractive options include: (1) a constant offset rate on gross income (50 per cent is the figure most frequently mentioned); (2) a constant offset rate applied to income net of taxes and net of loss of benefits from in-kind programs (housing subsidies, food stamps, day care), which cut off at certain income levels; and (3) a progressive offset rate on income (gross or net), increasing as income rises.

A progressive offset rate would be a helpful compromise between work incentives and program costs. The operation of one possible set of progressive offset rates, in terms of earnings and total income based on the 1976 cash-assistance level of $4,708 for a family of four, is shown on the next page.

Earnings	Offset Rates	
$0-3,000	35 per cent of income	
Over $3,000	$1,050 + 50 per cent of income above $3,000	

Earnings	Cash-Assistance Allowance	Total Income
$0	$4,708	$4,708
1,000	4,358	5,358
2,000	4,008	6,008
3,000	3,658	6,658
4,000	3,158	7,158
5,000	2,658	7,658
6,000	2,158	8,158
7,000	1,658	8,658
8,000	1,158	9,158
9,000	658	9,658
10,000	158	10,158
10,316	0	10,316

Low offset rates at low levels of earned income would make low-income jobs still relatively attractive since the worker would be able to keep most of his earnings. Under the scheme above, a worker earning $4,000 would have a total income of $7,158 or $2,450 over what he would have ($4,708) had he not worked at all. A higher offset rate for moderate levels of earning would keep costs down and not be too much of a work disincentive since the alternative—not working—would greatly reduce total income. Thus, a worker earning $6,000 would only be able to keep $500 of his next $1,000 of income; his total income would be $8,158. However, should he decide not to work at all, his total income would fall from $8,158 to $4,708—almost certainly enough to keep him working.

Unfortunately, this set of progressive offset rates combined with our basic cash allowance of $4,708 in 1976 would make the program quite expensive—more than $36 billion in 1976.

We are left to consider a flat offset rate of 50 per cent on earned income—a figure recommended both by the Heineman Commission and President Nixon in his 1970 and 1971 legislative proposals for a family-assistance program. The figure is a reasonable trade-off between work disincentives and total program cost. Assuming a basic allowance of $4,708 for a family of four and an offset rate of 50 per cent on earned income, a worker earning

$6,000 would have a total income of $7,708, whereas, if he had no income from employment, he would receive $4,708. The difference between working and not working, therefore, amounts to $3,000—or an increase in income of more than 60 per cent. This differential probably would not provide very much of a work disincentive.* The effects of a 50 per cent offset rate for a program with a basic cash allowance of $4,708 for a family of four would be as follows:

Earnings	Earnings All Cash-Assistance Payment	Offset Rate 50 per cent of Income Total Income
$ 0	$4,708	$4,708
1,000	4,208	5,208
2,000	3,708	5,708
3,000	3,208	6,208
4,000	2,708	6,708
5,000	2,208	7,208
6,000	1,708	7,708
7,000	1,208	8,208
8,000	708	8,708
9,000	208	9,208
9,416	0	9,416

The degree of work disincentive associated with the cash-assistance program is not solely determined by the offset rate. The provisions of other programs and laws (food stamps, housing subsidies, day care, state, local and federal taxes) also diminish the take-home value of an additional dollar earned, since the subsidies decrease as income increases. For this reason, we must look at the cumulative impact (the cumulative marginal tax rate on earned income) and attempt to relate the CAG program to other programs in such a way as to diminish the work disincentives.

One technique designed to reduce the cumulative marginal tax rates is to calculate some of the marginal taxes on individual programs on the basis of a dollar already reduced by other marginal

* Since work disincentives are not a consideration with income not obtained from employment, we recommend higher offset rates on such income—60 per cent on the first $3,000, 75 per cent on nonearned income between $3,000 and $5,000 and 100 per cent on any nonearned income over $5,000.

taxes. Thus, the CAG offset tax rate on earned income could be applied to net (after-tax) income rather than gross income.*

We recommend a system in which the CAG offset rate (50 per cent) *is calculated on earnings minus the amount lost through added housing and day-care payments; federal, state, and local income taxes; and the social security payroll tax.* Total costs for our program (with a basic cash allowance of $4,708) would be $28 billion in 1976.

In summary, our initial program would be very similar to the Nixon Administration's proposal. We would begin in 1972 with a basic allowance of $2,400 for a family of four and would cover only families with children. (States presently having higher public-assistance payments would be required to supplement the federal effort to that level. The federal government would provide 30 per cent of this supplement.) In 1973, the CAG program should expand to cover all households headed by persons under 65 or elderly persons with children. The basic allowance would also increase in stages until it reached the Census Bureau poverty level in 1975. The allowance would climb to 25 per cent above the poverty level by 1980.

Cash-Assistance Grants: Administration

The CAG program should be completely administered by the federal government, with a minimum of regulation and investigation. The model should be the income tax system rather than the present welfare system.

We have tried to ensure that the recommended program will not destroy incentives to work. The Nixon Administration's proposal went a step further and *required* employment or the seeking of employment by the able-bodied head of a family as a requirement for receiving assistance; if the recipient refused to work, his or her share of the family's cash assistance would have been cut off. The

---

* For example, instead of applying a 50 per cent offset tax rate to the next dollar earned by a family earning $4,000, the rate could be applied to that dollar minus 20 cents paid in federal income and social security tax. The CAG offset tax under this system (equal to 50 per cent of income after taxes, which in our example is 80 cents) would be 40 cents rather than $.50.

Nixon proposal did, however, specifically exempt women with pre-school children. The Heineman Commission suggested no work requirement.

We foresee no possibility of recipients choosing not to work in numbers large enough to affect either the cost of the program or the manpower supply of the nation. However, it is easy to imagine the demoralizing effect of even a few obviously able workers supported in idleness by taxpayers, particularly in times of rising taxes.

Thus, we recommend that administrators of the CAG be provided with reasonable means of dealing with possible problems caused by work disincentives: Unemployed recipients of working age (with the exception of women with children under 16) would be required to register with the U.S. Employment Service and would be expected to accept a decent job offer (not paying below the minimum wage) or, if lacking skills, to enroll in training to prepare for employment.

If a person refuses reasonable opportunities for employment or training, that part of the cash-assistance grant attributable to his or her presence in the family would be terminated. Needless to say, such a sanction will require sophisticated safeguards to assure that recipients are not subject to administrative prejudice. It is equally important that the procedures be fully spelled out and relatively automatic so that "enforcement" does not become an absorbing concern of program administrators.

SOCIAL INSURANCE: *
UNEMPLOYMENT INSURANCE ALTERNATIVES

Unemployment insurance is designed to provide cash benefits to regularly employed workers during limited periods of involuntary unemployment. Since it is an insurance program, benefits are based primarily upon previous wage levels rather than current income needs. Most states provide benefits for a maximum of twenty-six weeks, although during times of high unemployment, the period has been expanded temporarily to thirty-nine weeks.

There are several major shortcomings in the existing unemployment compensation program:

* Other than OASDI.

1. *Limited coverage.* As of 1969, over 57 million workers were protected by unemployment insurance, but 13 million (18 per cent) were not. By 1973, 1970 legislation will extend coverage to approximately 4.75 million additional workers in small firms, non-profit organizations, and state hospitals and institutions of higher learning. Farm workers, domestic workers, and most state and local government employees will remain uncovered. In 1968, 64 per cent of those persons unemployed during the year were, for one reason or another, ineligible to receive unemployment insurance benefits.

2. *Variations between states in benefit payments.* Benefit levels are set by individual states and consequently vary widely. The weekly benefit amount is a set fraction of the claimant's previous quarterly or weekly wage up to a maximum amount. Both the set fraction and the maximum vary by state. The maximum benefit ranges from 31 per cent of the average weekly wage of covered workers in Alaska, Michigan, and Washington to 61 per cent of the average weekly wage of covered workers in Hawaii. Benefits, as of May, 1970, averaged $49.30 per week, but state averages varied from $33.57 per week in West Virginia to $58.63 per week in Connecticut.

3. *Inadequate insurance benefits.* At least 40 per cent of claimants fail to get benefits equal to half of their weekly wage. The major reason is that maximum benefits in most states have continually fallen as a percentage of average weekly wage. Currently, more than half of all claimants are eligible for the maximum benefits. Repeated urgings to states by the President and Congress to increase benefits have so far been ignored. The goal, set first by President Dwight D. Eisenhower in 1954, that 80 per cent of covered workers receive, if unemployed, a benefit of one-half their regular wage, has not been approached.

4. *Inadequate duration of benefits.* Approximately 20–25 per cent of all workers who receive benefits have not found employment when their benefits end. This figure rises to 33 per cent during recessionary periods. The 1970 Employment Security Act included a provision to extend unemployment benefits an additional 13 weeks whenever national unemployment rates exceed 4.5 per cent for three consecutive months.

Clearly, changes are called for. *We recommend that unemployment insurance coverage be extended to farm workers and domestic workers. In addition, the federal government should establish a minimum federal benefit standard of 50 per cent of the worker's weekly wage loss, up to a maximum of $6,000 per year.* By this standard, average weekly benefits would increase from about $50 currently to $113 in 1976. The federal government should also require that no state have a maximum benefit of less than one year. The increases in outlays necessitated by these changes can be covered by raising the payroll tax base from its present level of $2,800 to $6,000.

Further, the federal government should drop the provision that allows states to vary their unemployment insurance tax according to "experience ratings." The desire to achieve lower state unemployment insurance tax rates provides an incentive to deny benefits to as many unemployed persons as possible. *We recommend that the federal government give states the option of either imposing on employers a 2.4 per cent (2.0 per cent after 1974) payroll tax on the $6,000 wage base, or not adopting the tax and having employers in the state pay a 2.7 per cent tax directly to the federal government.* Under either alternative, 0.4 per cent of the tax would go to support a federally administered U.S. Employment Service; the remainder would be more than sufficient to cover projected outlays for unemployment insurance benefits.

INCOME MAINTENANCE FOR THE ELDERLY

More than 25 per cent of Americans who have passed the age of 65 are now living in poverty. This rate is more than twice that of the entire population. To achieve our goal of ensuring that all elderly persons have at least a poverty level income by 1975, improvements and revisions are necessary in both Old Age, Survivors, and Disability Insurance (OASDI) and Old Age Assistance (OAA).

Social Insurance

"Social Security" has been and will continue to be the cornerstone of the present income maintenance system for the aged. The

OASDI program was constructed and has been since supported as a social insurance system. When an insured worker or his spouse reaches the eligible retirement age, benefits are paid to him in relation to his earlier payroll contributions. However, benefit payment patterns deviate from strict insurance concepts in several respects: (1) those who earned a relatively low income during their employment years receive a higher percentage of total benefits than their percentage of total contributions; (2) benefits are not financed solely from the total contributed by present recipients when they were employed, but also out of the contributions of present-day workers; and (3) benefits are reduced by some percentage of any income currently earned by recipients. In short, Old Age, Survivors, and Disability Insurance has taken on some aspects of income-support programs while continuing to operate as an insurance program.

The conflict between income-support and income-insurance objectives within the OASDI program suggests two different paths that might be followed: (1) return OASDI to a strict insurance program—something that could only be accomplished after either (a) an adequate cash-assistance grant program covering the elderly were enacted, or (b) OAA were expanded enough to ensure the elderly poor a decent income; or (2) maintain OASDI as a mixed-income, insurance-income support program and improve the program's benefit levels and eligibility requirements.

Accepting the second alternative, *we recommend several changes in the provisions of the Social Security Act, as amended. First, we recommend that the minimum benefit be raised from its present level of $64 per month ($96 per couple) to $100 per month ($150 per couple)*. This would guarantee all single beneficiaries a total of at least $1,200 yearly and would go far to reduce poverty among the elderly. *We also recommend that all OASDI benefits be increased 5 per cent immediately, an additional 5 per cent in 1973, and an additional 10 per cent in 1976.* These recommended increases should be in addition to automatic benefit increases as the cost of living (as shown by the Bureau of Labor Statistics' Consumer Price Index) increases.

To finance these benefit increases, changes will have to be made in the OASDI payroll tax. First, however, if we are going to maintain and improve the income-support aspects of our social security laws, we must diminish the regressive effect of the tax.

The payroll tax as of 1970, based on a flat rate on the first $7,800 of income, is an inequitable manner of financing what is, at least partially, an income-redistribution program. *We recommend that the OASDI wage base be increased immediately to $15,000 and be again raised to $16,000 in 1974, and to $17,000 in 1976.* The OASDI employee tax could then be decreased from its current 4.8 per cent level to 3.2 per cent in 1972, raising to 3.8 per cent in 1973, 3.9 per cent in 1974, 4.1 per cent in 1975, and 4.5 per cent thereafter. During 1972 and 1973, an additional 0.8 per cent payroll tax would cover the planned hospital insurance portion of Old Age, Survivors, Disability, and Hospital Insurance (OASDIHI). This tax will disappear when national health insurance goes into effect in 1974. The regular OASDI benefits, which totaled $36.0 billion in 1971, would then total $66.2 billion in 1976.* Contributions to the OASDI trust fund would total $60.6 billion in 1976.

Income Support: Old Age Assistance

In order to assure that every elderly person lives in a household with at least a poverty-level income, the income-support program for the elderly must also be greatly improved. *We recommend that federal benefit standards for Old Age Assistance (OAA) should be set so that by 1976 all single recipients will be guaranteed an allowance of $175 monthly ($240 for couples)*—the poverty-level income. These payments would be reduced 50 cents for every dollar of income earned and one dollar for every dollar of OASDI received. The program should be completely federally administered and, by 1974, all program costs should be borne by the federal government. Total OAA outlays under such a program would rise to $7.1 billion in 1976.

INCOME MAINTENANCE FOR THE DISABLED

The recommendations made above for the old-age (retirement) portion of OASDI should also apply to the survivor and disability

* Including railroad retirement.

portions. Other income-support programs for the disabled—Aid to the Blind (AB) and Aid to the Permanently and Temporarily Disabled (APTD)—must also be improved. A minimum benefit level of $110 per month should be instituted in 1972, at which time the federal government should assume full responsibility for administering these programs. Recipients of AB and APTD benefits also should be eligible to receive CAG or OAA help as well; their AB or APTD benefits would count as unearned income, reducing their CAG or OAA payments.

Veterans with service-connected disabilities and survivors of servicemen killed in service are eligible for veterans compensation. Outlays are expected to increase from $3.3 billion to $3.8 billion in 1976 as a result of Vietnam War deaths and disabilities and a newly enacted 10 per cent increase in benefits.

The veterans' pension program also acts as an income-support program, primarily for the elderly. Essentially, veteran's pensions are public-assistance payments made available to veterans as a reward for military service during periods of war. Veterans with a nonservice-connected incapacitating disability and with income below $1,800 ($3,000 with dependents) are eligible. However, veterans over sixty-five are automatically considered 90 per cent disabled for purposes of the program. Since the revisions recommended above in Old Age Assistance will provide elderly veterans with equivalent benefits, we see no need for this program to continue. *Accordingly, we recommend that veterans' pension payments be reduced $1 for every $1 of CAG or OAA benefits received.* Ultimately, this reduction will eliminate the veterans' pension program. By 1976, outlays will have fallen to $400 million from their present level of nearly $2.4 billion.

In-Kind Services

Food Stamps

The fact that millions of Americans are inadequately fed and suffer from various stages of malnutrition has been amply documented. According to a Department of Agriculture study, only 37 per cent of families with incomes under $3,000 maintain good diets. The Citizens Board of Inquiry into Hunger and Malnutrition in the United States in its April, 1968, report, *Hunger, USA,* estimated the number of Americans suffering from malnutrition at more than 10 million. Plainly, malnutrition is a major factor retarding the intellectual development of children, a primary cause of ill health, and a not unimportant contributor to lower productivity rates of workers.

The U.S. Department of Agriculture (USDA) food stamp program, the major "in-kind aid" federal food program, is quite inadequate. Food stamps are sold to families who may use them to purchase foods of greater value than the cost of the stamps. In calendar year 1970, over 6 million people participated in the food stamp program.

Another in-kind service, the USDA Commodity Distribution Program, distributes farm surpluses of certain nonperishable foods in order to supplement the diet of poor families. These commodities currently reach about 3 million people.

Participation in the two food programs has fallen far short of the total number in need and, indeed, of the total number eligible. In 1969, the Senate Select Committee on Nutrition and Human Needs reported that the two programs together serve only 44 per cent of those Americans so poor that they must have assistance if they are to escape malnutrition, and only 26 per cent of the 24 million Americans whose income falls below the official poverty line.

Neither program is designed to assure a participating household an adequate diet. Both are administered under local welfare requirements and, therefore, exclude many of the poor. The exclusions, plus the reluctance or inability of many persons to buy food stamps, account for the low rate of participation.

The cash-assistance grant program we have recommended would ultimately make both of the above in-kind aid programs unnecessary. People would have enough money to buy food. *Our immediate recommendation, however, is a temporarily expanded food stamp program covering all poor families.* Such a program could quickly eliminate hunger in the United States. This goal is both well within our reach and not inordinately costly.

Specifically, we recommend that, in 1972, every family of four be eligible for $1,200 worth of food stamps, to be reduced by 25 cents for every dollar of annual income above $840. (The cash-assistance grant would be counted as income). Recipients would not have to buy food stamps as they must in the present program; the stamps would be provided free. Since the basic CAG allowance would increase to the poverty level by 1975, the use of food stamps would gradually diminish. Total outlays for the food stamp program would rise from their 1971 level of $1.5 billion to $4.2 billion in 1972; by 1976, outlays would fall back to $680 million.

An alternative would be to provide a lower basic CAG allowance and to maintain indefinitely a separate food stamp program. We do not recommend this alternative because of our preference for cash rather than in-kind assistance. *However, since the health and well-being of children is a social concern, we recommend continued assistance in child nutrition. Our proposal is that the school lunch program be expanded and a new school breakfast program be instituted, thus ensuring school children at least one, and, in some cases, two well-balanced meals every school day.*

Social Services

The adoption of several proposals we suggest in the manpower, health, and education areas (see chapters 2, 5, and 6) would move many social services (like manpower counseling, family planning, and day care) from public assistance to new administrative settings. In addition, the institution of an effective income-maintenance program such as the cash-assistance grant would eliminate the investigative and eligibility-determination functions long performed by social workers associated with Aid to Families with Dependent Children.

Thus, the implementation of the CAG program can be expected to displace some of the estimated 85,000 present social workers in agencies largely supported by public-assistance funds. Many social workers would undoubtedly follow a professional speciality like day care to its new administrative domain. Others would continue casework related to other programs. *There should, however, be a major new effort to extend to all who need them the social services available in a community. We recommend the institution of a federally funded outreach program, building on several existing demonstration models.* Social workers would inform citizens about social services and, in addition, be advocates for their clients in dealings with various service bureaucracies in the community. The outreach program would be run from neighborhood service centers wherever they exist. The centers would house many of the available community services under one roof (see Chapter 8).

The outreach program could be financed by 75 per cent federal matching grants for operating costs to state and local public welfare agencies. Federal funds should also be made available to retrain present social workers who wish to participate in the outreach program. We estimate that a program gradually increasing to involve 25,000 outreach workers by 1976 would cost approximately $250 million by that year.

Major new federal initiatives are also needed in child welfare and services for the aging, as is a substantial increase in funds for child welfare programs. Locating children in adopted or foster families, group homes, or institutions are worthwhile services that more than pay their way in lessened institutional expenses and remedial programs later on. President Nixon in 1971 recommended a massive increase of federal funds for these programs as well as establishment of minimum national standards. We recommend that his proposals be accepted. We also recommend a major new program of adoption subsidies to encourage the adoption of hard-to-place children (see Chapter 12).

Budget proposals for Income Maintenance are summarized in Table 4:1 on the following page.

TABLE 4:1
INCOME MAINTENANCE[1]
(Outlays, in millions of current dollars)

	Administration			Urban Coalition Recommendations			
	Estimated 1971	Proposed 1972	1972	1973	1974	1975	1976
Social Insurance							
OASDI[2]	35,980	39,498	41,310	47,064	51,196	55,711	66,187
Unemployment Insurance[3]	5,439	4,586	8,369	6,756	7,628	7,928	8,546
Veterans' Compensation	3,323	3,582	3,582	3,640	3,670	3,730	3,760
Federal Retirement and Disability	2,923	3,266	3,266	3,628	4,005	4,385	4,775
Subtotal	47,665	50,932	56,527	61,088	66,499	71,754	83,268
Income Support							
Cash Assistance:							
Cash-Assistance Grant (CAG)		502	7,015	6,966	17,962	27,258	28,030
State Supplement			898	943	170	131	124
Old Age Assistance (OAA)	1,509	1,666	3,874	4,533	7,280	7,050	7,140
Aid to the Blind (AB)	60	62	103	121	146	134	150
Aid to the Disabled (APTD)	662	797	1,470	1,720	1,789	1,778	1,857
Veterans' Pensions	2,392	2,526	912	937	604	515	400
AFDC	3,002	3,719	-	-	-	-	-
In-Kind Assistance:							
Social Services	892	1,144	750	754	738	743	797
Food Stamps	1,490	1,941	4,154	3,682	1,922	938	680
Commodity Distribution	487	527	110				
School Lunch and Breakfast	673	667	641	666	691	718	746
Other	133	36	34	35	36	37	38
Subtotal	11,300	13,587	19,961	20,357	31,338	39,302	39,962
TOTAL	58,965	64,519	76,488	81,445	97,837	111,056	123,230

[1] Cost estimates for OASDI, CAG, OAA, AB, APTD, state supplement, veterans' pensions, and food stamps were derived through the Urban Institute's computer simulation model.
[2] Includes railroad retirement.
[3] Excludes conversion-assistance payments in 1972 and 1973.

5

Health

American health care presents a major paradox. No other nation provides better training for its doctors. Some U.S. citizens enjoy a quality of health care unsurpassed anywhere in the world. American hospitals particularly excel at providing crisis care for some serious illnesses; modern facilities and superbly capable technicians combine to keep alive patients who would die in any other setting. For the health practitioner, the U.S. health system provides the best working conditions and income in the world.

Yet, by clear statistical measures, the health care provided to American citizens is inferior. We rank thirteenth among industrial nations in infant mortality, seventh in maternal mortality, eighteenth for men and eleventh for women in life expectancy. Special geographical and cultural patterns may prevent the United States from ever ranking first in these and other health care indices. But what is alarming is that we were performing relatively better a decade ago and have been steadily falling back since.

A significant part of the responsibility for the current state of American health care rests with the most important person in diagnosis, prescription, and treatment—the American patient. The best way to improve our health is for us to take care of ourselves, but we don't or won't. This is partly because we receive inadequate health education. Worse, although we claim concern for our health, we hardly show it by our diets, our drinking and smoking habits, or our speeds on the highways. If these habits don't improve, the degree of improvement possible in American health care must remain limited. However, the current failures of health care extend far beyond personal health-care habits.

We receive a poor return from our investment in professional health services. Our annual per capita expenditure of $305 on personal health services is the highest of any nation. Yet, serious illness is synonymous with financial disaster for most Americans. Private insurance covers only 35 per cent of total health-care needs for Americans under age 65. An estimated 35–45 million people with incomes below or near the Census Bureau's poverty standard cannot pay for adequate medical care. When such families must have care, it is frequently of low quality provided under demeaning conditions. Higher-income families receive episodic care, often lavishly provided. Middle-class Americans as well as the poor are often defeated by the size and disorganization of the health-care institutions that purport to serve them.

The availability of health care to Americans is also seriously unbalanced. Many people, particularly those in inner-city and rural areas, lack the point of entry into the system—the family doctor.

SOURCES OF THE PROBLEM AND OBJECTIVES FOR CHANGE

In seeking the roots of these inadequacies, we tend to assign blame to one who personifies the health system to most of us— the doctor—much in the way the policeman personifies the entire law enforcement and criminal justice system. In both cases, we oversimplify greatly. The medical profession shares heavily in the responsibility for our current health situation, but not because of any lack of compassion, concern, or professional excellence of doctors as individuals.

The inefficiencies and decay causing our monumental problems rest in the entire health-care system—or, more accurately, nonsystem—of which doctors constitute only one important part. These problems generally can be summarized under four headings:

- an absence of national health policies out of which goals, objectives, and strategies can emerge;
- a shortage of manpower, equipment, and facilities;
- an uneven distribution of services; and
- spiraling medical costs that do not result in increased services.

Many institutions share responsibilty for creating these problems and allowing them to grow.

Private insurance carriers have failed to stimulate the organization of efficient health care—something they have the financial muscle to do through bargaining with providers of care or through simply broadening insurance coverage to encompass a wider range of services. Currently, most private health insurance plans artificially increase that proportion of care which is provided in expensive hospital settings and discourage less expensive ambulatory and preventive care.

Hospitals and medical schools have generally failed to work diligently to improve their efficiency. Medical societies and professional organizations have frequently limited access to health professions and limited advancement by people employed in health occupations.

The federal government's attempts to intervene—mainly Medicare and Medicaid—have proved by one measure counterproductive: they have inflated costs along the same perverse patterns as private insurance plans (that is, by pumping more funds into payments for medical services, particularly those provided in hospitals, without any compensating increase in the supply of providers of care) while failing to be the lever they could have been to bring about a balanced pattern of care. These programs also discriminate against the mentally ill in a variety of ways. (We will have more to say later about special assistance for the mentally ill and mentally retarded.)

Medicare and Medicaid provide the federal government with nearly as much purchasing power as all private health-insurers combined. Thus, the federal government is by far the most powerful and potentially the most sophisticated purchaser in the health field. If the government made effective use of its power as a purchaser, it could easily stimulate the health system to greater responsiveness.

Federal leadership must concern itself with "governing" the health-care system: building on the marvelous technology and skill that now exist a system to improve the health of all. Two fundamental objectives should guide our efforts at improving the health-care system during the next five years: (1) we must rectify the shortage of health manpower and facilities and create a resource-distribution pattern that ensures access to care for all; and (2) we must provide the financial means, and the incentives, for more efficient organization and utilization of these resources to make real the goal of comprehensive medical care for all U.S. citizens. One objective voiced without the other is an empty promise.

SUPPLY AND DISTRIBUTION OF HEALTH RESOURCES

Numbers and distribution of health personnel and facilities are of greater importance than financing schemes in determining the number of people who can receive health services and the quality of the services they receive.

Manpower

The more pressing supply need is for manpower. There is not enough trained health manpower to care for all Americans. The poor suffer most because health practitioners are generally less willing to practice in inner-city or rural areas, but everyone suffers the consequence—even if only through higher costs paid for health services.

The most urgent manpower requirement is for more paramedical personnel and nurses. Both can extend the reach of physicians by taking over some of the initial patient contact responsibilities. Although current government efforts support training of 85,000 paramedical personnel yearly, the U.S. health system could productively absorb trained personnel at nearly three times that rate; the training pace should be stepped up accordingly. Particular stress should be given to physicians' assistants, dental assistants (particularly dental technicians), mental health workers, and neighborhood health aides. As a critical prerequisite to such expanded training assistance, a companion effort must be made to overcome both physicians' and patients' resistance to treatment involving para-medical personnel.

The supply of nurses can be increased both through expanded training programs and through special efforts to recruit back some of the 550,000 qualified nurses who have dropped out of the labor force. Imaginative programs offering nurses opportunities for upgrading to positions of nurse clinician and pediatric assistant could serve both to fill pressing needs and to provide a powerful attraction in such a recruiting campaign.

Because of the long lead-time required for training, it is already too late to take actions now that will have much effect on the supply of doctors (including psychiatrists) and dentists during the next five years. But we must prepare now for more distant needs. The Carnegie Commission on Higher Education projects a need for expanding medical and dental school enrollment during the 1970's by, respectively, 50 per cent and 20 per cent. Many of these new places should be filled by women and members of minority groups. Currently, only 8 per cent of all medical students are women; only 2 per cent are black, even fewer are Spanish-speaking citizens.

These expansion goals could be attained through a combination of three measures advocated by the Commission: (1) shortening the curriculum from four to three years for an M.D. or D.D.S. degree; (2) expanding enrollment at existing schools an average of 10 per cent; and (3) founding ten new medical schools above and beyond the twenty-seven new ones being started. The new schools should be geographically located in areas now underserved. Medical schools and the university health science centers of which they are a part should assume broader roles in continuing education, training of other health-care personnel, and advising on improved ways to provide health throughout their regions.

Increased federal financial support, primarily in the form of cost-of-instruction supplements given directly to educational institutions, will be essential if medical and dental schools are to survive and shoulder these expanded responsibilities.

Altogether, we recommend that federal support for health manpower development should increase by 80 per cent during the next five years, increasing from its present level of $931 million to $1.7 billion by 1976. Nearly half of this total would be directed to the training of doctors and dentists.*

Construction

Not as critical a requirement to the improvement of health care as increased manpower, but still important, is a continuing program of federal assistance for the construction, purchase, and re-

* Years are federal fiscal years unless otherwise indicated.

modeling of health facilities. The Nixon Administration quite soundly has recognized that the Hill-Burton program has well served its original primary purpose of relieving hospital bed shortages. A much higher proportion of future federal hospital-facilities aid should be in the form of loan guarantees and interest subsidies.

There remains, however, a major need for renovation of existing hospitals and outpatient facilities and for additional new long-term and ambulatory care facilities, including those designed for the aged, mentally ill, and mentally retarded. *The largest dollar requirement will be for ambulatory care facilities serving widely diversified purposes*—from mobile dental clinics to nursing offices in public housing for the aged, as well as conventional multipurpose medical clinics. *We recommend only modest increases in federal assistance for construction of skilled nursing homes, now $12 million a year,* even recognizing the seemingly insatiable recent demand for such facilities.

Far too little is known at present about the best ways of serving the health and physical needs of the aged. There is some evidence which suggests that expanded home health care and other ambulatory health services make greater sense in many cases than placement in a skilled nursing home. Nursing homes may be treating the economic disorders as well as the physical ailments of the elderly; aged people who cannot afford decent housing end up being placed in nursing homes at government expense. For these people, our income-maintenance proposals combined with a recommended expansion of public housing programs (see chapters 4 and 9) will make possible a happier, perhaps healthier, alternative. Some careful social research is called for to guide federal investments in this burgeoning field—25 per cent of all U.S. health expenditures are incurred by the 10 per cent of the population 65 and over.

Distribution of Resources

Our recommended increases in the supply of health resources are necessary but far from sufficient responses to the fact that many Americans—mostly located in inner-city or rural areas—do not have adequate access to health services. Where these resources are distributed is also important. Currently, the federal government does little to assume effective resource distribution.

The most attractive way of meeting these shortages would be to persuade more physicians and other medical practitioners to establish private practices in these areas. The federal government can and should provide incentives (through Medicaid, national health insurance, location of federally funded health facilities, and other leverage points) for practitioners to locate in insufficiently served areas, but past experience suggests that there are limitations on how influential dollar incentives can be. Doctors and other health practitioners pick locations for environmental and cultural advantages as well as money. An increase in the total health-manpower supply, if deployed solely according to individual private market decisions, is likely to provide some relief to underserviced areas, but mostly to bolster the supply in well-served locales.

Given these limitations, a number of supplementary approaches should be attempted to bring professional care to residents of underserviced areas. Broader support should be given to: (1) special transportation programs to aid citizens for whom access is a serious barrier to care; (2) upgrading and expansion of selected existing outpatient clinics; and (3) a thorough trial of the helpfulness of primary-care diagnostic service facilities to screen and identify those in need of further care by a physician.

By far the most promising approach, though, in terms of quickly providing medical services to large numbers of people, is the community health center—a concept that has proven highly successful in government demonstration programs. *We recommend a sixfold increase—from 84 to 500—in the number of community centers.* A program of this scope would enable these centers by 1976 to serve 6 million people, most of whom otherwise would receive virtually no health services at all. The nucleus for such a network of centers could be provided by existing government generalized care centers—now operated by the Office of Economic Opportunity (OEO) and the Department of Health, Education, and Welfare (HEW)—and some autonomous mental health and mental retardation facilities. In order *to staff an operation of this magnitude, we recommend that a domestic health service corps be created. Support of the entire operation would require an increase* *in federal outlays for community health centers from $300 million yearly in 1971 to $1.5 billion in 1976.*

If community health centers are to succeed in providing appropriate, quality health services, their organization and operation must meet several important criteria. First, the centers must be linked wherever possible to private general practitioners, specialists, and hospitals; a community health center is only one link in the health-care network. Second, it is essential that the centers, backed up where possible by other local health resources, possess fully the same quality of facilities and mix of doctors, dentists, psychiatrists, and paramedical personnel as would be available in communities served by more fully private networks. Community health centers staffed by domestic health service corps personnel cannot be allowed to offer an inferior brand of health services to their clientele. Mechanisms to assure that quality services are provided must include a strong community role in decisions about the location of, services provided by, and manner of operation of the health centers.

FINANCING AND ORGANIZING HEALTH SERVICES

The above efforts aimed at improving the supply—both amount and distribution—of health services should receive our primary emphasis during the next few years. But two other changes are absolutely required before all Americans can hope to receive quality health care: (1) more efficient means of organizing the delivery of health care; and (2) some means of paying for the care of those citizens who cannot themselves afford it.

These two concerns are inextricably interwoven. Only through more productive use of the supply of medical manpower, which will be scarce in many localities even *after* the intensive efforts we recommend, will there be enough practitioners to provide care for every citizen. The most powerful single influence on how existing resources are utilized is the pattern through which health services are financed. We must eliminate financial incentives that encourage care to be chosen on criteria other than health need (e.g. hospitalization over outpatient care, crisis care over preventive medicine). Current financing methods created these warped incentives. Improved financing methods can be the lever for eliminating them.

It is clear that the invisible hand of the private marketplace has failed to work toward significantly lowering medical costs by improving resource utilization. And as long as we view adequate health care as a basic right that should be available to all citizens a private market responsive only to those who bid the highest for services will not be sufficient to perform the entire task.

None of these observations are new, but past and current efforts to develop solutions have proved inadequate.

New Alternatives

A number of new approaches—ranging from tax credits for consumers and minimal changes in the organization of health service delivery to a national health service—are being suggested to solve these problems. Most suggested approaches fall somewhere between these extremes, clustering around two basic new approaches to health insurance:

1. *A broadening of private insurance coverage—both as to the number of people and kinds of medical services covered—combined with enlarged federal government assumption of health-care costs for the poor and near-poor through an improved successor to the Medicaid program.* All Americans could be covered by these combined programs.

2. *A unitary national health insurance (NHI) plan including almost all Americans and covering almost all kinds of medical care.* NHI, which would be financed through a government trust fund and partially supported by new taxes, would replace Medicaid, Medicare, and private insurance coverage. This approach is advocated by the AFL-CIO and the Committee for National Health Insurance.

Certain features are common to both these approaches. Supporters of both recommend that coverage be limited to a package of basic services. There is considerable disagreement about precisely which services should be included (whether, for example, full costs of dental care, prescription drugs, or psychiatric care should be covered), but almost everyone feels that the coverage must be broader than current conventional private insurance coverage while stopping short of paying for expensive special treatment such as the use of kidney machines.

There is also agreement that all Americans should be eligible for coverage by broad health insurance. Most people also agree that the public, whether working though area-wide health-planning agencies or other similar community organizations, should have a stronger voice about the ways in which health services are provided in their communities, under whatever plan.

Thoughtful advocates of both approaches also suggest utilizing the government portion of financing to create incentives for prepaid group practice and other promising organizational forms for health-care delivery. Their objective is to orient the health system toward helping people to stay well—toward health maintenance, that is—instead of only toward getting well. The prepaid group-practice approach advances this objective by requiring a single fee, paid in advance by clients, covering most needed services. Conventional insurance plans really offer "sickness insurance," since they provide reimbursement only for a far more selective set of medical expenses.

Prepaid group-practice plans, in other words, assume broad responsibility for keeping their members sound of body. These plans can generally achieve such a result more efficiently than conventional plans—by encouraging preventive care, eliminating artificial biases toward expensive hospital care, and centralizing bookkeeping and other managerial functions. The prepayment feature of such plans also provides an incentive for efficiency, forcing the providers of medical care to share the financial risks of illness with the patient.

New health insurance approaches should be judged by how well they:

- provide access to care;
- prevent financial hardship as a result of illness;
- respond to consumer demands;
- retain an element of competition as to the type of service delivery;
- promote efficiency and economy by making all parties cost conscious;
- assure quality of care;

- provide for ease and economy of administration; and
- satisfy providers and consumers, generally.

Plans could be devised under either of the basic alternative approaches to meet all of the above criteria to some substantial degree. We feel that the NHI approach offers the best prospect for achieving the objectives of easy access, reasonable cost, and efficiency. The NHI approach offers greater opportunities and incentives for cost savings in several areas. It will:

- provide more health services in less expensive settings—notably more in ambulatory facilities and doctor's offices, fewer in hospitals;
- utilize less expensive personnel, especially senior paramedical personnel, to provide services and perform tasks that they can perform as effectively as doctors;
- eliminate profits and minimize administrative costs for the health-insurance function (a unitary NHI approach would cut red tape considerably because a single standardized set of forms would replace multiple sets) ;
- emphasize preventive care and thereby uncover many illnesses before they become serious (although cost savings here could well be initially offset by the fact that more illnesses would be discovered and treated) ; and, most important,
- control rates charged for medical services.

The most compelling argument for NHI is that it is an insurance program of sufficient scope to encompass cultural and long-term factors affecting the nation's health. For instance, the expectable benefits of preventive care in terms of over-all improvements in American health are fairly well established, but a private insurance carrier cannot justify including such services in his coverage. The initial costs would be high because many treatable conditions would be uncovered in preventive examinations, and the benefits would only be perceptible over a very long period.

However, NHI, functioning as both a social and fiduciary institution, might well encourage investment in the health of future generations and be concerned with such things as the health effects of the environment, food product manufacturing, and population pressures.

A system can be devised under the NHI approach that, in conjunction with the health-resource recommendations already discussed, will quickly make possible the provision of a basic package of quality health services to all Americans. Accordingly, *we recommend that a national health insurance plan be adopted, beginning nation-wide in 1974, following a one-year test conducted the previous year in three representative states in order to identify and develop solutions to operational problems.*

Admittedly, there is a large element of judgment in the timetable for implementing NHI, a schedule directly related to how rapidly resource and distribution improvements occur. Pressing that timing decision is the fact that the longer NHI implementation is delayed, the more expensive it is likely to become because of interim inflation of medical costs under present inefficient health delivery systems.

Interim Medicaid Reform

To extend immediately some minimum level of care to millions more citizens, we recommend an interim series of changes in the Medicaid program consistent with the suggestions of the 1970 HEW Medicaid Task Force. The most important of these suggestions are:

- Medicaid should be converted to a program with a uniform minimum level of health benefits financed entirely by federal funds, with a further federal matching of state contributions for certain types of supplementary benefits and for individuals not covered under the minimum plan.
- Additional groups should become eligible for Medicaid until all persons with incomes at or below the poverty level are covered.
- Medicaid, along with other government medical financing programs, must become concerned with promoting effective delivery of health care and encouraging the spread of innovative health-care systems, including group practice.

Medicaid was designed to assure the availability and financing of comprehensive health care to all the nation's poor and near-poor, but only one-third of that potential clientele is now being served. Program costs now are about $6 billion annually, of which slightly over one-half is paid by the federal government. Immediate full implementation of the Medicaid Task Force recommendations would require additional federal outlays of $6–8 billion during the coming two years. We cannot afford that much money so soon in view of other priorities; therefore, full attainment of the goals will have to await NHI implementation. *We do recommend, however, that the federal Medicaid contribution be increased by $1.5 billion in 1972 and $2.5 billion in 1973 and be used to advance the HEW Medicaid Task Force's goals as far as possible.* It is likely that this nearly 50 per cent increase in total funds for Medicaid will make possible full federal funding of minimum health services for all eligible persons reached; however, the benefit package will have to be slightly less broad than the Task Force envisaged.

Nature of the Proposed NHI System

At best, all revisions to Medicaid are stopgap measures, helping to smooth the way for the introduction of national health insurance, which can make a tremendous contribution toward improving the health status of Americans. *If this NHI contribution is to be realized, however, the kind of program is critically important. We recommend a plan that is financed on social insurance principles with a large contribution from general revenues and provides both resources and incentives for bringing about changes in the organization and delivery of care.*

Incentives must be arranged so that providers of medical services largely are reimbursed on a "capitation" rather than a fee-for-service basis. What the capitation approach means is that providers are paid so much for each person whom they agree in advance to provide medical services for during a set period of time, regardless of how many services that person actually requires. This approach, of course, differs from the more conventional fee-for-service arrangement, under which doctors charge patients for each specific service provided.

While capitation payment methods—normally the way payments are made under prepaid group-practice arrangements—

should be encouraged because they tend to encourage efficiency, choice-of-payment method can still be preserved for consumers and providers. One way would be to reimburse providers under any of several payment approaches, but in no case to pay them more than they could have been reimbursed on a capitation basis. Use of a variety of methods of organizing service delivery, with built-in standards of performance, can stir innovation and creative competition among different payment and delivery methods, thus maximizing the possibilities for continuing system-wide improvements.

The payment plans must also provide incentives for practitioners to locate in areas presently underserviced. The most direct incentive would be a bonus in addition to regular fees.

Without incentives such as the above to promote efficient forms of medical care organization and improved patterns of resource distribution, we risk repeating on a larger scale the disastrous impact of the introduction of Medicaid. In that instance, greater demand for health services was created with no companion provision either for increases in the supply of health resources or incentives for more efficient organization of health-delivery mechanisms. The result was predictable: spiraling costs and earnings of medical practitioners without comparable increases in services provided.

Coverage should be provided for a basic package of health services for all Americans—including full payment for maternal and child health services, annual physical check-up examinations, and active (as opposed to purely custodial) mental health care. The result of such coverage patterns should be a much more preventive-care-oriented system than we have at present. Prescription drugs and dental services should be initially partly paid for by NHI.

On the surface, NHI would seem to cost a great deal. We estimate that $64.6 billion of the $68.9 billion recommended for federal health programs in 1976 would go for this purpose. *We propose that funds for NHI be raised through employer contributions of 3 per cent of payroll, a 5 per cent surtax on individual incomes, and a residual contribution from general federal revenues.* Employer and individual taxes would raise $29 billion in 1976. The remaining $38 billion would come from general revenues, about half of that replacing what current federal health programs outlays would have been in 1976.

It is important to understand that the amounts we are talking about are not fundamentally additional to what our society now pays for medical care: rather, NHI financing would be largely in place of current financial payments to private health insurance companies or directly to doctors and other medical practitioners. Total personal health care expenditure in 1970 amounted to $67 billion.

It is also important to understand that the kind of national health insurance proposal we are recommending is a unique approach, building on our current medical-care system and tailored to specific American needs. We are *not* recommending adoption of socialized medicine, as practiced in Britain and several other European nations, with what that approach implies for government control over health practitioners.

All the foregoing programs and recommendations assume continued diligent attention to improving the quality of medical care. NHI needs to incorporate mechanisms for maintenance of professional standards, licensing of facilities, periodic retraining for practitioners, and public involvement in review of the system.

We recommend that support for development of improvements in the organization and delivery of health resources should immediately be increased by 25 per cent—from $188 million to $235 million—with the emphasis on benefits of the type expected from prepaid group practice. We also recommend provision for a modest expansion of funding for biomedical research to $1.4 billion in 1976 in order that better quality care will be possible in the future.

Impact of NHI on Other Government Health Activities

Many current federal government health activities—notably Medicaid, Medicare, Maternal and Child Health services, the crippled children's program, care for merchant seamen and American Indians, community mental health centers, and other federally supported health centers—would, beginning in 1974, receive their financial sustenance through NHI, although in some instances they would still require government-provided staff and facilities.

With the institution of NHI, the need for a separate Veterans Administration health-care network to provide care for a special population would largely disappear (the exception would be special care for injuries unique to warfare). Most Veterans Administration health facilities and personnel should convert to serving the general public; assets could be transferred to local nonprofit groups. A particularly important dividend from such a conversion would be broader use of the excellent VA professional and semiprofessional mental mealth manpower and manpower training facilities—both areas of strength within the Veterans Administration system, and badly needed nation-wide.

The Special Case of Mental Health

Mental health and mental retardation services historically have been the unwanted stepchildren of the medical establishment. Partly to compensate for this neglect, we are singling out these services here for special attention. Only during the last decade have these services inched into the mainstream of American health services. With the development of effective community mental health education programs, widespread use of tranquilizing and antidepressant drugs, extensive research, and numerous community mental health and mental retardation service programs, there has been a reduction in the severe incidence of mental health and mental retardation. In the area of mental illness alone, federal, state, and local governmental efforts over the past fifteen years have reduced the mental hospital patient load by nearly 50 per cent, saving an estimated $12 billion in care and construction costs. Of particular importance in reducing the occurrence of mental retardation has been better care and nutrition for pregnant mothers and very young children.

This recent experience justifies confidence that continued investments in such research, education, and treatment programs will provide significant social dividends. The mentally ill and mentally retarded draw heavily upon services of other programs—specifically, welfare, vocational rehabilitation, and education programs. Reduced occurrence of mental illness and retardation can lead to significant reductions in the costs of these public programs.

While progress has been made, not enough Americans requiring mental health or mental retardation services are being served. This inadequacy stems both from insufficient funding and poor coordination among the various federal agencies providing these services. The shortage can be met during the next five years by: (1) continued expansion of community mental health centers—probably double the currently funded 500 such centers will be needed—and mental retardation service programs; (2) expansion of mental health and mental retardation services in general health facilities; and (3) use of Veterans Administration facilities and personnel, now run on a total annual budget of $339 million, to help meet the needs of regions surrounding the thirty-nine communities in which they are located.

The implementation of NHI, along with our other recommended health program measures, would go far toward providing basic health care, preventive as well as curative, for all Americans.

Budget proposals for Health are summarized in Table 5:1 on the following page.

TABLE 5:1
HEALTH[1,2]
(Outlays, in millions of current dollars)

	Administration		Urban Coalition Recommendations				
	Estimated 1971	Proposed 1972	1972	1973	1974	1975	1976
Manpower Training and Education	931	1,010	1,130	1,310	1,390	1,520	1,670
Construction of Facilities	417	435	355	350	395	310	320
Community Health Centers and Other Resource Distribution Programs	550	621	705	970	255[3]	380[3]	405[3]
Care for Veterans, Indians, and Other Special Groups	1,867	1,939	1,960	2,075	100[3]	100[3]	105[3]
Medicare and Medicaid	11,395	13,254	13,820	14,445	—	—	—
National Health Insurance[4]	—	—	—	3,375	57,400	60,000	64,600
Biomedical Research	1,259	1,370	1,285	1,320	1,340	1,375	1,440
Disease Prevention and Control	239	233	210	200	200	200	200
Other	599	278	280	290	100	105	110
TOTAL	17,257	19,140	19,745	24,335	61,180	63,990	68,850

[1] Excludes health programs of the Department of Defense; specialized health activities of NASA, the Atomic Energy Commission, and the Department of Agriculture; and foreign health activities.

[2] Because health costs are expected to rise faster than either the consumer or the federal government price index, the following special price index was employed:

1971	1972	1973	1974	1975	1976
100.0	105.8	111.3	115.5	122.8	129.5

[3] A substantial portion of the costs of care provided in community health centers and care for government wards would be absorbed in these years by national health insurance.

[4] Based on cost estimates supplied by the Committee for National Health Insurance and developed with the help of the Social Security Administration.

85

6

Education

Education in the United States is a community concern. By far the major share of the cost of the U.S. public school system is paid from local and state taxes. Locally elected school boards are the policy-making bodies for schools throughout the nation. Only through such decentralized operation can the values, aspirations, and histories of the nation's various subcultures play the part they must in the education of the young. But one objective of education in America is to equip citizens to take part equally in the life of the whole nation. The federal government is the instrument that ensures the conditions of equality of opportunity for all citizens to take advantage of their full range of opportunities.

The federal policies recommended in this chapter are designed to stimulate basic changes in education. In all cases, they are designed to preserve and bolster the responsibility of the community to determine what changes will be made and how, or to elect not to change at all.

Our recommendations are grouped in policy categories corresponding to four segments of the education system. These are (1) early, elementary, and secondary education; (2) higher education; (3) adult education; and (4) the arts and humanities.

EARLY, ELEMENTARY, AND SECONDARY EDUCATION

A new conventional wisdom is emerging in American education circles. Growing numbers of teachers, administrators, and laymen concur in the belief that public schools must abandon many traditional education forms and attitudes if today's youth are to be prepared to participate fully in a modern, technological society.

86

Though no fundamental agreement exists over what ought to replace these traditional elements, schoolmen and concerned laymen alike concur in the belief that change and experimentation must be the watchwords for American education in the 1970's.

Yet very little change and experimentation actually are taking place in the nation's elementary and secondary schools. There are a few innovations based on a systematic reappraisal of school objectives and methods. However, most of what is masquerading as educational change is merely elaboration of traditional programs and techniques.

Why have most schools behaved so cautiously in the face of increasingly daring education rhetoric?

We believe there are two principal reasons. To begin with, few exhortations for change leveled at the schools have been accompanied by proven policy alternatives: it is clearly easier to call for better schools than to propose concrete steps for improving them.

Secondly, even with the introduction of sound programmatic and methodological alternatives to chart the future, the disincentives to change that currently confronts most school administrators and teachers would still outweigh the incentives to change. Over the years, delicate and complex relationships are constructed in school districts between boards of education, school administrators, teachers and teachers' unions, and other community institutions. Jurisdictions and spheres of influence are painstakingly negotiated to reduce conflict and create stability. There is understandable reluctance on the part of those whose positions and prerogatives are defined by this structure to alter it—whatever its educational merits or liabilities—because of the friction and insecurity certain to result.

Some critics have concluded that this stubborn resistance to the demand for change is possible only because of the public schools' monopolistic hold on education, a position that allegedly permits them to ignore public criticism without fear of losing public resources to competitors. Educational vouchers (a program for giving education tax dollars to children rather than institutions) and performance contracts with private concerns are frequently discussed as means of compelling public schools to change or perish by breaking their monopoly and making public education subject to the forces of competition in the marketplace.

Because some public school systems perform admirably, and because of important egalitarian values that only effective public education can hope to provide a democratic society like ours, we believe the public schools are worth saving. And in our view, no sustained, comprehensive, nation-wide effort to produce public schools capable of filling local and national educational requirements has yet been attempted.

The federal elementary and secondary education programs recommended in this budget constitute an attempt to define the federal government's role in such a campaign to reform public education. All of these programs have one unifying objective: *to offer school personnel sufficient new incentives for innovation and experimentation to make the benefits of purposeful change outweigh the short-term costs of abandoning the status quo.* Only after it has been demonstrated that the balance cannot be tipped in favor of change would we be willing to recommend support for alternatives to the present system of public education.

Defining the Federal Role

Federal aid to elementary and secondary education in 1971 is expected to be about $3 billion—less than 10 per cent of total public expenditures for elementary and secondary education in the United States. In order to exert a major influence on the shape of future educational development, this proportionately small federal contribution will have to be concentrated in a limited number of critical program areas.

Management of the aggregate aspects of the U.S. economy is by necessity a federal function. With enactment of the manpower training, public-sector-employment, and income-maintenance programs proposed in this budget, the federal government also will have accepted the full responsibility for matching supply and demand in the labor market and supporting those for whom no place can be found.

We believe this assumption of responsibilities will win for the federal government the right to insist on the inclusion of two specific objectives on every local education agenda:

- Every American leaving the public schools must possess the communication and mathematical skills required for successful participation in the national economy.
- Every student must acquire adequate information and experience in school to allow selection of a career objective consistent with his abilities and aspirations and the opportunity to pursue it through access to college, a job-training program, or a full-time job upon graduation from high school.

It is in pursuit of these two admittedly limited objectives that we propose to offer incentives for comprehensive educational change.

Early Education

Approximately 50 per cent of an individual's full intellectual development occurs during the first five years of life—before most children are placed in a planned learning environment. In addition, there is growing evidence that much of what is learned during the first five years is a necessary precondition to later intellectual and social development. By failing to provide planned, purposeful education for many of our children during their early years, we not only waste learning opportunities but may be destroying future opportunities as well.

Nearly 80 per cent of the 4 million five-year-olds in the nation now attend kindergarten. But, of the approximately 11 million youngsters aged two through four in this country, only 23 per cent of the four-year-olds, 9 per cent of the three-year-olds, and almost none of the two-year-olds are currently enrolled in pre-kindergarten education programs. Thus, about 75 per cent of these 11 million children will not experience so much as one year of formal teaching during the intellectually critical first five years of their lives. Present federal programs, primarily Head Start and Title I of the Elementary and Secondary Education Act, provide pre-kindergarten education to less than 5 per cent of these 11 million youngsters.

Because all children can benefit from pre-kindergarten education, and because many may require formal early education to realize their full intellectual potential in later years, we recommend making learning programs available to all children between the ages of two and four on a voluntary basis. This is consistent with the federal commitment to provide equal educational opportunities and with our objective of providing every U.S. child with the reading and math skills required for economic success in our society.

Two kinds of pre-kindergarten programs are needed: full-day child care programs (10–12 hours) for children of working mothers; and shorter programs (3–4 hours) for children of nonworking mothers. The full-day program, which would provide care for children between the ages of a few months and four years, would have a large educational component; the short programs, enrolling only two-, three-, and four-year-olds, would be completely educational. We estimate the cost of a quality full-day program for each child at $1,750 a year and the cost of the half-day program at $500.

Making early education available to all children could be approached in several different ways:

- by adding the provision of universal free pre-kindergarten education to state and local educational responsibilities;
- by establishing a state or federal subsidy for families that cannot afford the full cost of pre-kindergarten education for their children;
- by providing universal free pre-kindergarten education financed entirely with federal funds.

If a sufficient number of early-education teachers and paraprofessionals were available to enable all 11 million children in the age bracket two to four—as well as the 1.5 million children under two who have working mothers—to attend pre-kindergarten schools, the total cost of such a program is estimated to be $10–15 billion a year. This cost would be prohibitive, given available public resources and competing priorities, no matter which level of government assumed the responsibility for this program. The second alternative, then, which would restrict subsidies to those who could not afford to pay the full cost of pre-kindergarten education, would be the only fiscally feasible approach. And given the financial problems facing most state and local education agencies, this partial subsidy program would have to be funded federally.

In reality, we lack the training capacity to rapidly expand the number of early education personnel; it is estimated that only 4,000 to 5,000 pre-kindergarten teachers are being graduated each year. Therefore, a meaningful early education subsidy program would have to be coordinated with a federal plan to increase significantly the number of pre-kindergarten teachers and paraprofessionals trained each year.

We recommend spending $700 million for student aid and institutional support over the next five years to train an additional 80,000 early-education teachers and 160,000 new paraprofessionals. This would enable us to increase the national pre-kindergarten enrollment for two-, three-, and four-year-olds from the present figure of 1.3 million to 2.6 million by 1976* (See Table 6:1), while raising the enrollment of children of working mothers with children less than two years old to 500,000. The increases would constitute a significant step toward our ultimate objective of making quality pre-kindergarten education available and financially feasible for all who desire it.

The federal subsidy program we recommend would pay the full cost of early education for children from families earning less than $4,000 a year. Children from families with annual incomes between $4,000 and $16,500 would receive a partial subsidy determined by a sliding scale. In instances where applications outnumber available openings, preference would be given to children from families earning less than $6,000.

We would favor placing these pre-kindergarten programs under the supervision of the local public school system. Continuity between pre-kindergarten programs and elementary school appears essential if early education gains are to be sustained. Furthermore, since we would be holding public schools accountable for providing students with specific reading and math skills, these schools ought to be given every opportunity to contribute to their students' early education. However, in those instances when a public school system could not or would not be responsible for providing pre-kindergarten programs, state-accredited private schools would be eligible for federal subsidy funds. In either case—public or

---

* All references to years are to federal fiscal years unless otherwise indicated.

TABLE 6:1
EARLY EDUCATION (PRESCHOOL)
(Outlays, in millions of current dollars)

| | Administration[1] | | Urban Coalition Recommendations | | | | |
	Estimated 1971	Proposed 1972	1972	1973	1974	1975	1976
Development Programs[2]			1,164	1,492	1,657	2,145	2,606
Teacher Training			78	85	132	169	235
Research and Development			51	62	75	88	90
TOTAL	402	425	1,293	1,639	1,864	2,402	2,931

[1] The breakdown of costs in official budget documents was not available.
[2] Cost of child care programs and construction and facilities are merged into totals for development programs.

private—early education programs enrolling children with federal subsidies would have to comply with federal desegregation requirements and include federal reading and math objectives.

Finally, it should be made clear that good pre-kindergarten programs are no substitute for needed improvements in elementary education. Preschool learning cannot take the place of what should be learned in elementary school; it is preparation, just as what is learned in elementary programs should prepare a student for what he will encounter in secondary school.

Indeed, "preschool" is misleading. We suggest that education for two-year-olds be considered the first grade. School attendance would not be mandatory until the fourth grade (what is now kindergarten). But parents would be aware that children were undergoing definite intellectual and social development during the first three grades. Children not enrolled in early education programs should receive the equivalent education in the home. Viewing developmental programs for children aged two to four as early education instead of as preschool would do much to heighten awareness in this country of the importance of learning during the first five years of life.

Elementary School Achievement Program

According to the best estimates from the limited data available, approximately 20 per cent of the children in the United States fail to attain the level of literacy required for available employment. In certain poverty areas, this figure reaches 75 per cent or more. More than 9 million children now enrolled in the public schools eventually will enter the labor market as economic illiterates unless public education is changed. Performance figures in mathematics, the other skill area so essential for participation in the present American economy, are quite similar.

There is no existing federal program designed specifically to raise the reading and math performance of all U.S. children to the level necessary for real economic opportunity. Title I of the Elementary and Secondary Education Act does not specify what benefits children should receive from the programs funded. The framing of education objectives is left to the local school districts.

Furthermore, those Title I funds invested to date in reading and math programs have had no significant measurable impact on the reading and math performance of the great majority of students enrolled in these programs, according to Office of Education evaluations in *Title I/Year II* (U.S. Government Printing Office, 1968).

The five most frequently discussed federal alternatives for improving reading and math skills are:

1. Granting more time and resources to the present Title I program, which seeks to improve the education of "educationally disadvantaged" students by distributing compensatory funds under a formula reflecting the geographical distribution of school-age children from low-income families.

2. Continuing the present Title I program with more specific reading and math performance objectives.

3. Transforming Title I into a program providing strong financial incentives and operational support to induce elementary schools with children not making sufficient progress toward federally defined minimum reading and math performance standards to formulate plans to raise the performance of such children to at least those standards. Evaluation of local school performance would be by nationally devised and administered tests, and funds would be distributed on the basis of student performance deficiencies measured by those tests rather than by family income.

4. Shifting federal attention from existing education programs to the quest for new approaches by funding a large number of experimental schools that eventually might provide new models for the public schools.

5. Putting federal education dollars into programs such as educational vouchers and private performance contracting in order to stimulate the creation of alternative education institutions in the private sector to compete with and possibly supplant the present public school system.

We reject alternatives (1) and (2) in the belief that the present Title I emphasis on increasing education expenditures for the poor rather than improving the performance of all underachieving students fails to offer the incentives for change and experimentation that improved performance will require. Also, we find the Title I assumption that poor children should be singled out for help because they are "culturally deprived"—implying that the home life provided by poor parents is qualitatively inferior—a gratuitous and arrogant position that encourages many poverty-area schools to demand different children instead of developing different programs for the children they receive.

We would not favor the adoption of alternative (5) at this time because of our strong, previously stated preference for strengthening the public school system instead of creating a companion education system.

We recommend instead a new federal education program on the elementary level combining alternatives (3) and (4): a reading and math achievement-oriented Title I with incentives for change, together with a new federal role in developing and evaluating experiments in local schools that would serve as models for such change. The ultimate goal of this restructured and refocused Title I program would be to enable all groups of children in the nation to attain the same reading and math performance levels, independent of geographical, cultural, and economic differences. However, our more immediate objective within the five-year life of this budget is to assure that every American leaving the public schools possesses at least the minimum communications and math skills required for successful participation in the national economy, as defined in terms of absolute performance standards set by the U.S. Office of Education.

Allocations of funds would be based on reading and math achievement levels instead of family income. Each qualifying state would receive $300 annually for every child in kindergarten through the sixth grade not progressing at an acceptable rate toward the federal minimum math and reading standards.

To qualify for these new Title I funds, a state education agency would have to secure a comprehensive multiyear reading and math achievement plan from each public elementary school with eligible students in the state. Each school's plan—negotiated jointly by the staff of that school, parents from the school community, and representatives from the local and state education agencies— would have to contain specific reading and math achievement objectives that would meet or exceed federal minimum standards, a description of how the school intends to attain those objectives, and criteria for evaluating the success or failure of the plan, acceptable to all parties involved and consistent with U.S. Office of Education guidelines.

For the federal government legitimately to hold the states and individual elementary schools accountable for meeting the reading and math achievement objectives in their plans, the Office of Education would have to identify existing programs and develop demonstration programs in public schools able to raise the reading and math performance of students to national norms. Such school programs do exist in impoverished as well as affluent neighborhoods, but not in sufficient number or diversity to guarantee that each new Title I school would find a model that has succeeded in circumstances similar to its own. The Office of Education also would have to create a system of federal support teams to disseminate information about successful elementary school programs and about other federal research findings to state education agencies.

It is important to note that the federal role of testing and model development would not require a large bureaucracy. Technical support for individual schools and the administration of teacher retraining would be strictly a state task, thereby ensuring that the support and evaluation functions would be performed by different groups.

The timetable for implementing this new Title I program would be determined largely by the dispatch with which the Office of Education could identify and create successful experimental elementary programs. We estimate that some Title I schools would be prepared to put achievement plans into operation by 1974, while the majority would require an additional year of preparation. *In the interim, we recommend continuing the present Title I program with the added stipulation that all program funds be directed at improving reading and math skills.*

We believe the incentives provided by this new Title I program to change traditional elementary education attitudes, methods, and curricula would be compelling. The additional $300 in federal funds for every eligible student would assure widespread individual school participation in the program. State involvement would be secured by making active participation a condition for receiving funds under a massive federal general education-assistance program proposed later in this section.

However, participation in the program is not the objective. To attain our objectives, incentives to succeed would have to be present. Our Title I plan would create three such incentives.

First, to qualify for Title I funds, a state would have to agree to assume temporary control of individual elementary schools that fail to attain the objectives in their achievement plans. If, in turn, the state were unable to raise achievement in that school to national norms over a given period of time, the Title I funds received by the state for eligible students in that school would be given directly to the students in the form of federal educational vouchers to be used for supplementary instruction from other sources. At that point, the state and the local education agency involved would lose a proportionate share of the federal general education-assistance money they were receiving. Thus, the state, the local education agency, and the individual school would all share a financial incentive to succeed.

Second, since failure to meet achievement objectives would entail significant financial losses for both state and local education agencies, education bureaucracies would be more likely to reward administrators on the basis of their ability to create and direct successful achievement programs than has tended to be the case in the past. To the extent that this success required changes in educational forms and content, the current disincentives to change on the part of many school systems would be weakened and, let us hope, overcome.

Third, the Title I achievement objectives would give the public a yardstick for measuring one aspect of school performance. Elected education officials and administrators of school systems going to the voters for additional tax revenue would be under heavy political pressures to attain their individual school objectives.

Can we be sure that all participating schools would change, and change for the better?

It is conceivable that some participating schools would be able to meet achievement objectives without abandoning present rigid teaching patterns or altering the rest of their education program, but we would be providing children with important reading and math skills previously denied them.

In fact, we believe that concerted school efforts to teach all children reading and math skills would bring about fundamental and desirable changes in the entire program of most participating schools. Programs that in recent years have succeeded in significantly raising student performance employ a wide variety of teaching methods and forms of school organization. Clearly there is no *one* method or technique that ensures successful learning.

All of these programs appear to have in common three elements: (1) specific and sequentially defined achievement objectives, (2) the expectation that students can attain these objectives, and (3) regular support services for teachers and evaluation of student performance. Any school that approaches reading and math in this fashion would be almost certain to depart from the traditional practices found in most schools with underachieving students—a departure that would affect every phase of the school's operation.

Many education critics point out that changes are needed in the area of emotional development as well as in skill performance. We agree. We believe that the abilities this program fosters—to read, to use mathematics—contribute greatly to a person's self esteem in our society. And it is our hope that the expectation by school officials that children can learn, which appears to be a necessary condition for meeting achievement objectives, and parent participation in Title I planning, will combine to make schools more humane.

The federal cost of giving the states $300 for every public elementary school student not making adequate math and reading progress would be $2.1 billion by 1976. *We recommend providing an additional $100 million in Title I funds to the states to help develop and operate the state support teams the Title I achievement plans require.*

A federal Office of Education Evaluation, reporting directly to the U.S. Commissioner of Education, would be responsible for administering reading and math achievement tests to every public elementary and secondary education student in the nation at the beginning and end of every school year. The annual cost of this testing program would be approximately $500 million.

Funds for the identification and creation of model elementary programs would come from federal education research and development expenditures discussed later in this section.

Career Preparation for Secondary School Students

Selecting and securing an occupation has become an enormously complex task in the United States. As the demand for unskilled and semiskilled labor has diminished, success in the economy increasingly requires an understanding of the labor market, a set of specific skills, and enough basic education to permit later retraining to adapt to changing skill demands.

These requirements for economic success are of recent vintage, the products of the highly specialized and rapidly evolving American economy of the post–World War II period. Parents and many school counselors, the traditional sources of career education, no longer possess the expertise needed to prepare young people for entry into today's labor market. Most secondary schools, isolated as they are from structural changes in the economy, have failed to respond to this growing gap in their students' education, clinging instead to anachronistic curricular tracks and vocational programs designed for an America of fifty years ago.

The cost to the nation's young people of this failure to be relevant is staggering: an estimated 50 per cent or more of the high-school-age youth in this country are not securing the preparation and assistance they require to choose and enter an occupation commensurate with their abilities and aspirations, according to Ralph Tyler, in "Investing in Better Schools," in *Agenda for the Nation* (New York: Doubleday, 1968.)

One of every four young persons drops out of school before graduating, an act that condemns an individual to compete for one of the diminishing number of low-skill, low-paying jobs or to endure the bitter subsistence struggle of the hard-core unemployed. Perhaps even more tragic is the plight of the 25 to 50 per cent of our youth who do complete high school and who play the game by society's rules, only to experience the same failure in the labor market as their companions who drop out. For these young men and women, a high school diploma is a frustrating ruse, which raises expectations without providing the competence to realize those expectations.

There are two basic public policy alternatives for dealing with this national problem:

- We can ignore the school system and concentrate public resources on training and employing those men and women who fall into the pool of unskilled, unemployed labor after failing to find a place in the economy upon completing their formal education.
- Or we can attempt to stop the flow of people into this pool of the unskilled unemployed by restructuring the secondary school to ensure that all students receive the education, experience, and assistance needed to enter college, a job-training program, or a full-time job with a future *directly* upon graduating.

Currently, it is the first course we are pursuing. Only 10 per cent of today's high-shool-age students receive vocational technical instruction, and more than half of these students are receving this training in home economics and agriculture. Those in the academic curriculum are prepared for college only, despite the fact that many academic students either do not go to college or never graduate. And those pushed into "general education"—the third and most populated of the traditional high school curricula—are prepared for nothing.

The federal contribution to career preparation programs for the nation's 18 million public secondary students is expected to total $300 million in 1971. At the same time, the federal government will invest approximately $1.7 billion in 1971 in manpower programs to attempt to train and place 1.5 million people who have been left unskilled and jobless by the education system.

This present allocation of federal resources makes no sense in either economic or human terms. Training an adult who is likely to have a family that must be supported during the training period is far more difficult and expensive than preparing a secondary or post-secondary student already in school.

Therefore, *we recommend adopting the second of our two alternatives: a restructuring of secondary education to provide every student with the information and experience he needs to select a career objective consistent with his abilities and aspirations* and *the opportunity to pursue that objective through placement in a post-secondary education or training institution or in a full-time job upon graduating from high school.* Career preparation for all students would replace the traditional vocational track.

Making good on these new national rights for secondary school students will require the establishment of four separate but coordinated programs:

1. The revised Title I reading and math achievement program we proposed at the elementary level should be continued into secondary school for those students still lacking the basic education skills economic success demands. *We recommend a crash reading and math achievement program providing $300 in federal funds for each eligible secondary student in the nation, a sum sufficient to finance tutorials and other highly concentrated and individualized teaching forms.*

This new Title I secondary program, operating under the same federal procedures and requirements as its elementary counterpart, would cost $1.5 billion a year by 1976. As the elementary program took effect in succeeding years, this secondary effort would be reduced greatly in size and cost.

2. *We recommend the establishment of a Career Education Program for all of the nation's 18 million public secondary students.* The objective of this program would be to provide every young person with the information and experience required for realistic career planning.

On the junior high level, this program would consist primarily of in-school exploration of career alternatives. However, in the senior high school, the emphasis would shift to the placement of students in work-related adult activities outside the school. Here the objective would not be specific job training, but rather the opportunity for all students to learn about the labor market, employer expectations, career alternatives, and necessary educational preparation by observing and participating in real occupational activities in the community.

We recommend funding this Career Education Program with 70:30 federal-state matching grants. To qualify for these grants, which would allocate funds on the basis of public secondary school population, a state first would have to obtain a multiyear career education plan from each local school district, to be negotiated jointly by local school officials, parents, representatives of local business and labor organizations, officials of post-secondary education and training institutions in the area, and state education officials. Each plan would have to contain specific career education objectives consistent with federal guidelines, a timetable for attaining these objectives, and the means for measuring progress toward them.

The federal government's principal responsibility would be the identification and development of successful career education programs in a variety of school and community settings to serve as models for state and local school district plans. Ongoing support to assist local school districts to attain their objectives would be supplied by state education agencies.

We estimate the federal cost of this national Career Education Program, including expenditures for training and retraining teachers and counselors, at $2.5 billion a year by 1976.

3. *Present federal vocational education programs should be revised to complement the other secondary education programs we are proposing.*

In the course of their career education experience, we would expect many secondary students to discover occupational fields that capture their interest. When this happens, they should be able to obtain broad career preparation in these fields while still in high school. The main purpose of such career preparation would be to provide students with the information and skills required for success in the more specific training programs offered after graduation by employers and post-secondary schools. For example, students interested in the health field would all benefit from courses in physiology and laboratory practices, whatever their specific health career objectives.

Therefore, *we recommend using current federal vocational education funds to encourage states to develop these broad career preparation programs to replace many of the present narrow-skill programs.*

In those remaining instances in which specific skill training can be delivered most efficiently while a student still attends high school, precautions must be taken to ensure that this training will adequately prepare the student for a real place in the economy upon graduation. Too many present vocational education programs —particularly those in home economics and agriculture—are unrelated to the needs of the labor market.

In order to guarantee relevance in both the broad career preparation and the skill programs, *we urge the establishing of federal guidelines requiring the participation in formulation of vocational course plans of employers and educational institutions who are expected to receive the graduates of these programs.* The skill programs also would have to include provisions for actually placing students in related jobs upon satisfactory completion of the training provided.

4. *We recommend creation of a federally financed career placement program operating in all of the nation's public senior high schools to ensure that every graduating student has the opportunity to enter a college, a job-training program, or a full-time job with a future immediately following commencement.* This is the final bridge we propose building between the public school and the world for which it presumably is preparing its students.

Placement programs departing from present guidance and counseling methods currently operating in a few school districts around the country have demonstrated that virtually all of the students in a senior class can be placed within four months of graduating at a cost of less than $75 per student. In the program we are proposing, schools would be required to maintain contact with their graduates for a full year following initial placement.

We estimate the federal cost of this placement program at $293 million a year by 1976.

Like our proposed elementary programs, these four secondary-school-oriented programs are designed to attain a limited federal objective. However, in implementing these career-oriented proposals to break down the barriers between the school and the adult community that the high school graduate eventually must enter, we also believe the federal government would be providing the framework and incentives for introducing more relevance into the entire secondary program and for replacing the present rigid curricular system with a more flexible and functional structure.

Other Special Impact Programs

Education for the Handicapped: At present, 40 per cent of the 6 million handicapped children in the nation between the ages of five and nineteen are receiving special education services. *We recommend expanding current programs to increase the proportion of handicapped children served to 60 per cent by 1976.* This will require training 40,000 teachers for the handicapped each year for the next five years. The total cost to the federal government of expanding school programs and teacher training would be $183 million a year by 1976.

Indian Education: We recommend that the Bureau of Indian Affairs spend $1,000 for each of the 62,000 Indian pupils enrolled in the Bureau's schools, and an additional $3,000 per pupil for the 61 per cent of these pupils enrolled in boarding schools. We also strongly support the recommendation of the Carnegie Report that control of Indian education be transferred to Indian communities within five years. We estimate the federal cost of Indian education at $216 million a year by 1976.

Desegregation Assistance: The racial integration of students in elementary and secondary schools must remain a national goal of the highest importance, both because it is right in a society committed to equality and because it is beneficial to all of the students involved if implemented thoughtfully. *We therefore support President Nixon's proposal to provide $1 billion in federal funds to assist school districts in the process of desegregating their education systems.* To ensure that these funds are carefully and constructively used, *we recommend spreading their expenditure over the next four years.*

Bilingual Education: We recommend greatly increasing federal funds for bilingual education from the 1971 figure of $25 million *a year to $58 million in 1976.* Effective bilingual education is not a one-way street in which only non-English-speaking children are taught English; a program also must teach English-speaking children to understand and respect the language and culture of the non-English speaking peoples with whom they live.

Nutrition and Health: Malnutrition and poor health are unacceptable in a society as advanced as ours. They also are serious obstacles to learning. Therefore, *we recommend the enactment of a new title in the Elementary and Secondary Education Act to provide every poverty-area elementary and secondary school with federal funds to hire a staff person whose sole responsibility is to ensure that existing public nutrition and health programs are available to meet the needs of the children in that school.*

Research and Development: Under the new programs we recommend for early, elementary, and secondary education, *the federal government would assume responsibility for identifying and developing successful programs in a number of different educational areas to serve as models for schools attempting to improve their own programs.* This new responsibility, along with an increased commitment of resources for basic education research, would raise annual federal research and development expenditures for early, elementary, and secondary education to $500 million by 1976.

General Education Assistance: In order to help states and localities close the growing gap between education expenditure needs and revenues, *we recommend initiating a program of large-scale federal general education assistance to the states.* These block grants, which would total $4 billion a year by 1976, could be used for whatever educational purposes the states and localities desired.

However, to be eligible for this federal assistance, a state would have to meet the following conditions: (1) a state would have to assume at least 55 per cent of all nonfederal elementary and secondary education expenditures; (2) kindergarten attendance would be mandatory; (3) a state would be responsible for ensuring that all public schools with eligible children participate in the new Title I program we proposed; and (4) a state would be prohibited from

TABLE 6:2
ELEMENTARY AND SECONDARY EDUCATION
(Outlays, in millions of current dollars)

	Administration Estimated 1971	Administration Proposed 1972	Urban Coalition Recommendations 1972	1973	1974	1975	1976
Elementary Reading-Math Achievement (Title I)	1,275	1,415[1]	1,265	1,299	1,433	2,051	2,112
Secondary Reading-Math Achievement (Title I)			764	793	1,390	1,434	1,480
Career Preparation	262	286[1]	450	460	2,912	3,009	3,112
Staff Development	169	171	77	128	200	236	211
Desegregation Assistance	100	300	300	300	150	150	—
Indian Education	157	182	188	194	203	210	216
Bilingual Education	25	25[1]	25	30	44	56	58
Handicapped	34	34[1]	55	84	112	145	183
Impact Aid[2]	512	487[1]	—	—	—	—	—
Health and Nutrition	—	—	40	80	80	80	80
Research and Development	200	246	300	400	450	475	500
Other	779	712	514	538	565	591	625
TOTAL	3,513	3,858	3,978	4,306	7,539	8,437	8,577

[1] Included in Administration's revenue-sharing proposal scheduled to be implemented January 1, 1972.
[2] Urban Coalition recommendations are included under general education assistance in the fiscal relief for states and localities budget.

extending federal assistance to local school districts that fail to allocate resources and services equitably between schools in a district.

Funds would be distributed to the states on the basis of school population, state need, and state and local revenue-raising efforts. States would be required to allocate the funds equitably among their local school districts taking need into account. This inclusion of need as an allocation factor would ensure that localities now receiving impact aid (aid to school districts in areas with large amounts of nontaxable federal property) would qualify for a relatively larger share of the general-assistance money. The change would permit termination of the present impact aid program.

Recommended outlays for elementary and secondary education are summarized in Table 6:2.

HIGHER EDUCATION

Like so much in contemporary American life, higher education in the United States is both enormously successful and profoundly troubled. By providing intellectual excellence and creative scholarship in a system of mass education that accommodates 40 per cent of the nation's college-age population, our institutions of higher learning serve as the model of the democratization of higher education. At the same time, partly as a result of their rapid development and democratization, our universities and colleges are being torn today by the most basic conflicts over purpose, power, and structure.

The issues and questions raised by this dialectic of success and difficulty are central to the development of American higher education and, consequently, critical to the future character of our society. The central responsibility for resolution of these issues must be accepted by the universities and colleges themselves, in some cases aided by the states and localities that provide the major share of their financial support. The federal government, though, must contribute to the solution of these problems by structuring its higher-education-assistance programs in ways that nurture improvement and innovation in areas such as:

- *Structural organization.* The traditional four-year B.A. program increasingly seems an inappropriate frame of reference for many seeking higher education. Federal assistance should foster attempts to develop wider diversity of structures, including such forms as the Urban Grant University, one- and two-year degree programs, and continuing and vocational education.
- *Resource utilization.* Enormous capital, technological, and human resources are invested in the higher education system. For the most part, these fixed resources are incompletely and inefficiently utilized. Federal assistance programs should require innovative approaches (such as full-year and full-day use of facilities) to improve resource utilization.
- *Access.* For a variety of reasons, all Americans do not enjoy equal opportunities to receive higher education. Minority applicants still are stymied by discrimination in college admission and loan-approval policies at some institutions. Many intellectually qualified but financially poor students are unable to obtain the funds needed to pay for higher education.

It is our contention that the two principal federal objectives in the area of higher education during the next five years should be: ensuring equality of access to institutions of higher education; and expanding the capacity of those institutions to handle rapidly increasing enrollments.

Direct Student Aid

Increased student aid is necessary to eliminate the economic barriers that still prevent many qualified students from receiving the benefits of higher education. Currently, 48 per cent of all college students come from families in the top-income quartile in the nation, while only 7 per cent come from the bottom quartile. The chance for a student in the top half of the income range to go to college is three times as great as for one from the bottom half.

There are two alternative federal approaches for ensuring equal access to higher education:

- Directing federal financial assistance primarily to students prevented from attending college by inadequate incomes.

- Federal financing of the full cost of higher education for *all* Americans wishing to enter college, regardless of income.

The second approach—federal financing of universal higher education—is certainly consistent with our belief that higher education is a national resource of major importance. However, we estimate that such a program would cost $35-40 billion a year by 1976—a prohibitive price given the amount of federal resources we expect to be available during the next five years.

Therefore, *we recommend the first alternative, concentration of a smaller number of federal dollars primarily on those students who otherwise could not afford to pursue an education beyond high school.* Since the much discussed proposal of federal tax credits for education expenses would benefit higher-income families relatively more than lower-income families, we reject it outright. Instead, we counsel relying on more direct forms of student aid, such as scholarships, work-study grants, subsidized loans, and guaranteed loans.

In the past, the major emphasis of federal student aid has been focused upon students from lower- and middle-income families through a mix of scholarships, Educational Opportunity Grants, and work-study programs. The present Administration has sensibly attempted to increase the absolute amount and percentage of scholarships and subsidized loans to needy students, while restricting those in higher-income brackets to loans that the government simply guarantees against default.

We recommend that this shift in emphasis be continued and accelerated to provide $2.2 billion in total aid by 1976 to needy students (those from families with earned incomes below $8,500), a 350 per cent increase over current outlays. This amount of federal assistance in the form of Educational Opportunity Grants, work-study grants, and direct loans would enable approximately 1.6 million low-income students to receive an average of $1,250 a year in aid; today, roughly 1 million low-income students receive an average assistance allotment of only $450.

Students whose family income is above $8,500 should be aided through federally guaranteed loans obtained from private lenders (students from low-income families would also be eligible for such loans). During 1969–70, tight credit markets made it difficult for many students to obtain these guaranteed loans. To remedy this situation, the Administration has proposed creation of a National Student Loan Association (NSLA).

The NSLA would play substantially the same role in student loans as the Federal National Mortgage Association does in home loans (i.e., by buying loans made in the private sector, thus making more money available for additional private sector loans). Student loans would be made at market rates of interest, but NSLA, after purchasing the loan, would charge borrowers no more than 7 per cent interest. It is estimated that NSLA, purchasing new loans at an annual rate of $2 billion, would have $9 billion in guaranteed loans in its portfolio by 1976. This $9 billion could provide 4.5 million students with guaranteed loans averaging $2,000.

We also recommend that students be given the choice of repaying the NSLA through two different mechanisms:

- by repaying the actual value of the loan, plus interest, over a specified number of years in the conventional manner; or
- by agreeing to pay a small (but fixed) percentage of the student's annual income for every $1,000 of debt incurred.

The latter form of payment might prove particularly attractive to students from poor families, since it would greatly diminish their fear of not being able to repay debts incurred to finance their education. The same approach might also prove attractive to universities, since it might more readily make possible increases in tuition charges up to a level more fully approximating the total cost of the student's education.

Institutional Aid

The student aid programs we are recommending should induce an even greater number of students to enroll in college than is currently projected. The increased enrollment will exacerbate the financial crisis already facing many college and universities. Costs of instruction and operating costs will continue to rise faster than tuition receipts. Additions of buildings and facilities also will be needed. The Carnegie Commission has recently reported that state and local government will be unable to provide much additional support for higher education institutions. Many private institutions are already suffering from the inability to coax higher contributions from alumni and the private sector.

Therefore, *we recommend that the federal government reverse its recent trend away from institutional support, increasing its assistance from $850 million in 1971 to about $1,100 million in 1976 (excluding aid to medical schools).* Particular attention needs to be given to the astronomically growing network of community colleges.

. As the total amount of institutional aid grows, the form of that aid should change in order to improve educational access. Currently, about 60 per cent of federal institutional support is in the form of construction grants or loans, and 40 per cent is in grants for general operating purposes. We recommend that these proportions be reversed. General operating grants should be provided to eligible institutions in the form of a cost-of-education supplement on a dollar-for-dollar matching basis with Education Opportunity Grants. Those institutions enrolling students receiving Educational Opportunity Grants would automatically receive matching institutional aid. Colleges and universities would have a financial incentive to recruit qualified low-income students. Small absolute decreases in construction assistance are merited because universities are most readily able to raise funds privately for this purpose. All federal higher education construction assistance should incorporate incentives for improved utilization of facilities.

Research

The federal government currently supports 75 per cent of all university research. Of the $500 million in federal funds proposed for university research and training in 1971,* about $350 million (70 per cent) is for academic research, $101 million for teacher training, and $48 million for educational research.

We recommend holding the total amount of federal support for university research constant over the next five years in real dollar

* Excluding outlays for biomedical research, which are examined in Chapter 5.

TABLE 6:3
HIGHER EDUCATION[1]
(Outlays, in millions of current dollars)

	Administration			Urban Coalition Recommendations			
	1971	1972	1972	1973	1974	1975	1976
Direct Student Aid	2,489	2,762	2,604	3,177	3,877	4,506	5,014
Institutional Aid	849	699	888	935	1,014	1,081	1,112
Research	501	566	594	572	582	577	557
Vocational Education	124	200	200	250	300	350	400
TOTAL	3,963	4,227	4,286	4,934	5,773	6,514	7,083

[1] Excludes outlays for medical schools, which are covered in the chapter on health.

112

terms. But we believe funds for academic research should be reduced by $200 million; the $200 million should be reallocated to educational research ($50 million) and research in teacher training ($150 million).

Vocational Education

The two-year community college is the educational institution best situated to provide career training to high school graduates and members of the labor force seeking new occupational opportunities. Yet most of these schools continue to favor courses that prepare students to transfer to four-year colleges rather than career-oriented programs, despite the fact that only an estimated 15 per cent of all students entering community colleges ever transfer to four-year schools.

In order to stimulate the rapid growth of vocational education programs in community colleges, *we propose (1) that federal vocational education assistance to post-secondary institutions be increased from the present level of $125 million a year to $400 million a year by 1976; and (2) that preference be given to community colleges that emphasize career preparation programs—when distributing direct federal assistance—rather than to institutions of higher education, except when college-transfer courses are essential to fill an educational void in a particular area.* Federal guidelines also are needed to ensure that vocational programs in publicly supported post-secondary schools correspond to the realities of the labor market.

Recommended outlays for higher education are summarized in Table 6:3.

ADULT EDUCATION

Education traditionally is regarded in this country as an exclusive right of children and young adults. When Americans acquire the responsibilities of a family and a job, they tend to assume that the opportunity for further formal learning is automatically forfeited. This prevailing view of formal education as a youth activity is particularly damaging at a time when so many Americans

TABLE 6:4
ADULT EDUCATION
(Outlays, in millions of current dollars)

| | Administration | | | Urban Coalition Recommendations | | | |
	Estimated 1971	Proposed 1972	1972	1973	1974	1975	1976
Basic	80	83	90	120	140	145	150
Extension	160	171	175	180	185	190	195
Continuing and Career Upgrading	376	442	220	305	325	360	400
Other[1]	740	729	650	660	720	775	825
TOTAL	1,356	1,425	1,135	1,265	1,370	1,470	1,570

[1] Other includes support for training of federal professional employees and foreign students at U.S. educational institutions, assistance to educational institutions in foreign countries, support of the Smithsonian Institution and the Library of Congress, and several other miscellaneous educational activities.

already in the labor force are beginning to realize that more education is the key to protecting themselves against technological obsolescence and to improving their economic and social standing.

Therefore, *we recommend an expanded federal adult education program with two major objectives:*

First, *more Americans who are vocationally handicapped by deficient language, reading, and math skills should have access to adult basic education courses.* Because of the status higher education enjoys and because many men and women in need of basic education associate public elementary and high schools with past academic failing, adult basic education should be offered by community colleges and local universities whenever possible. More operational research is needed to develop better ways to convince people to enroll in such programs. *Federal support for these programs should increase from $80 million in 1971 to $150 million in 1976* (See Table 6:4).

Second, *support for continuing education should be revamped to ensure coordination with the increased emphasis on career upgrading for manpower training programs,* as recommended in Chapter 2. As a result, outlays for continuing education can be sharply reduced in 1972. *We recommend the establishment in 1973 of a program encouraging people already in the labor force to seek further vocational training.* This program would seek to build bridges between community colleges—and other post-secondary institutions that provide career training—and working men and women desiring new occupational opportunities. Funds would be used to inform adults of existing vocational programs and to provide incentives to post-secondary institutions to develop accessible courses for different segments of the working population.

ARTS AND HUMANITIES

We recommend long overdue increases in public support for the arts and humanities—increases that are essential if we wish to improve the quality of life for many Americans. This would mean increased grants to a highly diverse spectrum of professional American artists and cultural ensembles, with particular attention to raising performers' salaries to a level demonstrating acceptance of the "arts" as a valid occupation. A larger commitment of federal

TABLE 6:5
ARTS AND HUMANITIES
(Outlays, in millions of current dollars)

| | Administration | | Urban Coalition Recommendations | | | | |
	Estimated 1971	Proposed 1972	1972	1973	1974	1975	1976
National Foundation for Arts and Humanities	38	64	55	80	105	135	175
Public Library Services	51	34	45	46	48	51	53
Public Broadcasting	28	42	50	64	77	90	105
TOTAL	117	140	150	190	230	276	333

funds also would permit the accelerated development of community theater, art, and dance projects as well as an expanded public broadcasting program (See Table 6:5). *We recommend that federal support of the arts, humanities, and broadcasting increase fourfold—from $66 million to $280 million—during the coming five years.*

Budget proposals for Education are summarized in Table 6:6 on the following page.

TABLE 6:6
EDUCATION
(Outlays, in millions of current dollars)

	Administration			Urban Coalition Recommendations			
	Estimated 1971	Proposed 1972	1972	1973	1974	1975	1976
Early Education (Preschool)	402	425	1,293	1,639	1,864	2,402	2,931
Elementary and Secondary Education	3,513	3,858	3,978	4,306	7,539	8,437	8,577
Higher Education[1]	3,963	4,227	4,286	4,934	5,773	6,514	7,083
Adult Education	1,356	1,425	1,135	1,265	1,370	1,470	1,570
Arts and Humanities	117	140	150	190	230	276	333
TOTAL	9,351	10,075	10,846	12,334	16,776	19,099	20,494

[1] Excludes outlays for medical schools, which are covered in the chapter on health.

SOCIAL AND PHYSICAL DEVELOPMENT

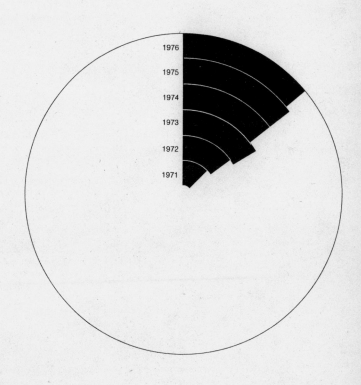

7

Fiscal Relief for States and Localities

Our large central cities are now caught in a financial crisis. Many of them may be unable to meet their present expenses. Rising costs and an increased demand for services in the face of a shrinking revenue base have brought about this imminent disaster.

Cities rely on property taxes for the bulk of their revenues. As inner-city property has declined in value, rates have had to be increased, with the result that city property taxes are now both overburdened and inequitable. In addition, the revenue base of our cities has diminished as jobs and middle-income families have moved to the suburbs. It has been difficult, if not impossible, for the central cities to tap their surrounding suburbs for revenue. To help meet this recurring crisis, federal and state aid to cities increased by more than 400 per cent between 1955 and 1968, yet such aid still amounted to only 23 per cent of city revenues in 1968, compared to 15 per cent in 1955.*

States, too, have seen drastic increases in expenditures over revenues. The fiscal dilemma of the states is due partly to their unwillingness to tax themselves either adequately or fairly. Forty-one states now have individual income taxes, but, in 1969, only $7.6 billion—less than 20 per cent of total state revenues—came from personal income taxes. (The federal government collects about 11.5 per cent of all personal income in income taxes, while states collect only 1 per cent of personal income. If state income taxes had averaged 3 per cent of personal income in 1969, the states would have collected an extra $15 billion.) Most state tax

* All references to years are to fiscal years unless otherwise stated.

revenues are collected from taxes that are not progressive in their impact, like the general sales tax. General and selective sales taxes accounted for $24 billion of state revenues in 1969.

STATE AND LOCAL REVENUE AND EXPENDITURE PROJECTIONS

Estimates of state and local expenditures and resources between now and 1976 represent little more than guesswork. Since 1965, there have been at least six studies projecting state and local expenditures and revenues for 1975.* The projections in these six studies have varied widely because of differences in basic assumptions (such as the rate of growth of the economy and the probable increase in prices), in evaluations of the effects of federal grants (the extent to which they stimulate or replace state and local spending), and in estimates of the degree to which state and local services will be improved and expanded. The most recent study, that of William Robinson of the Office of Budget and Management, is one of the few that projects expenditures to cover not only expansions in state and local services due to population and price increases but improvements in the quality of the services as well.

There is ample evidence that inadequacy of state and local services is a contributing factor in the decline of our cities. For instance, low-quality city schools are driving middle-income families to the suburbs, archaic transportation systems are choking commerce and industry in the cities, and inadequate police, fire, and sanitation services are forcing residents to live in fear and filth. These cities, regardless of size, cannot be rescued by slight increases in past levels of service.

In his study, Robinson set "aspiration levels" for the scope and quality of education and welfare programs and then projected the costs of achieving these levels. We have used Robinson's figures for the two services he projected (welfare and education) and, using a rather simpler form of his calculation method, we have set

* These studies were conducted by Professor Dick Netzer in 1965, the Joint Economic Committee in 1966, the Tax Foundation in 1966 and in 1968, the Committee for Economic Development in 1968, and William Robinson in 1969. Since all these studies used 1975 rather than 1976 as the year for their projections, we have also used 1975.

aspiration levels for other state and local services.* Assuming the levels of population growth, GNP growth, and price increases used throughout this book, we project total state and local expenditures for 1975 at $252 billion.

Robinson projects 1975 revenues from state and local taxes at $108.7 billion, assuming no change in present tax laws. He estimates that fees and charges will account for an additional $34 billion, and that the increase in net debt will total $15 billion. State and local revenues, excluding federal grants-in-aid, will total $157.8 billion in 1975, or $94.2 billion less than projected expenditures. Assuming that the present level of federal grants-in-aid to states and localities is maintained ($30 billion),** we estimate that the state-local revenue gap in 1975 will be approximately $67 billion.

Alternative Approaches for Remedying State and Local Fiscal Ills

The policies and actions of the federal government can determine, to a great extent, whether state and local governments will be able to meet the challenges the projected revenue gap will bring.

Clearly, the single most important federal responsibility is to ensure a healthy and growing economy. Economic growth alone

---

* Clearly, aspiration levels ought to be the relevant base for calculating expenditures. By projecting expenditures at the present level of inadequacy (or even at the same rate of quality increase), we would render the revenue gap an innocuous problem. States and localities could always avoid a revenue gap by keeping expenditures down and by providing less adequate services than previously provided (or services that do not improve at the same rate as they had previously).

Following Robinson's method, we have calculated the average annual rate at which various government services improved from 1962 to 1967, measured by the increase in expenditures not accounted for by population and price changes. This rate was then doubled to project the expenditures we estimate will be required for state and local governments to provide adequate services for these purposes in 1975.

We then added expenditures for preschool education and pollution control, services that states and localities were not providing to any significant extent during 1962–67 but should be providing by 1975. We estimated that annual state and local expenditures of about $15 billion by 1975 would be necessary to achieve high-quality preschool and pollution-control programs.

** Not adjusted for price increases.

accounted for 55 per cent of increased state revenues between 1966 and 1968. (The remainder resulted from new and increased taxes, mainly sales taxes.) Under the conditions of full employment assumed for 1973 and thereafter, state and local jurisdictions would receive, with no change in taxes or tax rates, a $6 billion annual "fiscal dividend" from economic growth.

The federal government can also intervene directly in state and local financing in a variety of ways. The major mode of federal assistance has been grants for specific purposes (categorical grants), usually accompanied by requirements to ensure that the federal funds do not supplant local funding (maintenance of effort) and that the recipient governments contribute some part of the total costs of the funded programs (matching money). Such assistance has the effect of greatly increasing the services offered through local governments—and of increasing their expenditures.

Still more federal efforts are needed to relieve state and local fiscal problems. A variety of new modes of providing relief have been proposed. The following are the major options, some of which could be combined:

1. *Revenue-Sharing.* Most of the numerous plans for revenue-sharing entail distributing a set percentage of annual federal revenues directly to the states. A recipient state would be required, in turn, to pass some of the funds directly to incorporated jurisdictions within its boundaries. The Administration's 1970 proposal would have provided states with $5 billion annually by 1976, approximately 30 per cent of which would go directly to local governments. Such a share would be a mere pittance to the large cities most in need. Under the Administration's 1970 plan, for example, Philadelphia, whose expenditures will be well over $1 billion by 1975, would receive $21 million—or less than 2 per cent of its budget—in revenue-sharing. Chicago would receive about the same amount, while Los Angeles would receive $18 million; Detroit, $13 million; Seattle, $4 million; and Indianapolis, $3 million.

It would, of course, be possible to structure a revenue-sharing program that would provide money directly to cities rather than states.

2. *Block Grants.* Under a block-grant arrangement, the federal

government could appropriate an amount of money yearly for cities and states in addition to present grant-in-aid funds. The block grant could be used at the discretion of the recipient government for a variety of purposes within broad federal guidelines. Currently, most federal grants are categorical, that is, they can be utilized by recipients only for specific functions set forth in law, such as Medicaid, vocational rehabilitation, and compensatory education. The current Model Cities program does provide cities with some discretionary funds.

3. *Expansion of Present Categorical Grant Programs.* The federal government could increase the funds of a large number of categorical grant programs to states and localities and institute new programs for specific purposes, as needed. Such an arrangement would ensure adherence to national guidelines, but would severely limit local discretion and preclude the application of funds to purposes other than those specifically designated in legislation. A variation of this scheme would be to consolidate various categorical grants in one functional area, such as manpower or education, thereby providing states and/or cities with block grants for each area. Total funding for the functional block grants could also be increased to exceed the sum of various previous program grants.

4. *Assumption of Costs.* The federal government could completely fund program costs now partially borne by the states. The two most important candidates for federal assumption of costs are the public-assistance and health (Medicaid) programs, both of which have proved quite expensive to the states. Assumption of welfare and health costs would save states about $11 billion in 1976.

In addition, a general aid program for education would relieve both states and localities of a part of their most severe burden. Localities, which currently finance more than 50 per cent of public school costs, would be greatly aided if states were to assume a much greater portion of these costs, and that assumption could be encouraged by federal incentives attached to a general aid program.

5. *Tax Credit.* States and localities find it politically difficult to make use of income taxes, partly because of high federal income taxes on their citizens. A tax credit allowing citizens to subtract a

percentage of their state and local income tax from their federal income tax liability would greatly encourage states and localities to tap their own revenue base more extensively. Alternatively, to avoid simply subsidizing citizens rather than governments, the federal government could provide a grant to states and/or localities equal to a percentage of total state or local income tax revenues.

A Package Approach

The recommendations in this report, if implemented, will affect state and local governments, and the problems they face, in several ways. A few will, in the short run, create more problems. For instance, a reduction in defense expenditures will create temporary unemployment, which, in turn, will place a severe strain on state and local resources. Special provision is made in the Counterbudget for federal assistance to such affected areas (see Chapter 3). Other recommended federal actions will have beneficial long-term effects, such as improving the health of Americans and eliminating poverty, which will eventually lighten some of the burdens state and local governments carry.

But probably the major effect implementation of the Counterbudget recommendations would have would be to increase the responsibilities of state and local governments to provide a higher quality of services.

Several recommendations of this report would have immediate effects on state and local governments—on the scope of their responsibilities, the quality of their services, and their ability to finance their activities—and have been designed with these effects in mind. These recommendations, summarized below, constitute an assistance "package."

The recommended programs will affect the finances of state and local governments in the following ways: (1) by supporting the conditions for economic growth; (2) by increasing present federal grants-in-aid; (3) by taking over some program costs presently borne by states and cities; and (4) by providing direct federal financial assistance to state and local governments. The net impact of our recommendations will nevertheless leave a substantial requirement for new funds to come from state and local revenues.

As will be seen from analysis of the assistance package, certain measures are designed to encourage and to assist states and localities to raise additional revenues through more equitable forms of taxation, particularly the graduated income tax.

The major elements of the state and local assistance package we recommend follow:

1. *Federal assumption of all state and local costs of present federal public-assistance programs and Medicaid* (about $8 billion in 1971). Both programs now flow entirely through state and local budgets. Under our recommendations, the federal government would not only assume full costs but would provide assistance directly to recipients. State and local expenditures would be reduced by some $20 billion annually, but nearly 50 per cent of that amount would be offset by the disappearance of $9 billion of direct federal aid for public assistance and Medicaid.

2. *Federal assumption of a portion of state and local education costs through a general aid to education program,* which would provide about $4 billion by 1976 (see Chapter 6). General aid to education would be available only to those states which provided at least 55 per cent of the state and local revenues raised for public elementary and secondary education. At present, only eighteen states meet this criterion; the average state share of state-local education costs is 44 per cent.

The formula for distributing the funds should be based on need (according to population and per capita income) and on the state's share of education costs (the higher the state's share relative to other states, the greater the funds received). The requirements and incentives built into this program to encourage states to assume a higher portion of education costs would result in reduced pressure on the overburdened local property tax.

3. *An increase in funding for a variety of present grant-in-aid programs to states and localities.* Presently, federal aid to states and localities amounts to about $30 billion, $10 billion of which is for public assistance and Medicaid. Under our recommendations, the federal government would take over all state and local spending for these two programs (see chapters 4 and 5). If federal aid, minus Medicaid and public assistance, were to be maintained at present levels, it would amount to $20 billion in 1975. Implemen-

tation of our recommendations would, by 1975, increase federal grants-in-aid to states and localities (excluding revenue-sharing, general aid to education, and Model Cities) to $39 billion, nearly a doubling of the present amount.

4. *A revenue-sharing plan that would automatically distribute 0.5 per cent of personal income ($5.4 billion by 1976) back to the states, which, in turn, would be required to pass 50 per cent of the funds directly to localities.* The funds could be used for any legal purposes. However, only states with graduated state income taxes (currently, thirty-six states) would be eligible to receive funds. The formula for distributing the funds among states would be based on need (according to population and per capita income), tax effort (states with a high ratio of revenue raised through taxes of state personal and corporate income would receive more funds), and reliance on state income tax (states that, relative to other states, collect a high portion of their tax revenues through an income tax would receive a greater share of funds). The last two criteria are particularly important.

5. *An expanded Model Cities program ($1.8 billion yearly by 1976) that would focus on the entire city rather than on only one neighborhood.* Unlike money municipalities receive from revenue-sharing, Model Cities funds would only be used for new program purposes and not for operating costs of ongoing programs. At least 60 per cent should be required to be spent in low-income neighborhoods. In addition, as an incentive for greater metropolitan planning and coordination, entire metropolitan areas ought to be eligible to submit applications.

Altogether this package would reduce the estimated state-local revenue gap in 1975 from $94 billion to $17 billion. (See Table 7:1.) States and localities will either have to forego this $17 billion of needed expenditures or to raise it through their own revenue systems. If they elect to raise it themselves, they will have to increase their revenues, over those projected under present laws and rates, by approximately 15 to 20 per cent. We have suggested a variety of strong incentives for states and localities to undertake badly needed tax reforms. Without more equitable tax systems, the prospects of raising $17 billion of added revenues are dim.

Between 1971 and 1976, we suggest an increase of direct federal

TABLE 7:1
PROJECTED STATE-LOCAL REVENUE GAP IN 1975
(In billions of dollars)

State and Local Expenditures	252.0	
State and Local Revenues (excluding federal aid)	157.8	
State-Local Revenue Gap[1]		94.2
Federal Aid		
Assumption of All State and Local Expenditures for Medicaid and Public Assistance	28.0	
Remaining Revenue Gap		66.2
Federal Grants-in-aid to States and Localities, Maintained at 1971 Levels (excluding aid for Medicaid and Public Assistance)	20.0	
Remaining Revenue Gap		46.2
Additional Federal Grants-in-aid Recommended	19.0	
Remaining Revenue Gap		27.2
Fiscal Relief Programs		
Revenue-Sharing	5.1	
Remaining Revenue Gap		22.1
General Aid to Education	3.6	
Remaining Revenue Gap		18.5
Model Cities (new funds)	1.3	
Remaining Revenue Gap		17.2

[1] Assuming present tax laws and rates.

aid to states and localities, in the form of categorical grants and fiscal relief programs, from $30 billion to $52.2 billion.* Recommended federal aid to states and localities would amount to $51.5 billion in 1972, compared to the Administration's estimate of $38.3 billion.**

STATE AND LOCAL BORROWING

About half of all state and local capital spending is financed through borrowing in the tax-exempt securities market. However,

* The 1976 total does not include any federal aid for public assistance or Medicaid, since these programs would have been replaced by a cash-assistance grant program and national health insurance, both fully administered and funded by the federal government.

** Although we recommend that complete federal administration and funding of public-assistance programs occur immediately, we have, nonetheless, included the federal costs of public assistance in our 1972 totals to make them comparable with the Administration's. Under our plan, federal public-assistance payments would go directly to families rather than to states.

it has become increasingly difficult for state and local governments to obtain funds in this manner. Interest rates on municipals have soared from 3.18 per cent in 1962 to over 6.5 per cent in 1970. As a result, some jurisdictions have been unable to borrow funds because the interest rates exceed the ceiling they are legally allowed to pay; others have hesitated to borrow because of the high cost of repayment.

State and local capital outlay needs are projected at $56 billion in 1976, compared to $34 billion in 1971. This jump suggests a need for approximately $28 billion of long-term municipal financing in 1976, an increase in net long-term debt of $13 billion over 1975 levels. Since interest rates on municipals are likely to fall from their present levels, it is impossible to forecast with precision where they will come to rest. A gross estimate is that rates will be between 4.5 and 5.5 per cent by 1976. *To permit states to acquire the funds they need for capital outlays, we recommend that the federal government provide subsidies to states and localities equal to one-half the difference between market interest rates and 5 per cent.* We assume that these subsidies will be necessary for new issues of municipals through 1974. Subsidy payments would, of course, continue for the life of the loan.

Budget proposals for Fiscal Relief for States and Localities are summarized in Table 7:2 on the following page.

TABLE 7:2
FISCAL RELIEF TO STATES AND LOCALITIES
(Outlays, in millions of current dollars)

	Administration		Urban Coalition Recommendations				
	Estimated 1971	Proposed 1972	1972	1973	1974	1975	1976
Revenue-Sharing	—	3,750	4,005	4,350	4,700	5,060	5,425
General Aid to Education	—	—	1,000	2,500	3,000	3,600	4,000
Interest Subsidy for State and Local Securities	—	—	95	145	175	175	175
TOTAL[1]	—	3,750	5,100	6,995	7,875	8,835	9,600

[1] Grants-in-aid are included in the budgets of the functional areas for which the grants were given.

8

Metropolitan Develoment

The daily life of most United States citizens is carried on within the unmarked boundaries of areas surrounding and including our large cities. Today, 65 per cent of our population lives in the country's 233 Standard Metropolitan Statistical Areas (SMSA's).* Metropolitan areas are growing, and, as they grow, they are irretrievably shaping the conditions under which most Americans will spend their lives.

America's population increased by 21 million between 1969 and 1970 and, according to Census estimates (Series D of the U.S. Bureau of the Census), is expected to increased by 80–100 million between 1970 and 2000. Nearly 85 per cent of the increase between 1960 and 1970 occurred in metropolitan areas. While the metropolitan population is increasing rapidly, both in absolute and percentage terms, most of this increase has occurred in suburban and outlying areas (30 per cent population growth between 1960 and 1969) rather than in central cities (only 2 per cent population growth between 1960 and 1969).

The desirability of further metropolitan and suburban concentration has increasingly been called into question. Several critics have suggested an immediate need to formulate a conscious policy

* The Bureau of the Census defines a Standard Metropolitan Statistical Area as follows: Except in New England, a Standard Metropolitan Statistical Area is a county or group of contiguous counties that contains at least one city of 50,000 inhabitants or more or "twin cities" with a combined population of at least 50,000. In addition to the county, or counties, containing a central city, or cities, contiguous counties are included in an SMSA if, according to certain criteria, they are essentially metropolitan in character and are socially and economically integrated with the central city. In New England, SMSA's consist of towns and cities, rather than counties.

on the distribution of future population growth. A number of alternatives have been suggested:

1. *Stem migration to metropolitan from nonmetropolitan areas by encouraging the growth of population in smaller regional centers.* However, in-migration from rural areas is a relatively minor factor in the growth of large metropolitan areas, amounting to abount 6 per cent of net metropolitan growth during the 1960's.

2. *Develop large numbers of self-sufficient new towns, predominantly in nonmetropolitan areas.* The National Committee on Urban Growth Policy, for example, has recommended that we build one hundred new cities of at least 100,000 population and ten new cities of at least 1 million population. However, it is questionable whether such new cities would be economically viable without imposition of strong central controls on business location decisions. They would also be quite costly, since they would not be able to take advantage of existing infrastructure. Even if these new towns and cities were constructed on the scale proposed, they would still account for less than 25 per cent of future population growth between now and the year 2000.

3. *Accept the fact that American citizens prefer to live in metropolitan areas and that 80 per cent of future population growth will occur there.* However, attempt to channel that growth into less densely populated metropolitan areas through incentives or even controls over business location.

4. *Accept the fact that 80 per cent of future population growth will occur in metropolitan areas and provide appropriate aid to ensure that development within those areas will be well planned to serve human needs.*

Americans have shown a preference for metropolitan living which, we believe, will be impossible to reverse. Accordingly, the most reasonable assumption for the future is that at least 80 per cent of future population growth will continue to occur in metropolitan areas. Most of the population growth in these areas will result from natural increase rather than migration. It would be useful to institute research and demonstration projects to determine what kind of incentives would be necessary to stimulate an increased movement of jobs and people from more crowded to less crowded metropolitan areas. However, we doubt that such research would reveal a panacea. It is clear we must become more concerned about the quality of development *within* metropolitan areas.

During the past two decades, our central cities have deteriorated physically, and their services have not kept pace with needs or expectations. Metropolitan areas have grown in an unplanned and inefficient way. Public policy should be devised to reverse these trends.

A major impediment to a concerted effort is that the needs of central city development are currently counterposed against the needs of suburban development as though the two were mutually exclusive. In reality, the cities and suburbs are integral parts of a larger system—the metropolitan area. Concentrating on either central city or suburban development to the exclusion of the other will merely result in greater problems for the entire metropolitan area.

Most people assume that the population of suburbs is drastically different from the population of cities. This is a misconception. The term "suburb" encompasses a vast diversity of municipalities ranging from high-income, low-density areas at the one end to low- and moderate-income high-density areas at the other. The latter are growing quickly as the central city population expands into contiguous suburbs. David Burch, in *The Economic Future of City and Suburb,* a study published in 1970 by the Committee for Economic Development, concludes:

> The effect of these shifts on the inner suburbs and, eventually, on the outer suburbs may be quite dramatic. Already, inner-suburb densities are approaching those of central cities, and increasingly this density growth is attributable to the poor and the Blacks. These inner suburbs can thus expect to experience many of the same problems experienced by the central cities during the first half of this century, and, in fact, they may resemble today's central cities in many ways.

AID TO CITIES

Two diametrically opposed alternatives have been suggested as public policy towards cities:

- maintain them at the lowest possible level of operating support; or
- rebuild them through both physical and social investment.

We strongly urge that the latter alternative—rebuilding—be the goal of federal policy toward cities, although we also caution against too great an emphasis on bricks and mortar. We would emphasize more fully companion programs serving human needs of city residents, programs that would make cities better places in which to live and work.

Model Cities

We have already suggested increasing the funding for the Model Cities program to $1.8 billion annually by 1976* (see Chapter 7). That program originally provided selected cities with discretionary funds (an amount equal to 80 per cent of the local share required for federal programs under a Model Cities plan) for use in a target low-income neighborhood. *The Model Cities program should be changed so that these discretionary funds could be used anywhere within the city's boundaries.* In effect, the Model Cities program could become a form of block grants to cities.

Entire metropolitan areas should also be eligible for Model Cities funds, with discretionary funds equal to 100 per cent of the local share. Such an arrangement would provide an incentive for more metropolitan-wide cooperation and planning.

We recommend expanded Model Cities funding, providing the following conditions are tied to the funds:

- a minimum of 60 per cent of the funds should be spent in low-income neighborhoods; and
- appropriate mechanisms for citizen participation should be utilized in determining how the funds be spent.

Community Action Agencies and the Office of Economic Opportunity

While Model Cities funds should be applicable throughout the entire city, community action programs should continue to be aimed solely at low-income areas. Local Community Action Agencies (CAA's) administer both national programs (e.g., Head Start,

* References to years are to federal fiscal years unless otherwise indicated.

Legal Services, Upward Bound) and local initiative programs designed by the individual CAA to meet the area's specific needs. The national programs are discussed throughout this volume. Many of the local initiative programs, developed through extensive citizen participation, have been quite successful; however, funding for them has remained nearly constant during the past several years at less than $300 million. *We recommend local initiative community action program (CAP) funds be increased to $750 million yearly by 1976.*

One of the most successful efforts of the local initiative programs has been the creation of neighborhood centers, many of which bring together under one roof information on the whole range of government and private services available to neighborhood residents. This is a highly desirable objective both because service delivery is more effective and because it fosters a sense of community. The Neighborhood Facilities Program of the Department of Housing and Urban Development (HUD) now provides municipalities a two-thirds federal grant for construction of multipurpose neighborhood centers and one-stop service centers. *We recommend that this program be expanded in the following ways:*

1. *Funding should be greatly increased from a present level of $40 million annually to $200 million annually by 1976.* Approximately 1,800 of these facilities could be established between 1971 and 1976, with federal funds committed totaling less than $1 billion.

2. *The grants should be utilized for building neighborhood city halls, which could be used by the mayor's office to provide liaison with neighborhoods.* The city halls could also be used to house ombudsmen-like city officials who would provide aid to constituents.

An experimental Office of Economic Opportunity program to encourage the establishment of local Community Development Corporations, run by a partnership of local business interests and target area residents, merits special attention. Since the program's inception in 1967, thirty-five corporations have been established to set up new business ventures and, at the same time, train local residents for managerial positions. It is hoped that after five years these corporations will become self-supporting. The program should continue on an experimental basis until these corporations have been operating long enough to be evaluated carefully.

Urban Renewal

Urban Renewal has been a disappointment to many of its early admirers. The program was originally intended primarily as a means of tearing down slums and providing standard housing for the poor. The 1949 act creating Urban Renewal authorized the building of 810,000 units of public housing on cleared slum land. Yet, Urban Renewal has actually resulted in a net loss of housing. The program has been criticized because it has too often destroyed well-functioning neighborhoods. It has ignored the needs of residents forced to move from these neighborhoods, who have often ended up in other slum areas.

Until quite recently, Urban Renewal was most frequently utilized to increase a city's tax base by building luxury apartment and office buildings on the cleared land. Although few would deny that this is one function of Urban Renewal, other objectives were lost in the almost total preoccupation with this function during the 1950's and first half of the 1960's.

Even in executing these distorted priorities, Urban Renewal was not a completely successful program. Regulations and administrative requirements were complex and time-consuming, and for a variety of reasons delays in programs were common. A study done by HUD revealed that of 288 Urban Renewal programs completed by 1966, the modal time for completion was between six and nine years. Furthermore, there were another 226 programs not yet completed in 1966 that had already been in existence more than nine years; 89 of these were more than twelve years old.

Widespread public discontent with the Urban Renewal program has resulted in several legislative and administrative changes of direction, which, in aggregate, now appear to make the program a more useful tool in the necessary task of rebuilding our cities.

First, HUD regulations issued in 1967 significantly altered the shape of the program. Priority of selection (there are always more applications than funds) was to be given to applications that:

contribute effectively to the conservation and expansion of housing for low and moderate income families; the development of employment opportunities and the renewal of areas with critical and urgent needs.

The Housing Act of 1968 reinforced this mandate by requiring that all future renewal projects: (1) be developed primarily for residential use, (2) provide a majority of units for low- and moderate-income families, and (3) reserve not less than 20 per cent of the total for low-income families. The Act also increased relocation assistance payments to displaced occupants and promised more assistance in finding suitable housing. The Housing Act of 1969 stipulated that for every unit of moderate-income housing removed during renewal, another low-income or moderate-income housing unit must be built in the renewal area. Unfortunately, all these provisions apply only to projects approved after the law was passed. *We recommend that these provisions be extended to programs already approved but still in the planning stage.*

An attempt to overcome the delays and administrative complexities that had plagued the program was also initiated in legislative authorization in 1968 for Neighborhood Development programs (NDP's) under Urban Renewal. NDP's are small-scale projects (often in noncontiguous areas) that can be expected to be completed within a year. The Neighborhood Development program is particularly useful for improving existing neighborhoods.

At the end of 1969, grant applications totaling $1.9 billion were being considered, with only $1 billion available for contract authorizations that year. *We recommend a moderate annual increase in the amount made available for new contracts, for both NDP's and longer-term projects, with NDP's receiving two-thirds of the total.* When expansion of these programs occurs, there will also be greater demand for other programs associated with renewal, such as code enforcement and demolition-assistance grants.

Recreation

HUD has recently focused its open-space program with emphasis on small parks and playgrounds in heavily populated central-city areas, particularly in low-income areas. In 1971, HUD spent $13 million to finance sixty-two such parks, far fewer than the number of applications. *We recommend that 500 of these parks be created annually,* an eight-fold increase over present efforts. Federal grants would cover the cost of acquisition, clearance, relocation, and development. The typical park would be about 2.5 acres, and grants would average $200,000 per park.

Although we recommend increased funding for urban parks, we strongly oppose transferring funds from open-space projects to urban parks. Open-space programs usually encompass more land (the average is 50 acres) in less densely populated areas of the metropolis. The need for open space is greater than ever; it is needed to provide recreation as well as ecological protection for lakes, forests, and water basins, all of which are threatened by urban sprawl. Outlays for open-space projects in 1971 (including small amounts for beautification and historic preservation programs) were $72 million. *We recommend that these open-space grants be increased so that they equal the amount spent on center cities*—a total of $121 million for each in 1976.

District of Columbia

Washington, D.C., is the only major city in the country that is forbidden an elected government. Congress should rectify this indefensible injustice immediately. Moreover, *federal payments to the District's budget—which amounted to $143 million, or 15 per cent of the D.C. operating budget in 1971—should be roughly doubled. Capital spending support also must increase during the next five years to finance construction of a subway system in the Washington metropolitan area.*

PLANNED DEVELOPMENT IN METROPOLITAN AREAS

We now commonly consider the United States as consisting primarily of a large number of metropolitan areas in which social, physical, and economic functions are highly interdependent even though there may exist a multitude of governmental jurisdictions.

The extent of U.S. metropolitanism can be measured by the increase in the number of Standard Metropolitan Statistical Areas (SMSA's) as well as the population growth within them.*

However, it is important to emphasize that, although the United States is a metropolitan nation by the Census definition of (SMSA's) as well as the population growth within them.* (which refers to incorporated municipalities of 2,500 or more), it is nonetheless *not* a nation dominated by large cities, as many people imagine. Richard Forstall's study in the 1966 *Municipal Yearbook* (issued by the International City Managers Association) makes this clear. Forstall breaks America's 1965 population into the following five territorial aggregates:

Territorial Aggregates	Per Cent of Total U.S. Population
Metropolitan Cities (50,000 or more)	30.4
Incorporated Suburbs of 10,000 or more	14.4
Metropolitan Remainders (suburban areas outside incorporated places of 10,000 or more)	17.1
Nonmetropolitan Urban Places of 10,000–50,000	29.0
Nonmetropolitan Remainders (towns and villages below 10,000 and rural areas)	9.2

At this time, America's large cities are just about balanced in population with its small towns. Even the sophisticated cliché— that we are, in reality, a suburban nation—is presently inaccurate. Clearly we are becoming one. However, suburbs with more than 10,000 residents now comprise less than 15 per cent of the population. A plurality of America's population is still small town and rural, although suburbs will soon become the plurality.

Despite the popular belief that metropolitan expansion and suburbanization have already largely occurred, the 1970's should witness an acceleration of these trends. Unless new policies are adopted, an unfortunate byproduct of growth will surely be the further proliferation of "urban sprawl," characterized by (accord-

* The number of SMSA's has increased from 170 in 1953 to 233 in 1969; residents of SMSA's now account for 65 per cent of the total U.S. population, compared to 42 per cent in 1900.

ing to *Urban and Rural Growth,* the report of the Advisory Commission on Intergovernmental Relations) "substantial bypassed tracts of raw land between developing areas and a scattering of urban development over the rural landscape."

Sprawl is usually condemned because of its ugly appearance. But its major deleterious effects are the increased costs of providing basic services, such as water, sewer lines, electricity, and transportation, and foreclosure of options for future efficient land use within an integrated metropolitan area.

The federal government should encourage planned development within a metropolitan area by making aid available only to jurisdictions and developers presenting plans consistent with metropolitan area plans. (Such plans are already required by the federal government as a condition of receiving many forms of federal assistance.) Plans should relate public facilities and services to projected residential needs; they should also include provisions for some housing for low-income and moderate-income families.

Aid to planned developments (including but not limited to new towns) must be sufficient to encourage such development but should not subsidize development costs that can be borne by the developer himself. Using these criteria, *new or additional federal aid is recommended in three areas: land acquisition and development, public facilities construction, and planning.*

Land Acquisition and Development

Developers often have enormous difficulty merely in assembling land at reasonable prices. Indeed, the spiraling cost of land is a primary cause for sprawl, since developers are forced to leap beyond closer, more expensive land to obtain cheaper land on the metropolitan fringe.

A variety of proposals have been suggested for dealing with this problem: land-tax reforms, possibly including a tax on land appreciation; a federally chartered public-private land development corporation; a federal land development agency; and federal aid to state land development authorities. *We prefer the last mentioned alternative—federal aid to state land development authorities—as the only one that is both potentially effective and con-*

sistent with America's tradition of decentralization. Federal aid in the form of grants and loans to partially defray the cost of acquiring land, particularly in metropolitan fringe areas, could be granted to state land development authorities upon their request.

The aid would have to be substantial enough not only to provide adequate means of financing the program but also to entice states to create land development agencies. Once land was acquired, the state land development agency could hold it for a period of years and then sell it to a developer (either public or private) for development according to a satisfactory plan. The developer would buy the land at cost plus a small profit to the state, a price far below what he would have paid had the land continued to appreciate on the private market.

Creators of planned developments and new towns also often find it difficult to obtain financing; even if they are successful in locating funds, they may find it difficult, at least initially, to repay even moderate-term loans. A well-planned development does not begin to produce income until several years after the heavy initial investment. A combination of federal loan guarantees and federal loans to cover interest costs (with a deferred repayment period) would first make it easier to obtain financing, since lenders would be assured repayment, and, second, would lift some of the overwhelming initial burden from the developer. Legislation establishing both of these programs was passed in 1970 but the programs have not yet been funded. Federal outlays should reach $240 million by 1976.

Federal loans guarantees are already available to new-town developers, but these guarantees, as well as new loans that would cover interest costs, should also be made available to other planned developments. It is the well-planned relationship of services and facilities to human needs within a metropolitan area that must be the goal; new towns, as they are typically envisioned, are only one of a variety of means of achieving that objective.

Public Facilities

A variety of federal programs exist to provide aid to communities for development of basic public facilities and amenities. Recently, the greatest need has been for additional water and sewer facilities. The development of metropolitan areas is currently being constrained because suburban jurisdictions are unable or unwilling to finance the cost of extending water and sewer facilities to relatively underdeveloped areas. Three possibilities exist for providing aid:

- a federally guaranteed loan program for water and sewer facilities;
- a direct federal loan program; or
- an extension of the present water and sewer grant program (up to 55 per cent matching grants) so that it is available to developers and small communities as well as to cities. Grants would be contingent upon the presentation of a satisfactory development plan.

We recommend primary emphasis on the last alternative—extension of the present sewer and water grant program—because it provides a high degree of incentive for planned development of metropolitan areas. The present grant program has been providing only about 30 per cent of total cost; *we suggest that the grant be stabilized at 50 per cent of cost and that the federal government guarantee loans obtained on the private market for the balance.* Such a loan guarantee program should be available as well to developers who do not qualify for the grants.

HUD estimates that an average expenditure of $2,000 for water and sewer facilities will be necessary for each new housing unit (13.3 million units projected for 1972–76), indicating that a significant expansion of the sewer and water grant program both for planned developments and for cities will be necessary.

In addition, nearly 60 million Americans, 40 million of them in urban areas, are not now served by any sewer system. Federal outlays averaging $585 million annually for 1973–76 would be sufficient to provide 20 million of these urban residents with sewage facilities by 1976. Total outlays for water and sewer facilities grants should reach $1.6 billion annually by 1976, a sevenfold increase over present outlays. It is estimated that these outlays would finance nearly 20 per cent of the total cost of water and sewer expenditures in that year.

Additionally, in order to encourage well-planned metropolitan areas, *it would be desirable—as the 1970 housing legislation proposed—that the federal government bear an additional 20 per cent of the total cost of all infrastructure programs qualifying for grant assistance, if the applicant is a planned development or new town.*

Planning and Coordination

In order to promote planned metropolitan development, grants for comprehensive planning assistance should be made available to developers who seek federal assistance. Comprehensive planning grants are already available to cities, states, metropolitan regions, and new-town developers. In some cases, receipt of federal aid is contingent upon development of such a plan. *We recommend that by 1975 all public and private bodies be required to present a comprehensive plan as a prerequisite for any federal aid and that use of the federal aid be consistent with that plan.*

Unfortunately, comprehensive planning by municipalities cannot, by itself, bring about a well-planned metropolitan area. A metropolitan area consists of a multiplicity of legal jurisdictions whose interests and policies sometimes coincide and sometimes conflict. Even when interests do coincide, policies and planning are often uncoordinated.

The federal government can provide incentives for better metropolitan planning coordination. *We recommend strengthening present federal laws that require that a locality's application for any federal assistance first be submitted to an area-wide planning agency for review.* Disapproval by the metropolitan agency should be binding unless specifically reversed by the federal government. At present, metropolitan agency review is only advisory.

Our emphasis on planning will require at least double the number and total cost of yearly planning grants. Additionally, there will be a need for more and better planners. Most municipalities simply do not have the capacity to undertake the kind of planning our policies would require. *We therefore recommend intensive efforts to train planners and urban affairs experts by federal offers of financial support to students attending graduate institutions in these fields.* Outlays averaging $18 million yearly could produce

15,000 professionals in a five-year period (assuming an 18-month graduate program with federal grants providing $4,000 per year). Currently, approximately 1,000 people receive professional planning degrees annually.

URBAN SOCIAL RESEARCH AND EVALUATION

One of the most cogent criticisms of federal social programs is that, when initiated, they are usually not based on empirically derived data and, when implemented, are not evaluated carefully to determine whether and how well they are doing what they were intended to do. Without such knowledge, policy choices may often represent little more than hunches or acceptance of fads. A concerted effort is needed to remedy this situation. Well-advised and evaluated experiments such as the income-maintenance experiment in New Jersey and the school voucher experiment in Boston, both under the auspices of the Office of Economic Opportunity, are excellent prototypes. Similar *experiments are needed in the area of criminal rehabilitation, manpower mobility, and population distribution.* In addition, *present programs must be regularly evaluated, not from the narrow Government Accounting Office "green eyeshade" perspective, but by well-trained social scientists, in order to determine program effectiveness and impact.* These evaluations should be conducted by a separate independent agency working in cooperation with the operating agencies. We have recommended outlays of $500 million for these purposes in 1976.

Budget proposals for Metropolitan Development are summarized in Table 8:1 on the following page.

TABLE 8:1
METROPOLITAN DEVELOPMENT
(Outlays, in millions of current dollars)

	Administration			Urban Coalition Recommendations			
	Estimated 1971	Proposed 1972	1972	1973	1974	1975	1976
Aid to Cities							
Model Cities	380	450	900	1,500	1,700	1,800	1,800
CAA Programs (Local Initiative)	240	225	400	600	650	700	750
Urban Renewal	1,082	1,300	1,500	1,938	2,336	2,536	2,322
Urban Recreation				106	110	117	121
District of Columbia	261	300	350	400	500	600	700
Other	113	108	157	244	322	338	432
Subtotal	2,076	2,383	3,307	4,788	5,618	6,091	6,325
Aid to Planned Developments							
Loans to Planned Developments	−3	−5	30	70	120	180	240
Water and Sewer Facilities Grants	226	284	500	1,030	1,250	1,590	1,615
Supplementary Public Facilities Grants	1	2	20	55	85	120	140
Planning Assistance	52	50	60	80	80	90	90
Planning Scholarship Grants		—	6	12	18	24	27
Open Space	72	100	80	106	110	117	121
Other	2	0	3	5	10	14	—
Subtotal	350	431	699	1,358	1,673	2,135	2,233
Urban Social Research and Evaluation	94	114	210	310	490	500	500
Community Development Special							
Revenue-Sharing	0	150					
TOTAL	2,520	3,078	4,216	6,456	7,781	8,726	8,858

9

Housing

The Housing Act of 1968 set a ten-year goal, which, if implemented, would assure sufficient housing for newly formed households and virtually eliminate substandard housing in the United States. The first-year (1969)* goal was met by changing the goal and including new mobile homes as housing starts. Second-year goals were revised downward, but the housing industry's performance still fell short by 60,000 units. Meanwhile, families continue to be formed at a high rate, housing continues to deteriorate, and the cost of adequate shelter continues to rise.

The President's first Annual Housing Report (1969) estimated ten-year needs at 26 million housing units, 6 million of which would have to be federally subsidized low-income and moderate-income housing. Thirteen million of these units were to be provided between 1972 and 1976, including 3.3 million of the subsidized units.

The ten-year goal would require an annual production of 2.6 million housing units. Housing starts have averaged only 1.5 million annually since 1960, and we have produced as many as 2 million units in only one year in the last two decades. Indeed, fixed investment in residential structures in constant dollars has not significantly increased over the last two decades and has fallen precipitously as a percentage of the GNP. During the past five years, housing investment has averaged about 3.2 per cent of the GNP. It has fallen below 3 per cent in the current year. Housing investment of 4 per cent of the GNP will be necessary to generate production of over 2.5 million units annually.

* All references to years are to federal fiscal years unless otherwise indicated.

Housing Goals and Actual Production

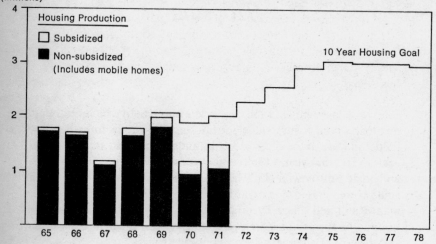

Housing Starts (Millions)

Housing Production
- ☐ Subsidized
- ■ Non-subsidized (Includes mobile homes)

10 Year Housing Goal

THE MORTGAGE MARKET

If investment in housing is to increase as a percentage of the GNP, something else must decrease; resources must be shifted from other areas to housing. This shift will, quite likely, be brought about only through government policy. Several alternatives exist:

1. *An increase in personal and corporate taxes sufficient to provide a sizable ($10 billion) annual surplus in the federal budget.* The federal government could then repay $10 billion of its outstanding debt, thereby making an extra $10 billion available for investment. Most of this repaid debt, it is hoped, would be invested in residential structures (other investment demand having been largely satisfied).

This alternative, implying a forced shift mostly from private consumption expenditures to housing investment, appears hopeless.

The demand for federal funds for other priority items makes a budget surplus of this magnitude most unlikely.

2. *A decrease of $10 billion in present federal outlays, which would provide the same situation as alternative (1)* (above) *but without any increase in taxes.* Resources would shift from the government sector to the investment sector, mostly to housing. This alternative appears undesirable, since the nation's aggregate needs dictate a rather significant increase in federal budgetary outlays rather than a decrease.

3. *Initiation of a government program providing $10 billion annually in direct housing loans.* Unlike the first two alternatives this would directly add $10 billion to federal outlays. However, the $10 billion would have to be raised in precisely the manner already discussed—either through raising taxes or cutting other federal expenditures. Rather than repaying public debt and hoping most of the repaid money would be invested in housing, no debt would be paid off. The extra $10 billion would be invested directly in housing by the government.

4. *Selective credit controls, which would ensure that more funds within the investment sector were invested in housing.* This could be accomplished in a variety of ways, such as an investment credit for housing analogous to the former 7 per cent investment credit for business, or a requirement that lending institutions (particularly private pension funds and mutual funds) invest a specified percentage of their funds in residential mortgages. The result would be a shift of resources within the investment sector from business investment and consumer credit into housing.

The last alternative appears to us to be the most attractive because it is both most direct and most workable. *We therefore recommend that selective credit controls be instituted if such a move should prove necessary to provide sufficient mortgage funds to meet the housing goal.*

During most of 1970, financial institutions were generally ignoring the mortgage market, primarily because interest rates for alternative investments were higher. Increasing mortgage interest rates in an attempt to make them competitive priced many Americans out of the market. During mid-1970, HUD Secretary George W. Romney estimated that 80 per cent of U.S. families could not afford the average cost of a new home. Recent actions taken to lower interest rates throughout the economy have reinvigorated the housing sector to some extent.

Historically, low-income families have not been able to afford new housing, occupying instead the housing vacated by higher-income families moving into new homes. Such used housing is often expensive to rehabilitate and to maintain and is located where public and private services are declining.

Several federal government programs—public housing, rent supplement, and home ownership and rental subsidy programs—provide low-income residents and moderate-income residents of specified housing units with subsidies. These programs produced an average of 60,000 new and rehabilitated units annually between 1964 and 1968. During calendar year 1970, however, nearly 400,000 units of federally subsidized housing were produced; it is estimated an additional 450,000 units will be built during calendar year 1971. An average of 660,000 units will be needed annually between 1971 and 1976.

Most federal housing activity, however, is directed toward providing assistance to families with middle-level incomes or above. FHA-guaranteed mortgage loans have literally financed the movement of the middle class to the suburbs. Since 1950, over 4 million single-family homes have been financed by FHA-insured mortgages, most of which have been loans to middle-income families. (The median family income of FHA loan recipients in 1968 was $10,597; less than 10 per cent of the borrowers had incomes under $7,000.)

Federal income tax provisions that allow homeowners to deduct their mortgage interest and property tax payments not only subsidize primarily middle-income families but also favor homeowners over renters. Low-income families are disadvantaged because: (1) they are disproportionately renters; (2) those who are homeowners usually take the standard rather than the itemized deduction, thus nullifying their subsidy; and (3) those low-income homeowners who do itemize find their deduction worth less than that of their higher-income counterpart with the same deduction because of the progressivity of the federal income tax.

These deductions cost the federal government $4.5 billion in lost revenue in 1969. To reduce this unwarranted subsidy to higher-income families, *we recommend that a ceiling be placed on the maximum allowable deduction for both mortgage interest and property tax payments.* The ceiling ($500 for mortgage interest and $300 for property tax deductions) would allow most low-income and middle-income families to continue to take full advantage of the deductions but would reduce the subsidy received by higher-income individuals. Such a provision would yield $1.5 billion in added annual federal revenues by 1976.

Several alternatives have been suggested for providing adequate housing for Americans with insufficient income to compete on the private housing market:

1. *Greatly expand the restructure present government housing programs.* Expansion of eligibility, change of subsidy formulas, program consolidation, and a broadening of program purposes to encompass social goals, such as racial integration, throughout a metropolitan area have all been suggested.

2. *Institute a new federal housing program in which the federal government, as the "houser of last resort," would build housing in areas where housing needs remain unmet.*

3. *Scrap present housing programs and provide all families below a specific income level with cash subsidies that could be applied to any housing unit.* The risk in this approach is that landlords would simply raise rents, thereby transferring a large portion of the subsidy to themselves. Rent control laws might very well be needed to make certain the subsidy benefited the recipient family.

4. *Encourage federal research and development into production techniques designed to cut housing costs.* HUD's present Operation Breakthrough program is an effort to determine how much costs can be cut through these techniques. Although these efforts are commendable, it appears extremely unlikely that costs can be cut enough to make a major difference.

Although in principle we prefer approach (3), we fear that adopting such an approach without first greatly increasing supply would mean a windfall to landlords. *We believe experiments with housing subsidies are in order, but, at least for the span of years under consideration, we fall back on alternative (1)—that present programs be restructured and greatly expanded.*

To produce the required 660,000 units yearly, annual federal outlays must reach a level of $3.5 billion by 1976. However, the

660,000 annual need estimate is based on an assumption of adequate performance in the nonsubsidized sector. Any shortfall in that sector would require increased production in subsidized housing, since the private market would not then be providing adequate used housing units to lower-income households. *If such a shortfall, for whatever reasons, should occur, we recommend increased funding for federally subsidized housing above the target level now specified. And if local obstacles block needed housing for low- and moderate-income families, the federal government should assume the responsibility as "houser of last resort"—alternative (2).*

The present programs also need to be restructured. First, housing must be viewed as service designed to serve social purposes rather than simply as physical structures. High-rise public housing projects that resemble concrete jails surely do not serve social goals. The recent de-emphasis on project-type construction should continue, as should efforts to allow tenants (in public housing as well as in other federally subsidized housing) the opportunity to purchase their dwellings. Public housing management must be upgraded and the rights and responsibilities of tenants made more explicit. Funding for tenant services and housing counseling for low-income families, programs now existing on a shoestring, should be greatly increased.

One of the most important social purposes to be pursued is integration of the entire metropolitan area. The moral imperative of integration, the relative scarcity of land in many central cities, and the increasing movement of employment opportunities to the suburbs all attest to the necessity of building a significant portion of the federally subsidized housing in suburban jurisdictions. These jurisdictions currently resist subsidized housing through a variety of legal devices, such as large-lot zoning laws, which make the cost of housing too high for low-income families. *Localities which either prevent or make no allowance for the provision of federally subsidized housing programs should suffer a cutoff of all other federal aid. If the cutoff does not provide the desired results, we recommend that the federal government be given the power to suspend local ordinances that prevent the building of federally subsidized housing.* (Secretary Romney supported such a proposal in HUD's 1970 legislative recommendations.) A further possibility would be federal acquisition of local land to be used for subsidized housing.

Present housing programs must be greatly simplified and rationalized. There are too many programs entangled in too much red tape. Eligibility requirements and subsidy levels differ for each program. A major criticism of these programs is that they neither reach down to the poorest families nor extend high enough to ensure adequate housing for families at all income levels. An expansion of funding ought to allow also for an expansion of coverage. In addition, both for administrative simplicity and for equity reasons, subsidy formulas should be changed so that they are similar for all programs. For instance, recipients might pay a set percentage of their income toward rent. Residents of all federally subsidized housing could, for example, be required to pay 20 per cent of their first $3,500 of income and 25 per cent of their next $6,500 toward the cost of their housing. A family with an annual income of $6,000 would pay $110 monthly for rent. A family with an annual income of $10,000 would pay $200 monthly.

RESEARCH

The housing industry has been notoriously slow in developing modern industrial production and management techniques. HUD, historically, has done little to come to grips with this problem; 1971 outlays for research and development (R&D) amounted to only $45 million (up from an infinitesimal $1.8 million in 1968).

HUD is now placing major emphasis on Operation Breakthrough, which is an effort both to test new housing prototypes and to encourage mass production techniques through the aggregation of markets. Unfortunately, Operation Breakthrough has been severely hindered by the unwillingness of Congress to appropriate adequate funds and by the fear of many local communities that Breakthrough projects will be an undesirable intrusion on their way of life. Nonetheless, Operation Breakthrough accounts for a major portion of HUD R&D funds.

The President's Committee on Urban Housing (Kaiser Committee) has recommended that HUD research and development efforts be funded at the level of $100 million. *We recommend that HUD's*

R&D spending level reach the $100 million level in 1974. Research and development priorities should be:

- The application of available technology—and to a lesser extent the development of new technology—to the physical, managerial, and planning needs of housing and urban development. This would include demonstration programs.
- The establishment of experimental municipal and metropolitan development centers to strengthen research and planning capacities at those levels.
- Continuous evaluation of ongoing programs and projection of likely consequences of prospective programs.

Budget proposals for Housing are summarized in Table 9:1 on the following page.

TABLE 9:1
HOUSING[1]
(Outlays, in millions of current dollars)

	Administration		Urban Coalition Recommendations			
	Estimated 1971	Proposed 1972	1972	1973	1974	1975	1976
Federal Housing Subsidies	1,653	1,948	2,074	2,393	2,619	3,161	3,653
Research and Development	45	25	65	80	100	100	100
TOTAL	1,678	1,973	2,139	2,473	2,719	3,261	3,753

[1] Excludes Department of Defense housing expenditures.

10

Transportation

The transportation system in the United States today clearly illustrates, in its marvels and its horrors, both the stimulating effects of bold federal programs and the chaos when government fails to consider the total impact of its policies.

The jet airways and interstate highways that criss-cross the nation are truly modern marvels, which would not have been possible except through nation-wide planning and massive federal spending. Travelers and goods can move from city to city with unprecedented speed and ease. But inside the cities—where most Americans spend most of their time and where most of the country's goods must be delivered—decrepit local mass-transit and congested traffic, even with proliferating expressways—threaten to cancel out the gains these programs have provided. It is now time for the federal government to complete the job so boldly started.

The importance of the transportation sector of our national life looms large in economic, as in other, terms. Operating transportation companies (railroads, airlines, trucking, barge lines, etc.) and their suppliers employ about 4.7 million workers and generate some $87 billion worth of Gross National Product. The auto industry and its suppliers and servicing networks represent an additional 4.7 million employees and $83 billion of the GNP. Government agencies employ another 800,000 in transportation activities. In total, about 10 million employees and $170 billion in Gross National Product make up the transportation sector of the economy, exclusive of transportation functions of national defense, education (school busing), and the like.

Historically, there has been more than ample federal budgetary support and public sanction for transportation programs. However, federal support for transportation has become heavily balanced in favor of highways and aviation. Other sectors—particularly mass transit and railroads—have suffered by comparison. (See Table 10:1.)

TABLE 10:1
FEDERAL AID TO TRANSPORTATION, 1971
(In millions of dollars)

	Outlays	Per Cent of Transportation Outlays
Mass Transit	215	2.8
Highways	4,880	62.9
Aviation	1,620	20.9
Railroads	48	0.6
Water	1,000	12.8
TOTAL	7,763	100.0

The heaviest transportation needs are now appearing in the sectors receiving the least federal funding, with the most critical and insufficiently met needs in urban areas, where the greatest number of persons suffer from the most severe problems deriving from transportation. These include pollution and congestion.

A greater portion of government transportation funding should go to urban areas. Moreover, the present allocation of resources within urban transportation, which greatly favors urban highways as opposed to urban mass transportation, needs to be drastically changed. A reallocation in favor of mass transport is critical if we are to make a serious effort to overcome traffic congestion and to provide urban residents, particularly those with low incomes, the mobility that they need to adjust to the exodus of jobs from the central city to the suburbs.

It should be noted that nearly 63 per cent of the transportation outlays during 1971 was for highway construction and improvement, most of it to be spent in nonurban areas. Although private automobile owners derive some benefit from these expenditures, the chief beneficiary is the trucking industry, inasmuch as highways are designed and constructed—at considerable additional expense —to meet truck use standards. And programs such as the supersonic transport (SST), airport development, Coast Guard aid to shipping and recreational boating, and Corps of Engineers navigation expenditures almost exclusively accrue to specialized, generally

Transportation Funding Priorities

1971

Mass Transit	2.8%
Highways	62.9%
Aviation	20.9%
Railroads	0.6%
Water	12.8%

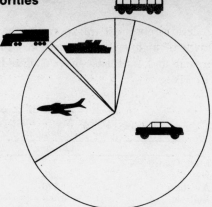

1973

Mass Transit	11.1%
Highways	49.2%
Aviation	27.6%
Railroads	0.5%
Water	11.6%

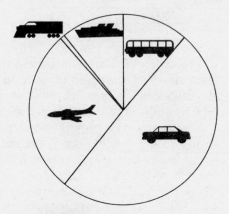

1975

Mass Transit	23.0%
Highways	36.1%
Aviation	32.4%
Railroads	0.7%
Water	7.8%

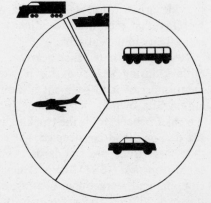

upper-income clientele groups rather than a broad spectrum of the population.

Federal participation in transportation is necessary and justified to assure transportation services deemed in the national interest. Direct subsidies to transportation can be economically justifiable if the marginal benefit to society as a whole exceeds the marginal public investment cost. However, user charges rather than a subsidy are called for when the beneficiaries can afford to support the service themselves or when the service is not considered socially important.

HIGHWAYS

Federal expenditures for highways in 1971 amounted to about $3.0 billion for the interstate program (cost shared 90 per cent federal, 10 per cent state and local), and another $1.9 billion for other federal aid programs, such as the ABC system of primary and secondary highways (costs shared, 50:50 with state and local governments) Traffic Operations Program to Increase Capacity and Safety (TOPICS), and highway beautification. Most of these expenditures are paid out of the Highway Trust Fund, which receives its revenues through federal highway fuel taxes.

Up to a point, highway construction is a major contributor to society's welfare. Today, however, we have by far the world's finest network of highways, while many of our other forms of transportation go crying for funds. As of October, 1970, approximately 30,595 miles of an originally proposed 42,500-mile interstate highway system were completed, and a good portion of the remaining part was in various states of progress, so that only 1,659 miles of the initial system remained to be initiated.

We therefore *recommend setting back the target date for completion of the interstate highway system from 1977 to 1980.* The system would eventually be completed as planned, but with smaller annual outlays. The first deferrals should be of those parts of the interstate system slated to pass through cities. In the past, these links have been built with disregard of community needs and often with wide-scale destruction of residences and property, particularly in low-income areas. Clearly, more time and effort are necessary to plan these routes, with participation of all interests, including the citizens whose neighborhoods are to be destroyed. As a result of this slow-down, total federal highway outlays (including the ABC system) should decrease from their present level of $4.9 billion to $3.1 billion in 1976. As outlays are divided nearly evenly between rural and nonrural interstate highway construction, the postponing of one-half of the urban construction would effect a $1 billion savings, in addition to providing additional planning time for consideration of urban social needs. A further result of these steps would be the growth of a large surplus in the Highway Trust Fund, should it continue to collect revenue under present laws.

Ideally, the Highway Trust Fund itself should be scrapped and all future highway funding should occur through direct appropriations. When it was inaugurated during the 1950's, the Highway Trust Fund provided a timely response to an overdue public investment need. The need has now been overtaken in priority by other, more pressing requirements, but since the monies are sheltered in a trust fund it is legally impossible to transfer them.

If it is not politically possible to end the Highway Trust Fund, we recommend that the law be amended to authorize the use of trust fund monies for mass transit and other urban transportation improvements. This broadened use of highway funds would not be a redirection of funds into unrelated areas. It would permit the federal government to obtain the maximum benefit from highway expenditures in the urban areas by funding transportation improvements, which will relieve traffic pressures on and promote more efficient use of federal highways.

MASS TRANSIT

Many urban transportation problems still await a concerted effort at solution. These include commuter problems (both getting people from the suburbs into the city and some city dwellers out to the suburbs), coordination between transportation systems, pedestrian circulation, the improvement of city streets, and goods movement.

A critical part of the solution to these problems will be improved and enlarged urban mass transit, both bus and rail.

Since World War II, public transportation has suffered from increasing operating expenses, decreasing profits, and a diminishing clientele. Fares have risen dramatically, driving away more customers, and operating income has turned to deficit. Private enterprise is withdrawing from transit as it perceives new capital and retained earnings to be inadequate for replacement of machinery and equipment. In 1969, at a time when the public transit system was certainly less than self-sufficient, the federal government spent thirty times more on roads than on all types of mass transit.

Federal outlays for mass transit programs have not yet begun to approach their needed size. They represent less than 3 per cent of 1971 federal aid to transportation. Estimated need over the next decade, according to the Rapid Transit Institute and the American Transit Association, is $20 billion—$17.5 billion of which is for rail transit. *A federal government program now exists to provide 60 per cent matching funds for capital outlays to mass transit systems, but less than $600 million has been spent on this program since 1965; we recommend that these grants increase from $215 million in 1971 to $2 billion in 1976—and we anticipate that outlays should increase further during the latter part of the decade. From 1971 to 1974, we recommend that outlays be used primarily for improvements in existing bus, rail, and commuter facilities and for planning and research* of the kind discussed below. We wish to avoid duplicating the mistake of poorly planning the location of highways in our metropolitan areas. From 1974 to 1976 and beyond, we envision most of the mass transit funds being spent for hardware and installation of new rail systems or extensions of existing systems.

Expenditures on research and development for mass transportation have been negligible. Among the topics needing further study are: appropriate use of the various transportation modes, means of cost reduction, improvements in vehicle comfort, reducing the emission of pollutants, transportation land use, and factors affecting transportation demand.

The federal government should expand research, training, and technological development in all its urban transportation programs. Rigorous attention needs to be directed to inadequacies in knowledge, technology, and trained personnel—all of which seriously impede transportation improvement.

OTHER TRANSPORTATION MODES

To the extent that transportation services benefit specific groups —particularly higher-income groups—and are not considered to be in the national interest, we recommend that they should increasingly be reimbursed by their beneficiaries through payment of user charges, rather than be paid from general revenues. *Included in this category, to varying degrees, are: aviation and airway systems development, Army Corps of Engineers navigation projects, Coast Guard aids to commercial navigation and recreational boating, and merchant-marine activities.*

The aggregate result of implementing this policy in each of the above areas would be to reduce net federal support for these activities from $2.8 billion in 1971 to $0.4 billion in 1976. More specific examination of two areas—inland waterway navigation projects and the merchant marine activities—will illustrate the wisdom and equity of such measures.

Inland Waterways Navigation Projects

The major navigation functions of the Army Corps of Engineers have included maintaining rivers for barge navigation, building harbors for shipping, and construction of dams and reservoirs for flood control. The Corps's navigation work literally makes it possible to have a large inland water carrier industry, but the operating costs of users are completely subsidized. Any boat or barge operator can pass through enormously expensive lock systems free of user charges. Since projects are not set up to produce sufficient revenue to be self-supporting, there is no way to determine which projects now do or could pay for themselves, which cannot (but are nonetheless in the national interest and deserving of subsidy), and which cannot stand such tests. *Instituting selective user charges for different forms of navigation usage would be the most effective way to determine both which projects are sensible undertakings and how much in operating subsidies is needed for each existing one.*

The 1971 level of spending for the program was $411 million. *We recommend that user charges be set at a level sufficient to collect at least $80 million annually.* This should be sufficient to discourage most unwarranted new capital spending and to cover a high percentage of operating costs.

Merchant Marine

The Maritime Administration awarded almost $230 million in ship construction subsidies and $188 million in ship-operating subsidies in 1971.

Construction differential subsidies (CDS) pay one-half of the difference between costs of construction in U.S. yards and foreign yards. The Merchant Marines Act of 1970 tripled the ship construction subsidy program, authorizing construction of 300 ships over the next ten years. Because of the new construction, the 1970 Act will add at least an additional $100 million yearly in federal outlays to subsidize the merchant marine, even though it will lead to gradually reduced subsidy rates (from 50–55 per cent to 35 per cent by 1975).

Operating differential subsidies (ODS) pay the difference in operating costs between U.S. and foreign ships. Because most of the operating cost difference is wages, about 80 per cent of every wage dollar paid by subsidized operators is ultimately paid by the federal government.

Two justifications are normally advanced for merchant-marine subsidies. The primary rationale is in terms of national defense considerations: the subsidies assure a large fleet of ships will be available to carry essential cargo during wartime. Charles L. Schultze in *Setting National Priorities: The 1971 Budget* (Washington, D.C.: The Brookings Institution, 1970) questioned this rationale on several grounds:

1. The operating and cargo preference subsidies keep some 400 U.S. flag ships engaged in foreign trade. But there are also 440 unsubsidized ships owned by U.S. firms operating under flags of conve-

nience (primarily of Panama, Honduras, and Liberia) that are contractually committed to serve the United States in time of emergency. In addition, there are the merchant fleets of our NATO allies, totaling 7,600 ships. While national security considerations do affirm the need for a U.S. flag fleet in case of war, that requirement needs to be put in the context of these other shipping assets.

2. Ironically, unless the President declares a national emergency, it turns out to be very difficult for the Defense Department to gain access to subsidized ships in limited war situations. During the early days of the Vietnam war, U.S. flag operators—subsidized all these years for national defense purposes—were most reluctant to give up their commercial business and carry defense cargo to Vietnam. Indeed, more foreign flag operators offered ships to the Defense Department than did U.S. operators.

3. Primarily because of naval work, the American shipbuilding industry is the largest in the world. However, of 110,000 production workers, only 7,500 are normally employed in building subsidized ships.

Efforts to justify the subsidies as a means of making the U.S. shipping industry competitive are even more questionable. There is no society-wide justification for subsidizing easy access to less costly foreign ships. Indeed, we do have easy access—only 6 per cent of U.S. trade is carried on U.S. ships.

However, *eliminating all maritime subsidies (immediately) would have an intolerable employment effect.* This would lead to an end of the U.S. merchant marine and the jobs of those presently employed and those who would have been trained for the future. Instead, *we support a staged phasing out over the next five years with the recommendation that some of the subsidy reduction be used for pensions and retraining for those who are displaced.*

The Supersonic Transport

The supersonic transport plane has recently become an object of considerable public controversy. It has been argued that it represents a grave atmospheric danger, particularly in terms of air and noise pollution. In addition, the SST has been termed technologically questionable in design and performance and commercially questionable in marketability, partly because it is expected to be inordinately expensive.

Proponents of the SST have built their case on the impact on our balance of payments if we do not produce the SST. They argue that the United States is a heavy exporter of planes. If the Concorde (the British-French competitor) grabs a large share of the market, we shall become a net importer. National status is also held up as involved in continuing SST research and production.

We recommend scrapping the entire SST project, after a phase-out in 1971. The negative repercussions weigh far too heavily against the public interest to allow the SST to be continued. The improvement in our balance of payments account from building the SST is far from assured; the Concorde may prove to be far superior to and more marketable than any U.S.-built SST. As for the prestige argument, national status hardly can hinge on so marginal a commercial achievement as the SST.

Railroads

The current financial difficulties of railroad companies have brought into question their continued existence. While freight service has remained economically viable, the devastating effect of the passenger service deficit has brought several railroads near the brink of bankruptcy. A number of plans to keep the railroads in operation have been advanced, including the following: (1) a $750 million loan guarantee program for weak railroads; (2) an $8–10 billion federal investment to modernize the railroads; (3) nationalization of the railroads; and (4) a federally chartered corporation to take over passenger service.

Congress has approved legislation to establish a federally chartered private rail passenger corporation that would provide essential corridor and long-haul passenger services. The corporation is supposed to revitalize passenger services and, by achieving both economies of consolidation and reductions in routes served, bring rail-passenger-service losses from the present level of $250 million annually to a hoped-for break-even point. Altogether, $40 million in government assistance will be provided to inaugurate the corporation. The corporation in turn will provide $100 million in loans to railroads that could not otherwise meet their required entrance fees, and $200 million in loan guarantees. Railroads participating in the corporation will be required to provide it with financial support (cash, equipment, or service) as a condition of ending passenger service.

The amount of federal assistance should be sufficient to maintain adequate railway passenger service along heavily traveled urban corridors. It will not be sufficient to maintain a national system. However, *the case for public subsidy of a truly national railway passenger system appears dubious in view of the existence of other effective competing transportation modes:* airplanes, buses, and private automobiles. *We* therefore *do not recommend significantly greater federal aid to the rail passenger corporation.*

Budget proposals for Transportation are summarized in Table 10:2 on the following page.

TABLE 10:2
TRANSPORTATION
(Outlays, in millions of current dollars)

	Administration		Urban Coalition Recommendations				
	Estimated 1971	Proposed 1972	1972	1973	1974	1975	1976
Mass Transit Capital Grants[1]							
Buses			160	154	129	134	139
Improvement of Existing Rail Transit Facilities			189	264	225	233	242
Extension of Existing Rail Transit Systems			120	162	196	233	103
New Transit Systems					281	1,166	1,413
Commuter Railroads			194	169	112	58	61
Research and Development			70	100	100	75	50
Subtotal	215	327	733	849	1,043	1,899	2,008
Highways	4,880	4,923	4,100	3,765	3,445	2,980	3,070
Civil Aviation	1,387	1,553	1,850	2,115	2,380	2,680	3,010
Supersonic Transport	233	281	10	0	0	0	0
Other[2]							
Coast Guard[3]	233	243	243	243	258	273	288
Merchant Marine	356	467	315	282	225	147	125
Inland Navigation (Corps of Army Engineers)	411	428	386	349	306	224	169
Railroads	48	57	70	42	50	60	65
TOTAL	7,763	8,279	7,707	7,645	7,707	8,263	8,735

[1] The breakdown of Administration costs was not available.
[2] These figures are gross outlays not offset by revenues from recommended user charges.
[3] Includes Coast Guard search and rescue, aids to navigation, and safety components.

11

Environment and Natural Resources

In 1970, national attention for the first time was focused directly on the deteriorating condition of the environment. It is now recognized that pollution not only degrades the quality of American life, but threatens health and property as well. Accompanying this new consensus is increasing awareness that the national economy is not oriented to protect the environment and the natural resources that sustain contemporary civilization and life itself. Ecological laws cannot be suspended. Resources are not unlimited, although we have treated them as if they were.

Pollution is actually only one element among many in all production and consumption cycles. The generation of products from raw materials eventually results in wastes; it is only when these waste materials are not successfully recycled (broken down to become the raw materials of new production processes) or when they accumulate in dangerous concentrations that pollution emerges as a major problem. As a result, maintenance of tolerable levels of pollution involves more than removing wastes from fouled water or air; it also requires effective recycling, limiting wastes formed during production (or creating waste in its most advantageous form), and recognzing that the price of some production processes may be too high if individual and environmental health are at stake.

POLLUTION CONTROL

We have been slow to recognize the effects of various forms of pollution on human health. But nowadays, with increasing frequency, consequences can be and are being measured in terms of illness and attendant higher health costs. The U.S. Public Health Service has estimated that air pollution costs the average American $65 a year. Those living in heavily polluted areas may lose $200 annually to higher medical bills, household maintenance, and other expenses. Total costs to the nation are enormous: air pollution is estimated to cost Americans $13.5 billion annually just in property damage from soiling, corrosion, and abrasion of materials. Water pollution costs the country at least an additional $12 billion annually.

There is indisputable need to control the factors causing pollution and degradation of the environment. But the price of control will be high. The Federal Water Quality Administration has estimated that during the next five to seven years Americans must spend at least $35 billion (and perhaps $70 billion) to control water pollution alone. The National Air Pollution Control Administration estimates $15 billion in expenditures are needed to control air pollution during the same period.

Costs borne by the federal government will be determined by the policies and programs adopted in the immediate future. *In view of the many other unmet needs also competing for federal resources we have serious reservations about spending large sums on pollution control at this time.*

We believe that meeting these more immediate human needs ought to have top priority in the near future. Massive spending at this time would almost certainly involve false starts and waste of effort and money since the nation has so little experience in the technology, economics, and organization of pollution control. A crash program based on today's scanty knowledge and preparation could do damage to our economy and result in political backlash that might well retard pollution-control progress.

The program we recommend is designed to bring under control those pollutants that are recognized to be an immediate threat to personal health; to provide adequate surveillance and control to ensure that conditions do not worsen to the extent that they will be uncontrollable five or ten years hence; and to begin the establishment of an effective, nation-wide pollution-control mechanism based on comprehensive knowledge and integrated with our political and economic systems. Human health must be protected now and future calamity averted, but the slow, expensive process of repairing the damage already wreaked on our part of the globe must wait until the 1970's, when research has produced the means and the economy the funds, to handle that task.

Policy alternatives for dealing with pollution problems vary according to what society is willing to pay in order to achieve certain levels of control, and to whom the bill is delivered. Among suggested alternatives—not all mutually exclusive—are the following:

1. *Strict enforcement of present pollution laws and of standards based upon health criteria.* Federal activities now reflect this policy, but standards are not strict enough, and enforcement attempts have been characterized by arbitrariness and lack of enthusiasm. Enforcement techniques need considerable strengthening.

2. *Initiation of a pollution-discharge fee system.* Such an approach would focus more of the social costs of pollution on the polluters themselves (private and public) and would serve as an incentive to limit pollution. As pollution fees were added to production costs, producers would be encouraged (in order to lower fees and thereby cut expenses) to reduce pollution to the point at which any further efforts to abate would be more expensive than the fees themselves. Desirable levels of pollution reduction could be attained by raising or lowering fees as required. Under this approach, most of the costs would probably be passed eventually to consumers in the form of higher prices.

3. *Payment of federal subsidies or tax write-offs to businesses, either for purchase of pollution-control equipment or for development of new equipment and alternate production methods resulting in less pollution.* This proposal would place the cost of pollution more directly on the American public as a whole, since subsidies would be financed through increased federal taxes. Presently the federal government allows a tax credit ranging from 33 to 44 per cent for every dollar of capital investment undertaken for pollution-control purposes.

4. *Granting of federal matching funds or loans to states and localities for construction of new pollution-control facilities.* A federal program now provides up to 50 per cent in matching funds for liquid waste treatment facilities construction, but funding has been limited (see Chapter 8).

As Congress has recognized, the foremost consideration in pollution-control programs at this time must be protection of human health.

Discharge Fee System

New legislation as well as more vigorous enforcement of present laws will be required to ensure that pollutants are not permitted to accumulate in dangerous concentrations and that individuals are compensated for health injuries resulting from pollution. But these actions alone will not stop environmental deterioration. Nor would it be sufficient to limit federal efforts to cleaning up pollution after it has been produced. Accordingly, *we recommend that planning begin immediately to establish a mechanism for operating a pollution-discharge fee system. Fees should be levied on all pollutants discharged into air or water after 1976.* *

The fee system would put the costs of pollution into the calculations that now guide our decisions to produce and consume.

Because environmental costs have, as a whole, been ignored in the past, pricing and output decisions have not reflected the full costs to society of production of goods. As a result, in many cases consumers have purchased more goods produced by high-pollution processes than they would if these very real social costs were included in the prices of products on the market. A discharge-fee system would ensure that the costs of pollution were included in production costs, and, as a supplement to federal health standards, would provide a powerful incentive to curtail production of excessive wastes.

Too rapid a changeover to a fee system could have undesirable effects upon the national economy. Some firms might be forced out of business with consequent hardship for employees and commu-

* Years are federal fiscal years unless otherwise indicated.

nities; sharp price increases could occur as businesses passed pollution costs to consumers.

To minimize these possible consequences, *the fee system would be phased in over a two-year period, beginning in 1975, in order to permit the orderly development of workable standards and to give producers time to alter production methods or find other means of controlling their emissions of pollutants.* The most severe pollution problems would be attacked first, with the result that some producers would have less time than others to prepare to operate under the fee system. *We recommend that all the fees paid during the first two years of the program be held in escrow,* and that the producers required to pay fees during that period be entitled to get back those fees earmarked to defray the actual costs they incur in reducing emissions. Unreturned fees would revert to trust funds at the end of the two years.

Regional Associations

Because the effects of pollution frequently extend beyond state jurisdictions, a regional mechanism is required to deal with pollution-control problems. *Regional associations should be established to administer the discharge fee system and set acceptable pollution levels in their areas.* Representatives of involved states and municipalities would make policy decisions. Prior to establishment of the associations, the Environmental Protection Agency would set standards for permissible emissions and minimum fees for pollutants and would authorize research to assess pollution-control needs. States and some interstate blocks have already been designated as regional jurisdictions to set and enforce air emission standards. In the future, these regions should be redefined in terms of water, air, and waste-management needs.

Under the fee system, corporate and municipal polluters would be required to apply for permits through state licensing bureaus; without a permit, any level of pollution would be illegal. Permits would specify types and amounts of discharges produced by each source. Levels of discharge would be verified by inspections, and penalties would be instituted for exceeding limits. Each regional association would adjust fees for various pollutants in a pattern related to that region's pollution-control objectives (though fees could never drop below the national minimum). Charges would be subject to semiannual review.

In some cases, either when nonpolluting production techniques are readily available, or when production of goods with little social importance creates great amounts of harmful wastes, pollution should be forbidden entirely.

Facilities Grants

By means of financial incentives, the federal government should encourage regional associations—rather than municipalities—to apply for pollution-control facilities grants. Grants to associations would cover 60 per cent of capital outlays for facilities construction; grants to individual jurisdictions, only 40 per cent of costs. To receive any funds at all, municipalities or associations would have to guarantee that participating firms would pay a fee for services commensurate with the cost of treating their wastes. An additional 10 per cent grant would be awarded to regions that institute nonregressive taxes to defray waste treatment costs and that require local elections of officials to serve as directors of the regional associations.

Some have objected to the fee system as a "license" to pollute, seeking instead total cessation of polluting activities. They suggest that damages can be remedied and the quality of life restored by vigorous enforcement of new, strictly prohibitive laws. Pursuit of that goal, however, would reduce the American standard of living to a level most people would not and should not have to accept. The real question is: How much pollution are we willing to permit in order to enjoy our technological advantages, once health threats have been eliminated?

Immediate Control Measures

Ultimately, a discharge-fee system would reduce pollution to levels deemed nationally acceptable and would provide a portion of the funds needed to construct pollution abatement facilities. But the federal government should not remain inactive while awaiting the completion of research and organizational efforts for the new system. Despite limits on immediate federal spending, certain actions must be taken at once to prevent pollution from becoming so serious a problem as to defy control later in this decade.

We recommend that the government be permitted to seek injunctions forcing polluters to cease operation if they have not rectified violation of standards within 72 hours of receiving notice. Also needed are expanded federal enforcement staffs, a responsive citizens' complaint mechanism, and reorganization of federal administrative offices to improve efficiency within agencies as well as to make it possible for the Environmental Quality Council to assess present programs effectively.

Immediate federal actions are also required in the following areas:

Water Pollution: Many municipalities, burdened by insufficient revenues and high interest rates, badly need new or improved waste treatment facilities. Estimates of total expenditures required for municipal treatment facilities during the next five years range from $10 billion to more than $25 billion. However, recent innovations that may greatly increase the efficiency of existing facilities raise hopes that by 1976 additional processes may also be available, lessening necessary capital requirements for new plant construction. *We* therefore *recommend that until 1975 when regional associations can assess needs for new facilities, only grants funding improvements in existing facilities or those providing facilities for new towns and planned developments be awarded.* Two billion dollars in federal contract authority would be obligated for these purposes between 1972 and 1974, sufficient to meet more than 55 per cent of the need as estimated by the Federal Water Quality Administration. By 1975, when regional associations are to be in operation, grants would be made available for new facilities construction as well. Federal outlays would average $925 million annually during the five-year period. In 1971, outlays were only $422 million.

Air Pollution: The primary federal role in air pollution control should be to provide increased funds for research. Study should focus upon development of pollution-control devices suitable for installation on internal combustion vehicles, lesser-polluting engines; and more efficient incineration systems. Research must also provide additional information concerning the effects of air pollutants on human beings and plant and animal life, as well as the levels of emissions injurious to human health.

Additional funds will be required to enlarge the staff of the National Air Pollution Control Administration. Manpower training expenditures should be stepped up from an estimated $3 million in 1971 to $11 million by 1976 in order to provide sufficient qualified technicians to properly enforce pollution-control legislation. Research expenditures, estimated at $55 million in 1971, should be increased to $90 million by 1976. Abatement and control expenditures (including costs of control equipment, prosecution of charges, and administration of programs) should rise to $150 million by the same year.

Solid Waste Treatment: The total cost of disposing of our solid wastes each year has been estimated at about $4.5 billion. In addition, an estimated investment of $835 million annually for five years would be required just to upgrade existing collection and disposal operations to acceptable sanitary levels. *Included in federal waste-management programs should be a major research effort to increase the efficiency of solid waste collection and disposal by municipalities. Research spending should increase from its 1971 level of about $5 million to $68 million by 1973.* If new, successful techniques have been developed by 1975, construction grants for solid waste treatment facilities would be awarded to regional associations and municipalities, requiring a federal contribution of about $125 million in 1976. Funds for abatement and control, primarily to finance demonstration projects, would increase from $7 million in 1971 to $110 million in 1974, and level off at $100 million in 1976.

Noise Abatement: Before laws can be proposed to protect Americans from irritating, often dangerous levels of noise, it will be necessary to conduct research leading to the establishment of permissible limits of noise production and the development of materials and techniques for containing or protecting from noise. We need to determine what degree of noise is tolerable—and safe —in aircraft, urban mass-transit systems, heavy and construction equipment, and automobiles. Further, noise limits should be included among performance standards applied to household appliances, toys, and office machines. These criteria should be developed with consideration of the hidden costs of noise pollution, such as loss of property value, damage to health (including hearing), and the nuisance cost of unnecessary noise. *We particularly recommend a federal program financing research into the effects of excessive noise on human health, in order to facilitate institution of noise standards.*

Within three years, airplanes should be required to meet stricter noise standards for engines, set and enforced by the National Aeronautics and Space Administration (NASA).

NATURAL RESOURCES

America's richness in natural resources—land, water, timber, and minerals—has been the foundation of our marvelously productive industry and agriculture. The federal government has long been concerned with husbanding some of these resources. Its responsibility to ensure that all resources are utilized wisely and economically and for the good of all is growing as our growing population and standard of living multiply the nation's demands for the relatively fixed supply.

Land Use

Until a land use policy or set of national development priorities is established in the United States, it will remain difficult for the federal government to encourage economic growth and to protect the environment as well. Present land laws promote neither of these goals efficiently.

We recommend that Congerss determine a basis for land use priorities—a flexible set of goals toward which resources management, protection, and development can be directed. While these goals are being formulated in the course of the next two years, we recommend that necessary information be gathered for determination of which federal lands should be sold or purchased, which should be improved, and what uses would be most advantageous for the various tracts of the federal government's more than 750 million square miles of land (about one-third of the nation's land).

Other land use problems must also be solved if the public interest is to be served.

Indian and Alaskan land claims must be settled and satisfactory compensation provided; water rights legally belonging to Indians must be restored. We should study the feasibility of moving all Indian programs out of the Department of the Interior into a separate federal corporation, run by Indians.

A portion of the monies in the Land and Water Conservation Fund should be directed toward development of urban parks (see Chapter 8). Outlays from the Land and Water Conservation Fund for purchase and maintenance of national and state park lands should remain constant until the research recommended above is completed and analyzed.

Research should be directed toward improving damaged lands, developing more effective forest fire and flood control techniques, and controlling insect damage without use of long-life pesticides.

The Forest Service should be moved from the Agriculture Department to the Interior Department in order to eliminate duplication of services and to reduce some costs. Funds spent for certain projects under the 1902 Reclamation Act should be halved as Corps of Engineers irrigation and flood control activities are merged with similar Bureau of Reclamation activities (see Chapter 13). Mining operators and other users of public or private land should be required by law to rehabilitate the lands they use.

Public Works—Irrigation and Water Resources Projects

Water resources projects have made a significant contribution to American development. But while national needs have changed, budget allocations for construction of these projects have continued to expand. As a result, enterprises of questionable justification have been undertaken, and in some cases, federal programs have worked at cross purposes.

Costs-to-benefits ratios are utilized by the Corps of Engineers to measure anticipated benefits against expected construction costs;

projects for which benefits would not at least equal costs are rejected. The Corps has been criticized by economists for misusing cost-benefit analysis; furthermore, cost-benefit ratios projected by the Corps have not in the past proven to be very accurate. The 1967 report of project costs revealed cost "overruns" of more than 300 per cent.

Corps flood control projects in areas where investments should never have occurred have at times stimulated development in those areas beyond that which the projects could protect. Bad floods have later damaged expensive buildings, causing losses more extensive than those that would have occurred if the Corps projects had not been constructed. Irrigation projects have also been criticized; projects approved between 1964 and 1967 cost an average of $122,000 per farm served, according to economist Charles L. Schultze. Many of these projects have subsidized high-income farmers by providing facilities to increase agricultural output, while other federal projects simultaneously pay to reduce output.

Corps nagivation projects should be transferred to the Department of Transportation when the Interior Department assumes the Corps of Engineers' flood control, irrigation, and power projects. The transfers would eliminate numerous duplications of resources and personnel (for instance, the Corps in 1971 spent $462 million for flood control and irrigation projects, while Interior's Bureau of Reclamation spent $70 million for similar activities). *With centralized responsibilities and stricter standards to determine necessary projects, irrigation and flood control public-works budgets could be reduced by 50 per cent for the Bureau of Reclamation and by 30 per cent for the Corps of Engineers.* These cuts would not become effective, however, until 1973, when the economy is expected to be better able to sustain reductions in construction activity than during the current period of high unemployment. *In addition, user charges should be instituted for flood control project construction and for all federally constructed waterways* (see Chapter 10).

Ocean Policy

Oil, sewage, and chemical wastes spilled into the ocean in recent years, both from the nation's river system and directly from ships, oil rigs, or off-shore dumping, have caused widespread pollution. Many fish and shellfish have been destroyed, and others made unsafe to eat. The American fishing industry has been commensurately damaged. One million of the nearly 11 million square miles of America's shellfish producing waters have already been declared unsafe due to pollution. *Highest priority now should be given to prevention of further ocean degradation,* by (1) development of effective countermeasures, now virtually nonexistent, to protect life against oil spills, (2) banning of all pesticides with long life periods, and (3) studying marine life to determine possible techniques to counteract effects of these pesticides, oil, and other dangerous pollutants already in the biosystem.

The Sea Grant program providing monies to universities for marine-resource related studies should be funded at $30 million annually for 1972 and 1973 and $50 million thereafter, with the stipulation that research be directed toward the goals mentioned above. The program was funded at $20 million in 1971. An additional $80 million should be spent in 1973, and $150 million annually by 1976, for research and experimental projects aimed at organizing a coastal management system, determining efficient means of counteracting the pollutants mentioned above, and developing technology to prevent and correct oil spills and other exploitive damage.

Until these problems are solved, funding levels for development programs should increase only incrementally. To guarantee ocean protection, the Coast Guard's functions (excluding transportation and defense activities) should be moved to the National Oceanic and Atmospheric Administration (NOAA). There the Coast Guard should serve as an enforcement arm, prosecuting violators of new stricter regulations against dumping solid wastes and pollutants, and of regulations guaranteeing that oil rigs meet stringent safety specifications, with $50,000 daily fines for violators of these regulations even if oil spills do not occur.

Budget proposals for Environment and Natural Resources are summarized in Table 11:1 on the following page.

TABLE 11:1
ENVIRONMENT AND NATURAL RESOURCES
(Outlays, in millions of current dollars)

	Administration			Urban Coalition Recommendations			
	Estimated 1971	Proposed[1] 1972	1972	1973	1974	1975	1976
Pollution Control							
Water:							
Grants for Construction of Waste Treatment Facilities	422	1,000	570	975	1,000	1,025	1,050
Air	49		105	131	147	155	162
Solid Waste	10		42	83	123	199	254
Noise			5	13	22	20	17
Research[2]	181		221	287	323	380	405
Other	29		74	111	130	138	176
Subtotal	691	1,358	1,017	1,600	1,745	1,917	2,064
Natural Resources							
Land Use and Recreation	1,493	1,576	1,578	1,536	1,579	1,678	1,723
Oceans[3]	650	722	827	903	915	973	1,033
Public Works:							
Flood Control and Irrigation[4]	540	460	460	313	342	353	363
Subtotal	2,683	2,758	2,865	2,752	2,836	3,004	3,119
TOTAL	3,374	4,116	3,882	4,352	4,581	4,921	5,183

[1] Administration figures only available for waste treatment facilities and pollution-control subtotal.
[2] Includes research in air, water, solid waste, noise, radiation, and pesticide pollutions.
[3] Includes NOAA and Coast Guard funds not covered in transportation budget.
[4] Corps of Army Engineers and Bureau of Reclamation.

12

Family Planning and Population Growth

Population growth has become an issue of major concern within the United States and throughout the world. But it is an issue difficult to confront in public policy. As Robert McNamara, president of the World Bank, observed in an address at the University of Notre Dame on May 1, 1969:

> It is an issue that is so hypersensitive—giving rise to such diverse opinion—that there is an understandable tendency simply to avoid argument, turn one's attention to less complicated matters, and hope that the problem will somehow disappear.

Indeed, only during the past five years has the federal government acknowledged population as an issue demanding public attention. Emerging federal policy addresses the issue in three problem areas: domestic family planning, U.S. population growth, and international family planning and population growth control. Since the federal budget tends to reflect these divisions, we shall examine each of them individually.

Domestic Family Planning

Social scientists Larry Bumpass and Charles Westoff ("The Perfect Contraceptive Population: Extent and Implication of Unwanted Fertility in the United States," *Science*, September 4, 1970) have estimated that 20 per cent of all children born in the United States during the nine-year period 1960–68 were not desired by one or both of their parents. This expression of un-

181

wanted fertility was found in all socio-economic groups in the United States. Without doubt, it carries high individual and social costs.

Because the inability to plan the size and spacing of a family often forces women to have children too early or too late in their childbearing years, or results in inadequate spacing between pregnancies, unplanned childbearing produces an increased incidence of infant and maternal mortality and of premature births. A recent program analysis by the Department of Health, Education, and Welfare (HEW) concluded that provision of family-planning services in the form of information and contraceptives would prevent 2,173 infant deaths for every 500,000 women served each year.

There is also a high correlation between unwanted fertility and poverty in the United States. Unwanted children often cause an overextension of limited family resources or necessitate the withdrawal of the mother from the labor force, driving many families below the poverty line and blocking the escape route from poverty for others. American families with five or more children are 3.5 times more likely to be poor than families with only one or two children.

Finally, the inability to plan the size and spacing of a family severely restricts personal and career options available to American women of all income groups.

Taking into consideration both the sizable costs of unwanted fertility and the relatively small expense required to eliminate it, *we declare, as have Congress and the President, that the opportunity for every American to plan voluntarily the size and spacing of his or her family is an important national goal.* We support this goal in the belief that the opportunity to voluntarily plan one's family is a fundamental human right, independent of any national policy to increase or to decrease the birth rate.

An effective federal policy to eliminate unwanted fertility must focus on the three factors responsible for most of the involuntary childbirths in the United States today: (1) Inadequate incomes that prevent many poor and near-poor women of childbearing age from purchasing the information and the most effective contraception techniques currently available to more affluent Americans through the private health system; (2) Shortcomings in existing contraceptive technology; and (3) Obstacles to the acquisition of family-planning information and techniques, such as inefficient or purposely obstructive hospital and clinic administrative practices, inadequately trained medical personnel, insufficient or poorly distributed public health information, and archaic state and local laws.

Federal programs now exist on a small scale to eliminate some of these obstacles to family planning. Through the Center for Family Planning Services of the Department of Health, Education, and Welfare and the Office of Economic Opportunity, the federal government will spend $57.5 million in 1971 for grants to public and private organizations to subsidize the delivery of voluntary family-planning services to predominantly low-income women. Another $28.3 million will be given to the Center for Population Research in the National Institutes of Health (NIH) for biomedical and behavioral research, with $14 million of the total to be spent on contraceptive development.

To implement an effective national family-planning policy, we recommend:

1. *The provision of family-planning services on a voluntary basis, beginning in 1974, to all Americans under the national health insurance (NHI) plan* (see Chapter 5). This course is most consistent with our objective of making the opportunity to plan family size available to the entire population rather than to specific groups.

2. *An expansion of existing federal grant programs to meet President Nixon's objective of eliminating all barriers to family planning by 1974.* Serving all of the estimated 5.4 million women of childbearing age who are prevented by inadequate incomes from purchasing family-planning services will require an annual federal expenditure of $304 million by 1973. Beginning in 1974, this program would be replaced gradually by NHI.*

3. *A concerted federal effort to develop a variety of contraceptive methods that are effective, safe, inexpensive, reversible, self-administered, and acceptable to various groups in the population.*

* Special family-planning grants could not be phased out until it was certain that low-income women actually were receiving services under NHI.

Improving the rhythm method should receive high priority. Such an effort would cost a minimum of $100 million a year. More research funds are also needed to study the health effects of contraceptives now in use and to conduct operational research to improve the delivery of family-planning services and the dissemination of related public health information.

4. *A program to train 15,000 paraprofessionals to assist in providing family-planning services through neighborhood health centers, hospitals, and clinics,* at a cost of $30 million.

5. *The establishment of a Population and Family Planning Administration in the Department of Health, Education, and Welfare on a par with the Food and Drug Administration, the National Institutes of Health, and the Health Services and Mental Health Administration.* Combining all federal service and research programs concerned with population growth under one administrative head would encourage the coordination that has been lacking.

All of these recommendations assume public and private efforts to adjust health administrative practices, medical training, public education programs, and state and local statutes to reflect the intent of Congress and the President to remove all economic, technical, and organizational obstacles to the practice of voluntary family planning.

Until the obstacles to family planning are eliminated, abortion on demand should be available for those who desire it to prevent unwanted births. We believe that abortion is a matter best left to individual conscience. The state should not be given the power either to compel a woman to have an abortion or to constrain her from doing so. Easy access to completely effective contraceptives in the future should reduce the need for abortion as a course of last resort in family planning.

U.S. POPULATION GROWTH

In his message on population delivered to Congress on July 21, 1969, President Nixon said:

Only recently has it come to be seen that pressing problems are also posed for advanced industrial countries when their populations increase at the rate that the United States, for example, must now anticipate. Food supplies may be ample in such nations, but social supplies—the capacity to educate youth, to provide privacy and living space, to maintain the processes of open, democratic government —may be grievously strained. . . . I believe that many of our present social problems may be related to the fact that we have had only fifty years in which to accommodate the second hundred million Americans.

If the present rate of growth in the United States continues, we shall have only thirty years to accommodate the third hundred million Americans, for our population will grow from 207 million in 1970 to roughly 300 million by the year 2000.

Stopping population growth in the United States today will not eliminate any of the serious problems we face. Our central cities will still require rebuilding. The environmental crisis will remain unsolved as long as the current high levels of consumption are combined with a sophisticated and powerful but untethered technology.

However, it is increasingly clear that a growing population makes the solution of nearly all of our problems more difficult and more expensive. (Many of the benefits traditionally attributed to national population growth have disappeared as technology, rather than manpower, has become the principal source of military might and the stimulus behind economic growth in industrialized nations.) The reconstruction of our cities during the next thirty years will be rendered considerably more complex and costly by the appearance of 75 million additional Americans in our urban areas. And, since population growth is expected to account for nearly 40 per cent of increased consumption in the next fifteen years, according to Census Bureau figures, cleaning up our air and water by 1985 will be much more expensive with 250 million Americans than with 207 million.

But one fact is incontestable: Population stabilization is inevitable in a nation with finite space and resources. Mathematics, not social policy, dictates that conclusion. Although there are differences of opinion concerning the ultimate population capacity of the United States, and the time it will take to reach that capacity, there is no real debate over the eventual need to stabilize U.S. population size.

The issue is, rather, when and how, measured against our stated commitment to steadily improve the quality of life for individual Americans and our responsibilities as a cohabitant of an increasingly crowded planet.

There have been numerous policies to deal with population growth suggested to date. They include:

- Accepting future population growth and concentrating on redistributing the population and preparing states and localities to serve more people.
- Attempting to stabilize U.S. population size by relying exclusively on efforts to eliminate all unwanted fertility by means of voluntary family-planning programs.
- Supplementing voluntary family-planning programs with noncoercive education programs and incentives to encourage a reduction of average family size to a level consistent with a stable population.
- Implementing coercive measures, such as laws regulating maximum family size, to stabilize the population size.

The first alternative mentioned, redistribution of the population, is a short-term ameliorative at best and by no means an easy one to implement. The last alternative appears to us as both unnecessary and inimical to the values of a free society.

But the problem of uncontrolled population growth is so pressing that we believe conscious, noncoercive policies aimed at lowering the birth rate in the United States to replacement level (the level at which births balance deaths) are essential if coercion is to be averted in the future.

An effective policy for national family planning to eliminate involuntary childbearing may reduce the birth rate significantly. (Some demographers predict that voluntary family planning may be sufficient to reach replacement level.) But, there is no way to determine a priori the exact impact of effective family-planning programs because such programs give families only the means to limit the number of children they have—the programs do not affect the number of children families desire. We therefore believe that the most prudent policy is one that supplements voluntary family-planning programs with noncoercive programs, with the aim of encouraging as desirable a family size consistent with a stable national population.

Developing effective noncoercive public programs to bring average desired family size to the current replacement level of 2.3 children, however, will require a great deal more information than we presently have. Little is known, for example, about the social, economic, and psychological determinants of family size. Why does one family want two children while another wants six? *We therefore recommend that federal funding for behavioral population research to determine the causes and consequences of population growth be expanded from a 1971* level of $5 million to a 1976 level of $50 million.*

Two programs to encourage small natural families and voluntary family planning should be established immediately while we await further research findings. *We suggest establishment of a federal adoption subsidy program, modeled after the successful Maryland Plan, that would offer families annual adoption fees to encourage adoption as a substitute for additional natural births.* The costs of such a program would be $30 million a year.

We also recommend the establishment of a population education fund of $10 million a year, to be administered by the Population and Family Planning Administration, to encourage the development of public school curricula, mass media presentations, and adult education programs to inform the American public of the known costs and benefits of family, national, and global population planning.

International Family Planning and Population Growth

Serious as the consequences of population growth in this country may be, the problems raised by the global population explosion are much more pressing. Only nuclear weaponry casts a more threatening shadow over mankind's prospects for a better tomorrow.

* All references to years are to federal fiscal years unless otherwise indicated.

For most of man's recorded history, world population doubled only every thousand years. By 1650 A.D., this plodding geometric process had pushed the earth's population to an estimated 500 million people.

Since then, modern medicine and public health programs have been rapidly reducing population "doubling time" from one thousand years to the current rate of thirty-five years. If present population growth rates persist, the planet that now houses 3.5 billion people will contain over 7 billion people by the year 2000—with the 8 billion mark reached a scant five years later.

Failure to check this rapid growth of population poses a serious threat to the survival of all living things and a virtually insuperable obstacle to progress in the developing nations of Asia, Africa, and Latin America, where 90 per cent of projected world population growth will occur over the next three decades. With populations in many of these nations doubling as rapidly as every twenty years, resources that would otherwise be available to raise living standards and increase capital formation are diverted in a tragically unsuccessful effort to keep the growing dependent population of children alive. (In 1971 alone, 4.5 million children are expected to starve to death.) The Pearson Commission report on international development, *Partners for Development* (N.Y.: Praeger, 1969), stated: "It is clear that there can be no serious social and economic planning unless the ominous implications of uncontrolled growth are understood and acted upon."

At present, the most effective American contribution to international efforts to slow world population growth would be the immediate implementation of a policy to stabilize U.S. population size. Such action would reduce, albeit to a small degree, the number of people our planet would be forced to support in coming decades. Far more importantly, it would constitute a dramatic statement to many of the developing nations still not committed to population stabilization policies that the wealthiest nation in the world considers a national population policy essential to its future progress and well-being.

There is a more direct way in which the United States can help ease the world-wide population crush. U.S. foreign assistance can support public family-planning programs and population research in those developing nations, such as India and Pakistan, which are striving to bring their soaring population growth rates under control. In 1971, the Agency for International Development will spend $100 million to aid population programs in developing nations. We recommend increasing this program by $50 million a year through 1976. The details of our recommendation are described in our foreign economic assistance chapter, Chapter 19.

Budget proposals for Family Planning and Population Growth are summarized in Table 12:1 on the following page.

TABLE 12:1
FAMILY PLANNING AND POPULATION GROWTH
(Outlays, in millions of current dollars)[1]

	Administration		Urban Coalition Recommendations				
	Estimated 1971	Proposed 1972	1972	1973	1974[2]	1975	1976
Family-Planning Services	59	101	175	304	96	33	9
Population Research	28	38	80	125	175	175	175
Manpower Training	—	—	11	33	23	25	26
Population Education	—	1	5	11	12	12	13
Adoption Subsidy	—	—	16	33	35	25	26
TOTAL	87	140	287	506	341	270	249

[1] Because health costs are expected to rise faster than either the consumer or the federal government price index, the following special price index was employed:

1971	1972	1973	1974	1975	1976
100.0	105.8	111.3	115.5	122.8	129.5

[2] Beginning in 1974, family-planning services will be paid for through national health insurance. The funds for family-planning services for 1974, 1975, and 1976 are for transition expenses.

13

Rural Development and Agriculture

The poverty of rural America is often overlooked in the contemporary discussion of domestic social problems. Poverty brings to mind images of deteriorating urban slums and unemployed central-city dropouts. Too few of us are aware that findings of the Census Bureau in 1965 indicated that one-quarter of all rural residents are officially classified as poor, compared to only 15 per cent of urban residents. Only one of two rural houses was in sound condition or had adequate plumbing in 1960, though four of five urban houses met these criteria. Educational and health services available to residents of rural areas, too, have been shown to be of lesser quality than those available to residents of urban centers.

Moreover, few people realize the magnitude of the technological revolution that has transformed American agriculture since the inception of farm price-support programs in the late 1930's. As a result of this revolution, fewer farmers are needed to produce America's food. In 1950, one farm worker supplied sixteen persons with farm products; in 1969, his counterpart supplied forty-three persons. It is not surprising, then, that 1 million farmers moved off farms in the 1960's. Yet, these farm migrants have often been unable to find adequate nonfarm employment in depressed rural areas. Their alternatives are underemployment in the country or migration to already overcrowded cities.

RURAL ECONOMIC DEVELOPMENT

Our recommended programs in income maintenance, education, health, housing, and manpower will provide needed basic services

191

to the rural poor (providing these programs are equipped with the mechanisms and the specific mandates to assure that benefits are fully extended to rural areas). In addition, the federal government should act to specifically build a healthy rural economy through a program of rural economic development and a reform of agricultural policy.

Rural economic development is particularly important. Wisely spent federal funds can revitalize the economy in rural growth centers and move the rural sector toward self-sustaining prosperity. Intelligently planned development can "pull" excess human resources away from the farm sector and help to create the nearly 2 million new jobs needed in rural areas. Indeed, federal support of growth centers, through the Economic Development Administration, is proving to be an effective way to help stem the flow of jobless rural residents to large metropolitan areas burdened with staggering economic and social problems. But, if this strategy is to be effective on the scale required, increased funding is essential. *We therefore recommend allocating $4.4 billion during the 1972–76* period for rural economic development.*

These increased funds would be spent to expand the industrial infrastructure in small and medium-sized cities, chosen both for their growth potential and for their proximity to rural areas of substantial employment need. Communication networks, water and sewer lines, transportation facilities—the elements of social overhead capital—combined with appropriate technical assistance can provide a solid base for a revitalized rural sector. In addition, the existing program of the Department of Agriculture's Extension Service, now directed primarily toward the needs of farming, should be reoriented toward the servicing of rural industrial requirements.

This economic development strategy is based on the argument that the concentration of public investments in the principal growth centers of rural areas, each within convenient commuting distance of surrounding rural households, can contribute more to development than can dispersion of funds over hundreds of communities. It is not a new strategy. Neither does it run counter to existing

---

* All references to years are to federal fiscal years unless otherwise indicated.

economic trends. There is evidence that business is increasingly willing to move from traditional centers of industrial concentration to rural regions: nearly half of the new manufacturing jobs from 1960 to 1970 were in nonmetropolitan areas, although these areas have only about one-fourth of the total jobs.

Nor is rural economic development prohibitive in cost. We estimate that an average outlay of less than $1 billion yearly would provide the necessary base for 1.75 million new jobs in rural growth centers by 1976. These cost estimates are modest for two reasons. First, much of what could properly be called rural economic development (manpower training, education, health) is included in other budgets. Second, the cost figures are discounted to allow for the so-called multiplier effect. Our estimates make the implicit assumption—a conservative one—that the government-financed creation of two industrial jobs will spawn a third job, as the "original" two workers spend their incomes on food, housing, and other goods and services.

In addition, *we recommend that the federal government complement this infrastructure development strategy by using its own position as a contractor and employer to influence the location of job opportunities.*

FARM POLICY

Linked to rural economic development is the need for a reform of farm policy. The dramatic transformation of agriculture has led to a farm sector in which, by calendar year 1968, 33 per cent of all farms produced 87 per cent of total agricultural goods, while the least productive 50 per cent of all farms produced only 6 per cent of output. Not all of these small farms are operated by full-time farmers; nonetheless, there are about 500,000 farms in this country (17 per cent of all farms) with owners who work full time at farming but get so small a return that they are classified as poor.

The problem, in sum, is that the United States has an excess of human and land resources devoted to agricultural production. We estimate that nearly half of the 3.3 million U.S. agricultural workers could be freed to work in nonfarm occupations with no sacrifice in food and fiber output.

Price-Support and Land-Diversion Programs

Government response to farm poverty and to potential agricultural overproduction is embodied primarily in farm price-support payments. These payments consist of an income-supplement component and a land-diversion component (compensation to the farmer for diverting part of his cropland from production). Price-support payments, however, were not originally designed and are poorly suited for easing the economic hardship of low-income farmers—the richest 10 per cent of all farmers receive more than 50 per cent of price-support payments. Our proposed programs of rural economic development and income maintenance are more sensible ways to meet basic income needs of the rural poor. Moreover, the land-diversion effort is extremely costly since payments are made annually to keep acreage out of production. This stop-gap annual land-diversion scheme is not a sound long-range policy since it does not act to permanently reduce excess capacity. Annual land diversion is analogous to bailing water from a boat in preference to fixing the leak.

As an alternative to existing farm policy, we recommend movement toward a more market-oriented farm economy: a farm sector in which the price system could work with less restriction to ensure an efficient allocation of farm resources. A first essential step in that direction would be the elimination of the income-supplement component of price-support payments. That change would reduce federal farm outlays by more than $1 billion annually and would end an unneeded and inequitable government subsidy to the wealthy. But, that step alone will not remedy the supply-management problem. A workable program must be developed to replace the costly annual land-diversion program.

Several alternative approaches merit consideration. Perhaps the three most important are: (1) tight farm-product marketing quotas, expressed in volume terms; (2) long-term land retirement of whole farms; and (3) an easement system under which the government would buy in perpetuity the rights to grow crops for market on particular plots of land.

Of these alternatives, marketing quotas would be the least expensive in dollar terms. But, their implementation would involve arbitrary, forcible limitations of production on American farms through government mandate, without any compensating measures. We feel such an approach, so blatantly inimical to the private entrepreneurial values upon which our economy is based, extracts too large a price to be acceptable.

Long-term land retirement and an easement system bear many similarities to each other, the chief one being a broad familial relationship to current short-term land-diversion programs. Like those current programs, long-term land retirement and an easement system would work by paying farmers money in return for agreements not to grow crops on their land. But there are important differences both between these new plans and between them and existing programs.

These new plans would be less expensive in the long run than are the current land-diversion programs. Under present programs, the government must renew its land-diversion payments each year in order to curb excess agricultural capacity. At the expiration of the annual contract, the landholder is still actively farming and is prepared to plant all his cropland if not paid again to divert a fraction of it from production. Under long-term whole-farm retirement, the need for government subsidized land diversion would gradually decrease. At the expiration of the long-term contract (ten years would be a reasonable period), the government would make no effort to divert the land of landholders who were no longer engaged in farming and who were, therefore, not potential contributors to excess agricultural production.

An easement system, generally considered a variation on long-term whole-farm retirement, would work in a similar fashion and achieve similar results. The key difference would be that the easement approach would involve permanent government purchase of crop rights on particular parcels of land rather than agreements limited to a fixed period such as ten years.

Both an easement system and long-term whole-farm land retirement would "fix the leak in the boat" in place of the costly "bailing water" programs now in existence. Farmer participation would be voluntary under both approaches, but those who chose to participate in the program would be required not to engage in farming themselves during the life of their agreement as well as to remove their land from commercial production during this period.

Choice between easement and long-term land retirement is difficult because the two schemes share more similarities than differences. Of the two, an easement system would be less expensive to operate and would more conclusively achieve the desired result of supply limitation. However, *we favor long-term land retirement*, and for two important reasons.

First, the easement approach would put additional millions of acres of land under permanent government control. Government land-holdings may be highly desirable on a smaller scale for recreation, conservation, or metropolitan land-use planning purposes, but central control of property does not seem desirable on such a broad basis. Second, we think it would be healthy to create a logical point, even ten years away, at which any new land-diversion program could be re-evaluated. A long-term land-retirement program would enable such re-evaluation; an easement system would not.

We recommend retiring 70 million acres of farmland by 1976, under ten-year contracts. A somewhat similar approach was tried during the 1950's, but our proposed program differs from that attempt in three crucial respects:

1. The proposed plan would not concentrate land retirement in a few communities, forcing them to bear the entire weight of the adjustment.

2. The proposed plan would retire whole farms, unlike the earlier scheme in which most participants retired part of their land and remained in farming.

3. The long-term land-retirement effort envisioned here is tied to a major program of rural economic development.

Other Supply-Limitation Measures

Still a third important step in a movement toward a more market-oriented agricultural industry is readjustment or elimination of a series of small programs that have outgrown or subverted their original purposes and now aggravate the agricultural capacity problem.

A $230 million Interior Department irrigation program stems from the 1902 Reclamation Act, designed primarily to help develop the West by encouraging the irrigation of arid lands. About half of the current outlays for this program go with projects that are at cross purposes with Department of Agriculture programs aimed at limiting agricultural capacity. We believe the out-of-date irrigation programs should be ceased.

The $152 million Department of Agriculture Agricultural Conservation Program (ACP) often subsidizes projects that farmers would undertake even without such encouragement, and a considerable amount of the ACP monies are used to increase crop production. This pork-barrel program should be eliminated.

A considerable portion of the $371 million spent by the Department of Agriculture on research and development is aimed at increasing agricultural productivity. Increased productivity, unfortunately, adds to the overcapacity problem. The smallness of most individual producing units provides justification for continued government support of agricultural R&D, but greater emphasis needs to be placed on diversification of products and on improvement of quality—and less on increasing yields.

Farm Cooperatives and Migrant Workers

The needs of two special farming groups merit a final word. Instead of off-farm migration, there are small farmers who would prefer, as is their privilege, to remain on their farms and to organize into agricultural cooperatives to permit them to operate more efficiently and more profitably. As the government should assist off-farm migrants through aid to rural economic development, so should it assist these rural residents in establishing thriving, well capitalized farm units. A loan program such as the one offered through the Small Business Administration is well tailored to the needs of these agricultural cooperatives. *We recommend the creation of an agricultural cooperative loan program that would operate at levels of $5 million of outlays in 1972 and $10 million during the following four years.*

The second group with special needs are the nearly 1 million migrant farm workers who constitute one of the most economically and socially deprived groups in the United States. The average migrant family of four earned $2,700 in 1970, a sum $900 below the official poverty level. Migratory labor is excluded from minimum-wage legislation, and in most states, migrants are neither eligible for unemployment insurance nor covered by labor-protection laws. Migrants' use of medical care is about one-seventh that of the general population. Their estimated per capita annual expenditure for health services is $11. In addition, 80 per cent of migrant children never enter a high school classroom.

Correcting the appalling conditions underlying these facts is a task that will require many approaches and many years. An important start should be made by ensuring that migrants are eligible for the manpower training, income-maintenance, and national health insurance programs described in earlier sections of this book. But supplementary, specialized programs will continue to be required to ensure access to health care, to provide remedial education and English-language courses, and to encourage investment in migrant housing. Programs focused on these needs already exist, but they are inadequately funded to reach all needy migrants. *We therefore recommend an increase in aggregate funding of these special programs from $107 million in 1971 to an annual level of $205 million in 1976.*

Finally, migrants should be guaranteed all the rights of the majority of American workers, including unemployment compensation, the right to organize and bargain for wages, and inclusion under labor-protection laws including the prohibitions against the use of child labor. And, to prevent the artificial reduction of wages, offered to migrant farm workers there must be more effective enforcement against illegal entry of workers into the United States at the Mexican border.

Budget proposals for Rural Development and Agriculture are summarized in Table 13:1 on the following page.

TABLE 13:1
RURAL DEVELOPMENT AND AGRICULTURE
(Outlays, in millions of current dollars)

	Administration		Urban Coalition Recommendations				
	Estimated 1971	Proposed 1972	1972	1973	1974	1975	1976
Rural Development							
Rural Industrial Development	501	504	813	947	968	881	747
Extension Programs	160	171	175	180	185	190	195
Agricultural Conservation Program[1]	179	150	—	—	—	—	—
Other	79	129	114	117	120	124	128
Subtotal	919	954[2]	1,002	1,244	1,273	1,195	1,070
Agriculture							
Price-Support and Related Programs	3,203	3,624	1,657	653	668	684	700
Long-Term Land Retirement[3]	78	70	1,200	2,288	2,340	2,394	2,450
Research	381	390	390	400	410	420	430
Soil Conservation Service	136	136	165	168	172	176	180
Consumer-Protection, Marketing, and Regulatory Programs	210	227	225	235	245	250	260
Special Migrant Programs	108	115	128	150	172	189	205
Other	836	620	686	678	663	660	650
Subtotal	4,952	5,182	4,451	4,572	4,670	4,773	4,875
TOTAL	5,871	6,136	5,453	5,816	5,943	5,968	5,945

[1] The Agricultural Conservation Program is really an agriculture supply management program. We list it here under rural development in order to conform with the category employed in the 1972 Administration budget.

[2] The Administration proposes that, beginning January 1, 1972, all the subsidiary categories contributing to this total be merged into a single revenue-sharing fund.

[3] Outlays for long-term land retirement would decrease in future years due to a shrinking need to renew contracts with persons who have retired whole farms.

14

Research and Development

Research and development—R&D in current cant—is still a young area of government responsibility. World War II demanded the first massive mobilization of organized knowledge in the pursuit of a national goal. When the process began, no one could have foreseen that the 1970* federal budget would earmark $15.9 billion for research and development—an amount 215 times greater than the $74 million allocated in 1940.

The past few years have shown that the explosive growth in federal support of R&D has reached a plateau. And there are indications that troubling reassessments of technological "breakthroughs" in terms of the quality of life are diminishing public enthusiasm for continued unquestioning support of research activities. Such misgivings should not be allowed to lead to neglect of science and industry as a national resource to be developed but should be given full weight in planning a national policy toward technological progress in the 1970's.

Reassessment of the assumptions, objectives, and institutions behind the nation's science policies is required. The most inviting challenge is the chance to employ the potential of science and technology in pursuit of social goals.

R&D has come to embrace all basic and applied research and engineering, as well as the design and development of prototypes. Some activities of the federal government are almost totally devoted to it: among these are space, oceanography, and nuclear energy. Other activities, such as defense, transportation, housing,

---

* Years are federal fiscal years unless otherwise indicated.

and health, have substantial R&D components. We address research and development as a separate topic because its size, its scattered nature, its effects, and its potential require integrated thinking and planning.

A close look at the federal budget reveals about $16 billion labeled "Research and Development." The total has hovered around this level for several years, but there have been significant changes in its distribution. A shift away from defense and space toward socially oriented activities is clearly discernible. Seventy-three per cent of federal R&D funds still go for defense and space studies, reflecting the extremely high costs of developing new weapons systems and space vehicles. But funds for defense, space, and atomic energy research nevertheless *have* declined, while R&D funds for housing, transportation, protection of the environment, health services, education, and criminal justice have received increased attention and resources.

In order to develop recommendations for future R&D funding allocations, we surveyed research needs and capacities in major program areas and the effectiveness of different means of organizing research activities. Consideration was given to R&D needs of functional activities (such as health or pollution) in relation to a government-wide strategy. Our review led us to two general conclusions:

First, we found that mission-oriented agencies—such as the National Aeronautics and Space Administration (NASA)—have been successful in generating and applying technological advances in the service of well-defined policy objectives but that these same agencies have often paid little heed to the ways their programs affect, and often disrupt, other sectors of society.

Second, we found that, in the social areas, policy goals are harder to reach, partly because they are relatively abstract and partly because new mechanisms are needed for the better integration of natural and social sciences in pursuit of those goals. The argument that technology can be put to use rebuilding cities in the same way it has been used in sending men to the moon rests on shaky ground. Increasingly, we learn how small the technical component of social problems is, and how large and complex are the political issues. Greater funding of research in these areas is

TABLE 14:1
RESEARCH AND DEVELOPMENT
(Outlays, in millions of current dollars)

	Administration		Urban Coalition Recommendations				
	Estimated 1971	Proposed 1972	1972	1973	1974	1975	1976
Military							
Department of Defense	7,281	7,540	6,400	6,290	6,415	6,525	7,360
Atomic Energy Commission	669	630	555	670	685	695	705
Subtotal	7,950	8,134	6,955	6,960	7,100	7,220	8,065
Economic Growth							
Bureau of Standards	42	46	46	49	52	55	58
Patent Office	52	56	56	59	62	65	68
Agriculture	381	390	390	400	410	420	430
Other	8	8	8	8	9	9	9
Subtotal	483	500	500	516	533	549	565
Infrastructure							
SST	233	281	10	—	—	—	—
Mass Transit	35	63	70	100	100	75	50
Nuclear Energy Reactors	365	366	470	545	460	450	450
Other Energy	40	50[5]	72	124	167	187	207
Subtotal	673	730[5]	622	769	727	712	707
Environment							
Pollution Control[1]	(274)	(300)[5]	(325)	(415)	(475)	(535)	(560)
	181	200[5]	221	287	323	380	405
Space (NASA)	3,368	3,151	389	437	446	480	525
Marine Science and Technology[2]	265	304	3,100	3,200	3,400	3,600	3,800
Subtotal	3,814	3,655	3,710	3,924	4,169	4,460	4,730

Social Programs							
Urban Social Research	94	114	210	310	490	500	500
Health[3]	1,259	1,370	1,285	1,320	1,340	1,375	1,440
Education	200	246	300	400	450	475	500
Housing	45	25	65	80	100	100	100
Law Enforcement	42	59	60	67	97	125	150
Family Planning and Population	28	38	80	125	175	200	225
Subtotal	1,668	1,852	2,000	2,302	2,652	2,775	2,915
Basic Research							
All Agencies[4]	(2,700)	(2,900)[5]	(2,905)	(3,125)	(3,360)	(3,610)	(3,900)
National Science Foundation	313	425	450	675	1,000	1,300	1,500
Subtotal	313	425	450	675	1,000	1,300	1,500
Other							
Central Administration and Strategy Development	2	2	5	10	15	20	20
Other Activities	1,057	960	1,033	1,065	1,097	1,130	1,164
Subotal	1,059	962	1,038	1,075	1,112	1,112	1,184
TOTAL	15,960	16,258	15,275	16,221	17,293	18,166	19,666

[1] Numbers in parentheses represent total outlays recommended for pollution control. Some of these funds were included under "Nuclear Energy Reactors" and "Other Energy" and are therefore excluded from the total.

[2] Civilian activities only.

[3] HEW, Veterans Administration, and the NSF only.

[4] Numbers in parentheses represent total outlays for basic research. Funds for basic research for all agencies except the NSF were included under budgets for the agencies concerned.

[5] Staff estimate.

needed, but it would be unrealistic to seek a rapid build-up of socially oriented R&D to the level, for instance, of defense and space programs.

Over-all, our recommendations in all areas of federal research activity—for the period from 1972 through 1976—suggest average annual increases in total federal R&D expenditures of 4 per cent. This rate is simply derived from the sum of the various recommended federal research and development activities that, in our opinion, are necessary to the continued pursuit of national goals. Whether or not it is an appropriate rate is a matter of judgment. It is not so low as to threaten any portion of the government's research capability, nor so high as to give an increased emphasis to science and technology in the nation's affairs. It is within our ability to pay in relation to other needs. In the context of historical experience, our recommended 4 per cent rate of increase seems reasonable, particularly when contrasted with an estimated *decline* in federally funded R&D expenditures of about 2.5 per cent (about 6 per cent in real terms) between 1968 and 1971.

Although defense, space, and atomic energy would continue to dominate federal R&D spending under our recommendations, their share would decline from 73 per cent to 63 per cent of total expenditures.

A major part of the recommended increases should go toward the exploration and protection of man's environment: *pollution-control R&D should be more than doubled (to an annual level of $405 million), and civilian oceanography should be brought up to $525 million per year from its current $265 million level. Space should be allowed to reach a ceiling of $3.8 billion, which would then change only with economic growth.*

Altogether, we recommend the pattern of federal R&D funding set forth in Table 14:1. Most of the research and development recommendations are discussed in other chapters as part of particular functional area programs. The remainder of this chapter will focus on a few R&D activities—those associated with economic growth, nuclear energy, space, and basic research—that either are not part of functional categories discussed or have implications well beyond the functions they support.

Economic Growth

During the past century, American industry has developed effective ways to use science and technology to improve manufacturing techniques and to create new products. By and large, this "know-how" serves the public interest by producing increased wealth and a higher standard of living.

Government, for its part, encourages industrial innovation by granting temporary monopoly rights to inventors and by allowing the deduction of R&D costs from taxable income. The indirect public support given to industry R&D efforts through tax deductions amounts to something more than $5 billion a year—a considerable sum that does not show up in the federal budget.

In recent years, new dimensions have been added to government's responsibility for industrial innovation. They result, in part, from the extremely high costs of ambitious new technological ventures, such as the development of nuclear energy and the construction of a supersonic transport (SST). And they pose some difficult policy choices: Under what circumstances, for instance, and to what extent should the government guarantee risks or provide incentives that will enable private industry to undertake new activities?

Direct government support of civilian technology is small. Compared to the indirect support provided by military and space programs, it is almost nonexistent. The Department of Commerce, with responsibility for all manufacturing industries, will have an R&D budget of $99 million in 1971. Most of these funds support such organizations as the Bureau of Standards and the Patent Office. Almost none supports industrial innovation. In general, funds for the National Bureau of Standards and the Patent Office should grow in proportion to total research efforts since these agencies provide services for which demand parallels the rate of innovation and economic growth.

Some perspective on the meager federal research support given civilian industrial technology is provided by a comparison to agricultural research aid. The Department of Agriculture will have a 1971 R&D budget of $371 million. While questions can be raised about the appropriateness of this particular amount, the principle of government support for agricultural R&D is soundly justified because individual producing units are small.

Industrial corporations have sufficient resources to invest in R&D and are encouraged to do so by tax write-offs. Further federal assistance does not appear warranted. There is one exception. *When innovations come along that are too costly to be privately financed, we believe that government should step in—but only if the public interest will be broadly served in a way that goes beyond a general increase in productivity and wealth.* The SST, for example, does not meet this test, whereas nuclear power does, since its potential benefits would be spread across most of society.

ATOMIC ENERGY

Two developments have created a crisis in the field of energy: an unprecedented increase in power demands, and a growing concern about pollution from installations that generate power. Without new technology and a reorganization of governmental structure regulating the energy field, we cannot get what we need —more power with less pollution.

Dramatic increases in fossil fuel research—concentrating on removal of sulfur pollutants from stack gases and including sharply increased research activity by the electric power industry itself— are critical to the alleviation of this problem, particularly over the short term. For a long-term solution, though, development of nuclear energy increasingly appears to be the most promising solution. Fossil fuel supplies are limited, and new reactor technology holds a prospect for fewer environmental hazards than either fossil fuel installations with pollution-control devices or present-day nuclear installations.

All federal work on nuclear energy is conducted by the Atomic Energy Commission (AEC). While our prime concern here is with a civilian activity, the production of electricity, it must be noted that the military and civilian activites of the AEC are related. Reactor developments, for instance, have both naval and civilian applications. The AEC military activities budget recommendations, which follow, are shaped by the defense posture recommendations described in Chapter 18.

Research in the promising nuclear energy field is expensive. Without government funding of early research, it is doubtful the technology—very much in the interest of society—would be developed. The civilian nuclear power industry is still young and beset with problems. Only 2 per cent of U.S. electric power is produced by nuclear-powered plants.

Primary research efforts should continue to be focused on the early stages of reactor development. Deciding when it is appropriate to cut off government support is difficult, but far from impossible. The AEC, for example, considers that reactors utilizing uranium-235 are now developed to the point that further development can be conducted by private industry without government assistance. We argue, on the other hand, that *the AEC's effort to develop breeder reactors (so called because they permit the conversion of unusable uranium-238 into usable plutonium) should continue at the funding levels established by the AEC. So should advanced work on thermonuclear fusion as a source of power.*

Complete funding for the Atomic Energy Commission should be as in Table 14:2.

SPACE

By the end of fiscal year 1971, the United States will have spent a cumulative total of $61 billion for its space program—most of it during the previous ten years. During its peak years, the NASA budget almost matched the R&D effort of the Department of Defense, thus reaching a level of expenditure that no other civilian R&D activity had previously approached.

Within broad boundaries established by the typically large scale and long duration of space ventures, spending on space projects is highly adjustable in relation to the relative claims of other national needs. The space program does offer a practical technical and scientific yield—in communications, navigation, monitoring of the environment, physics, astronomy, medicine, and management of complex systems. But ultimately its justification depends heavily on less concrete standards—leadership among nations, the quest

TABLE 14:2
ATOMIC ENERGY COMMISSION
(Outlays, in millions of current dollars)

	Administration[1]		Urban Coalition Recommendations				
	Estimated 1971	Proposed 1972	1972	1973	1974	1975	1976
Military							
Weapons	1,002	984	950	890	825	765	700
Naval Propulsion Reactors	168	170	175	190	205	215	225
Special Nuclear and Raw Materials	187	184	185	170	160	150	135
Subtotal	1,357	1,338	1,310	1,250	1,190	1,130	1,060
Civilian							
Reactor Development	365	336	470	545	460	450	450
Special Nuclear and Raw Materials	217	213	210	225	235	250	260
Basic Research: Physical and Biomedical Sciences	501	460	480	480	480	480	480
Subtotal	1,083	1,009	1,160	1,250	1,175	1,180	1,190
Administration, Receipts, and Miscellaneous	-165	-29	-65	-110	-175	-230	-285
TOTAL	2,275	2,318	2,405	2,390	2,190	2,080	1,965

[1] Some allocations among subcategories are based on staff estimates.

for adventure, and exploration of our universe. Certainly the resultant boost to technological progress and improved management of our environment are useful ends. But, as in most other areas of research, judgments of appropriate funding allocations are highly subjective.

Even though NASA is currently experiencing some comparatively lean years, the space program continues at a level that surpasses any other civilian R&D operation. President Nixon recommended, early in 1970, that the space program should be kept on a steady course, but with less funding than in the peak years. We agree with that basic decision, and conclude that *NASA budgets in the $3 billion to $4 billion range are appropriate, given the magnitude of our past investment and the challenge of the tasks ahead.*

A decision must be reached toward the middle of the decade concerning further manned exploration of the planets. Until then, no new peaks in spending or dramatic cuts below present levels are anticipated. The main consideration with regard to manned planetary exploration is a balancing of the quest for adventure against competing national priorities. Most of the gains in technology and knowledge of our environment stemming from the space program could be reaped even if the program lacked a manned mission component.

Considering these factors, we feel *the nation should not mount during the 1970's a man-to-Mars program, which would cost several times as much as the $24 billion Apollo moon program.* Budget constraints and pressing domestic needs will not permit such a luxury. On the other hand, to maintain any space capability at all requires the maintenance of a relatively vast and expensive technological complex. With the investment already made in that complex, we can now expect substantial returns from continued, incremental expenditures.

But the emphasis of our space program should not remain unchanged. When the United States made its strong commitment to an intensive space program in the early 1960's, it did so for a variety of reasons: the Soviet challenge, the bolstering of our stature as a world leader in technology, the adventure of placing a man on the moon, the desire to increase our understanding of the cosmos and the earth's resources, and the scientific "sweetness" of mastering a new environment. These same elements will be present in the future, but they should be assigned different weights.

In the second decade of space exploration, the excitement of space adventure needs to be replaced by a more rational approach. The overemphasis on manned exploration must give way to the less exciting, but scientifically productive, automated missions. Greater priority must be given to activities designed to advance scientific knowledge and yield practical benefits.

A package of such automated scientific knowledge missions could be mounted at an annual funding level of around $2.5 billion. The major policy issue is the degree of support for supplementary manned missions—fundamentally the space shuttle, space station, and Mars expedition options.

With total annual space funding boosted to $5 billion, NASA estimates that the space shuttle and space station objectives—both directed toward advancing man's ability to spend extended periods of time in space—could be achieved by 1977. Each of these programs is expected to cost $6 billion.

In view of other pressing national needs, we do not feel that a $5 billion level of effort is appropriate. *We recommend instead a 1972–76 space-spending peak of $3.8 billion a year.* Such a spending rate would force either a slippage of the 1977 achievement date or sequential (rather than concurrent) development of the two systems. *If program costs turn out to be higher than these initial $6 billion estimates, we urge a further stretching of the timetable and not higher budgets.*

In view of the enormous cost of manned flights to Mars, we recommend that the United States defer such an undertaking until it can be designed and carried out on an international scale. This would require a new organizational framework. But it would be a historic achievement if the nations of this planet could work together on man's most ambitious extraterrestrial adventure.

BASIC RESEARCH

In order to achieve mission-focused research and development, the United States must be able to tap a pool of fundamental scientific knowledge and capabilities. Basic research is undertaken for the purpose of constantly replenishing that pool of fundamental knowledge. Although the line of demarcation between technological advance and basic research is usually fuzzy, new scientific technology and research breakthroughs generally are accomplished through utilization of techniques or relationships discovered in basic research activities.

Funded in 1971 at a level of $2.7 billion, basic research is one of the most difficult and controversial issues to arise in the relationship between government and science. This is largely because the relationship between investment and return eludes precise analysis.

In 1950, the National Science Foundation (NSF) was established to provide a central mechanism for the support of basic research. It was to become the general science agency of the government and the government's principal mechanism for the support of nonmission related scientific activities. After a difficult beginning, the challenge of Sputnik brought the NSF rapidly increasing budgets between 1960 and 1967.

During this period, NSF funds for basic research rose from an annual level of $68 million to $235 million. Since then, funds have increased only moderately. But even during the period of rapid growth, the NSF has never come close to being the government's principal supplier of funds for academic research. NASA, the AEC, and the Department of Defense consistently had—and still have—higher budgets for basic research than the NSF. So did the National Institutes of Health for biomedical research. What this means is that NSF never has controlled sufficient funds to serve, through the distribution pattern given those funds, as a balancing agent among the various scientific disciplines.

The major need, in our view, is not so much for substantial increases in total federal basic research funds as it is for stabilizing funding of research according to a reasonable strategy for future growth. If funds vary wildly from year to year, as they have in recent years, work is unproductively disrupted. The ultimate effect of such uncertainty is to discourage people from entering scientific professions. One way to provide stability of funding would be to establish multiple-year financing.

Because of relative neglect for it in recent years, we do feel *spending for basic research should grow at a faster rate during the 1970's than spending for other kinds of research and development; we recommend an annual rate of 7.5 per cent.* To help give the National Science Foundation the larger role in basic research that its architects intended, *we recommend that basic research in all other agencies remain virtually at current levels during the next five years and that most of the growth be channeled through NSF.* This approach would permit an increase in NSF basic research from $300 million to $1.5 billion. Thus, by 1976 the country's central science agency would ˙oversee more than one-third of federal funds for basic research.

Budget proposals for Atomic Energy, Space, and Basic Research are summarized in Table 14:3 on the following page.

TABLE 14:3
ATOMIC ENERGY, SPACE, AND BASIC RESEARCH
(Outlays, in millions of current dollars)

| | Administration | | | Urban Coalition Recommendations | | | |
| | Estimated | Proposed | | | | | |
	1971	1972	1972	1973	1974	1975	1976
Atomic Energy Commission	2,275	2,318	2,405	2,390	2,190	2,080	1,965
NASA	3,368	3,151	3,100	3,200	3,400	3,600	3,800
NSF Basic Research	313	425	450	675	1,000	1,300	1,500
TOTAL	5,956	5,894	5,955	6,265	6,590	6,980	7,265

SOCIETY UNDER LAW

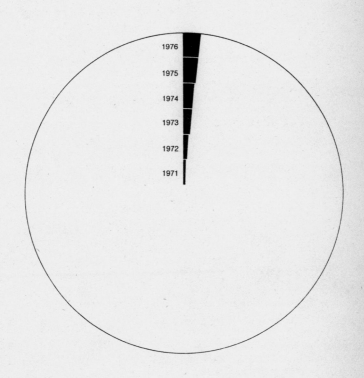

1976

1975

1974

1973

1972

1971

15

Law Enforcement and Criminal Justice

Crime, the cost of crime, and the fear of crime have become major factors in American life. At the same time, many of the measures advanced to cope with this increasing threat challenge our commitment to basic concepts of justice.

Even when the demagogic overstatements that this subject seems to inspire in many public officials are discounted, there remain indicators that crime is limiting the freedom of many Americans: Businesses fail under the weight of thefts; families move out of high-crime neighborhoods; parks and public gatherings are avoided; and, most important, millions live in fear and distrust their fellow citizens. The United States is not what it ought to be when normal existence includes fear of crime and violence.

Statistics reveal the magnitude of the problem:

- Nearly 5 million crimes were reported in 1969—and the Department of Justice estimates that only half of the crimes committed are actually reported.*
- The 1969 total of violent crimes—murder, rape, robbery, and aggravated assault—was 11 per cent higher than in 1968.
- The total of reported crimes rose by 12 per cent from 1968 to 1969.

* The crime rate is measured by reported crime. Clearly, more crimes are now being reported as a result of improved reporting and recording techniques. Therefore, to some extent the increase in the crime rate represents a statistical artifact. However, nearly all professional observers agree that a large percentage of the increase is real and cannot be accounted for by improved reporting techniques.

217

The cost of crime to the nation is staggering. Each year, losses of $20 to $25 billion burden American society, with a disproportionately high percentage falling upon those who can least afford it—poorer members of minority groups.*

A disproportionate burden is carried by residents of large cities (population over 500,000)—the location of less than 18 per cent of the population, but of almost half of the reported crimes. According to the FBI Uniform Crime Reports, urban areas have experienced a 120 per cent increase in reported crime (adjusted for population growth) since 1960.

The criminal justice system, if such a fragmented apparatus can be called a system, is presently ill prepared to deal effectively with the crime problem. Primary responsibility for law enforcement lies at the state and local level, but almost without exception, state and local expenditures for criminal justice are insufficient. These expenditures totaled just over $6 billion in 1971. Furthermore, state and local funds are allocated primarily for police. The courts and corrections and treatment components of the criminal justice system are seriously shortchanged.

Federal assistance to states and localities for law enforcement amounted to only $447 million in 1971. Nearly $340 million of this aid was provided by the Justice Department's Law Enforcement Assistance Administration. The LEAA share consists primarily of block grants to states, 75 per cent of which are earmarked for local jurisdictions. Each state's share is determined by population. A National Urban Coalition survey of twelve states found that most (74 per cent) LEAA funds in 1969 were spent on police forces—mostly for equipment. The emphasis changed somewhat for 1970, as the percentage spent on corrections—probably the most poorly funded part of the criminal justice process—doubled to 26 per cent of the total, and the amount for police dropped from 74 to 49 per cent.

The ultimate objective of federal actions should be the reduction of crime, through

- programs (recommended elsewhere in this report) that may reduce the social and economic causes of crime and

* Federal Reserve Board Governor Andrew Brimmer estimates that the direct cost of crime to Negroes in 1969 was $3 billion.

- a coordinated effort to improve the entire criminal justice system, primarily through increased federal assistance to states and localities and through incentives and requirements for reform attached to such assistance.

In the immediate future, federal assistance should provide aid for state and local criminal justice systems with incentives encouraging these jurisdictions to upgrade their police departments and to improve their court, corrections, and treatment systems.

POLICE

Crime statistics measure only a part of police effectiveness. The policeman's job more often entails social work activity, such as reconciling family disputes, rather than apprehending criminals. Although police performance is difficult to measure, recent assessments have made clear that many police departments suffer from chronic shortages of manpower, poorly trained manpower, and poor organization and administration.

Increasing the quality of police manpower is now perhaps the most important need. Although police professionalism is gaining, nearly one-third of all police departments still do not require their applicants to be high school graduates, and fewer than twenty-five departments in the nation require a college degree. Furthermore, although police departments spend almost 90 per cent of their funds on wages, salaries are still not high enough to attract the quality of men needed. Those factors, together with the poor public image of the police (related in many instances to the lack of professional attitudes on the part of policemen themselves), are clearly preventing many well-motivated and qualified people from considering police work as a career.

However, increasing the educational levels of recruits would only partially improve the quality of police departments. Greater emphasis should be given to the training of recruits, in-service training for all policemen, and special training for high-ranking officers.

The federal aid to local and state police departments through LEAA grants (requiring 60 per cent matching funds) amounted to $282 million in 1971.* Although some grants have been used

* Years are federal fiscal years unless otherwise indicated.

to assist students enrolled in college law-enforcement programs and policemen taking college courses, no direct federal incentive is provided to encourage local departments to raise educational standards for recruits.

Therefore, *we recommend that federal aid to police departments be directed toward upgrading the quality of police personnel.* Two types of programs appear necessary: (1) a salary supplement aimed at attracting better-educated recruits; and (2) assistance of police departments for recruiting and in-service training, minority recruitment, police-community relations, and similar purposes.

Police Salary Supplementation

We suggest, as a long-range goal, that all local police department professionals should have at least two years of college education and all chiefs, supervisors, and administrators should have a college degree. *A program of federal aid is necessary to encourage local departments to raise the educational level of police manpower. Local jurisdictions should be eligible for direct federal grants, starting in 1972, in the amount of $4–5,000 for each college graduate on their force,* provided police departments:

- establish a minimum education requirement for recruits of a high school diploma or its equivalent;
- provide incentives for college graduates and others with higher educations to enter the force by offering direct entry into jobs at higher skill and salary levels; and
- establish a promotion policy that gives a greater weight to ability and achievement than to the amount of time spent on the force or in various positions on the force.

The federal grants could be used either to supplement the salaries of college graduates and those on the force with some college education (as some departments do now) or to raise all police salaries within the department.

We believe that this program will enable departments to attract at least a greater share of the graduates of college law-enforcement programs. Currently, only one-third of graduates from four-year programs and one-half the graduates of two-year programs enter local police departments. Better salaries would also encourage students in other degree programs to consider police work. Assuming that the program is moderately successful, we estimate that the number of college graduates on police forces would increase from 40,000 to 86,000 by 1976, when outlays would total approximately $355 million.

Many departments could use nonpolice manpower to relieve trained officers of such routine jobs as issuing parking tickets, directing traffic, and handling office duties. *Use of paraprofessionals or police aides for routine tasks would not only make police work more attractive to college graduates but would also represent more efficient use of manpower. Federal assistance for funding such programs would be available through our recommended public-service employment program* (see Chapter 2).

Block Grants for Upgrading Police Departments and Personnel

We also *recommend that block grants be made available to states and localities for upgrading police departments and personnel through programs including training of recruits, in-service training, minority recruitment, and police-community relations.*

Federal funds for training recruits must be tied to minimum program standards, including classroom instruction in social and behavioral sciences and actual street experience. The funds should also be available for teacher training courses, such as those required of recruit teachers in the FBI.

In-service training to keep policemen abreast of new developments in law enforcement techniques, and refresher courses in such subjects as social sciences, community relations, and law are virtually nonexistent except in the largest police departments. Federal funds for in-service programs should be granted only to departments that agree to require all patrolmen to participate in these programs at least once a year.

States and localities could also utilize block grants for training of local police department supervisory and command personnel, particularly in administrative management techniques. To qualify for these funds, departments would have to agree to require satisfactory completion of appropriate courses as a prerequisite for promotion to any rank above sergeant.

Programs to improve police-community relations, including more intensive efforts at minority recruitment, should also be eligible to receive federal funds.

Peculiar problems exist for a predominantly white police force that must relate to nonwhite communities. At the present, many police forces are in this position. For example, although Detroit's population is 47 per cent black, its police force is only 8 per cent black; in Newark, which is 46 per cent black, the police force is 10 per cent black. Increased recruitment of minority members could be expected to improve significantly police-community relations in many localities with large minority populations. As a prerequisite to receiving federal aid, discrimination in promotion policies must be eliminated.

Federal grants to upgrade the quality of policy personnel under our proposals would increase to $300 million by 1976.

COURTS

Operating inefficiencies throughout our courts have created a major snag in the U.S. criminal justice system. Court dockets are overloaded with criminal cases, and overloading delays and diminishes justice. Crimes committed by people awaiting trial have aroused public clamor for pre-trial detention, despite grave civil liberties questions. Such measures would not be suggested if we were willing to tackle the tough, real task of reducing court backlogs.

Another critical problem is the disparity in the quality of justice from lower to higher courts. Ninety per cent of criminal cases are heard in lower courts. The President's Commission on Law Enforcement and the Administration of Justice's *Task Force Report: The Courts* (Washington, D.C.: Government Printing Office, 1967) points out that division of the criminal courts has produced lower standards of judicial, prosecutorial, and defense performance in the misdemeanor and petty offense courts. The Report states:

No program of crime prevention will be effective without a massive overhaul of the lower criminal courts. The many persons who encounter these courts each year can hardly fail to interpret that experience as an expression of indifference to their situations and to the ideals of fairness, equality, and rehabilitation professed in theory, yet frequently denied in practice. The result may be a hardening of antisocial attitudes in many defendants and the creation of obstacles to the successful adjustment of others.

In addition, almost all studies concerned with court reform have pointed out the need for better administrative procedures such as computerization of records and improved management. Relieving judges of the routine work that they now handle would free them for more important judicial responsibilities. Lower-level tasks could be handled by paraprofessionals or less-skilled, lower-paid officials.

The federal government is limited in what it can do to improve state and local courts. Maintenance of a fair system of criminal justice is the responsibility of state and local governments, but the federal government should encourage and finance reform.

First, however, *the federal courts must evaluate and improve their own procedures, so that the entire federal court system becomes a model for upgrading, improving, and expediting the administration of justice. We would double funding for federal courts by 1976, from $60 to $120 million.*

A second goal should be to encourage creation of federally funded model and experimental court systems in three or four states. The models should demonstrate methods for: handling court backlogs; improving physical facilities; computerizing court administration; upgrading court personnel and defense counselors; and training paraprofessionals. We estimate a total annual cost, beginning in 1973, of $25 million for these model programs. In addition, the federal government should provide funds for state surveys of court problems.

Finally, states and localities should be granted 75 per cent federal matching grants specifically for court reform. In order to receive grants, states would submit to the federal government plans for reform, based on the problems revealed by the surveys. Nearly $300 million would be available for this purpose in 1976.

LEGAL AID TO THE POOR

The Office of Economic Opportunity's Legal Services program now operates 800 field offices and employs 2,200 lawyers—and it is reaching only a fraction of those who need assistance.

Although the American Bar Association estimates that the poor have a minimum of 5 million legal problems each year (other authorities estimate the number is closer to 10 or 15 million), OEO lawyers deal only with approximately 600,000 cases annually. *We recommend an increase both in the number of Legal Service projects (from 265 to 500 by 1976) and in staff, to expand existing operations. Greater use should also be made of paraprofessionals, particularly law students, in the program.* To make these improvements, outlays for Legal Services should be increased from the 1971 level of nearly $61 million to $131 million by 1976.

We also recommend that the program particularly emphasize assistance in cases involving policies and administrative procedures of public agencies dealing with the poor and in cases that may alter the law, affecting significantly the lives of thousands of the poor by a single ruling. Failure to do this, in our opinion, will mean that the most important goal of this program—that of changing social institutions to make them more responsive to the needs of the poor—cannot be realized.

THE CORRECTIONS SYSTEM

Today, the enlightened public believes that the primary purpose of our corrections system should be to rehabilitate offenders. Yet, the traditional demands for punishment—deterrence of crime and protection of the public by isolating socially dangerous individuals —have left us with a system in which rehabilitation is almost impossible.

The chances that a former convict will make a successful transition to normal life are poor, and those chances clearly decrease the longer that a person is imprisoned. There is evidence that the detrimental effects of exposure to prison subculture actually encourage recidivism (further offenses after release).

There are about 200,000 inmates in federal and state institutions and approximately 80,000 serving sentences in local jails. If present trends continue, 60–70 per cent of these persons will commit crimes upon release and will eventually be returned to prison, according to Richard W. Velde of the Justice Department's Law Enforcement Assistance Administration. In remarks made at the American Correctional Association's Centennial Congress of Correction, October, 1970, Mr. Velde said that we are not yet able "to identify with any certainty the kinds of institutional programs that can be depended upon to rehabilitate any reasonably great number of persons exposed to them."

A number of states and localities have begun to experiment with minimum security institutions and community-based centers for the rehabilitation of misdemeanants, particularly juveniles and first offenders. Various graduated release programs, such as work-release (in which offenders work in the community but live in an institution), and halfway houses (small residences in the community where the offender is "boarded" rather than imprisoned) have been tried for those who have completed part, or all, of their sentences.

Unfortunately, despite enthusiastic claims, there is no clear indication that offenders who participate in these programs have a lower rate of recidivism than others merely placed on probation or parole. In a 1969 article in the *Information Review on Crime and Delinquency,* published by the National Council of Crime and Delinquency, Eugene Doleschal, assistant director of the Council, reported seemingly contradictory conclusions after he reviewed studies of graduated release programs:

> With minor reservations, the majority of agencies administering the programs report that graduated release is beneficial to the offender and to society and should be expanded; and
> Of the research and experiments undertaken in the areas of work-release, pre-release and halfway houses, the more rigorous the methodology used, the more ambivalent or negative are the findings regarding the efficacy of these programs.

We recommend that the federal government support research and demonstration projects on community-based rehabilitation and

assign LEAA responsibility for collection and evaluation of data.
Funds for this purpose should increase from an estimated $58 mil-
lion in 1971 to $100 million by 1976.

Our corrections efforts must satisfy two goals: (1) protection of
society from socially dangerous individuals and (2) the rehabilitation of offenders. Yet incarceration—the surest manner of protecting
society—seems to inhibit efforts at rehabilitation, and partial incarceration or graduated release programs do not appear to be more
effective in terms of rehabilitation than probation or parole programs. These latter procedures are far less expensive than other
corrections programs. Probationers and parolees cost society between $350 and $1,000 per year, while those imprisoned in penal
institutions cost between $3,000 and $8,000. Yet probation and
parole programs would seem to offer the least protection to society.

Probation and Parole

The majority of those convicted of less serious offenses are not
in fact a very serious threat to society, and studies indicate that
those who do pose a threat can be identified relatively easily. In
many instances, then, probation or early release on parole may
provide the best chance of rehabilitation. But many states make
inefficient or little use of probation and parole procedures. About
28 per cent of state prisoners are released on parole each year
(figures for local jails are not available), compared to 40 to 50
per cent of federal prisoners. There are also wide variations in
probation procedures.

Some states have virtually no services, or at best, fragmentary
services. Although the number of people placed on probation is
quite high (LEAA estimates as many as 800,000 at this time),
many of the offenders sent to institutions could also have been
placed on probation.

We therefore *recommend three federal programs encouraging
local corrections systems to rely more on probation and parole.*
First, for each offender placed on probation who, because of the
seriousness of the offense, could have been sent to a state prison,
a local jurisdiction should receive a federal grant of $2,500. This
amount is intended to exceed the actual cost of probation, thus
acting as an incentive for states to rely more upon and improve
probation systems. We estimate that, in 1976, 30,000 offenders

would be placed on probation as a result of this program, at a cost of $75 million in federal outlays.

The federal government should also provide all jurisdictions with a $500 nonrecurring grant for every person put on probation in each year. We estimate that nearly 1.3 million offenders will be placed on probation in 1976; federal probation subsidies would be nearly $650 million. Money from both of these grants would have to be spent on the corrections system, but not necessarily on probation services.

In 1970, the federal share of state and local probation and parole costs was $5.3 million. Under our proposals, this share would rise to $755 million in 1976.

By adopting these proposals, we hope to reduce the number of persons committed to prison, but the prison population will very probably remain high. Institutions at all levels require renovation and reform, but the problem is most acute at the local level. Almost without exception, the nation's 4,000 jails are underfunded, overcrowded, and poorly operated; very few offer any rehabilitation services.

We have already pointed out that there is little evidence to suggest that we know how to rehabilitate offenders incarcerated in institutions. However, job training programs, by satisfying the prisoner's most urgent need upon release, have proved moderately successful in easing the transition to a normal life. Therefore, federal support for inmate rehabilitation programs (currently estimated at approximately $7 million) should be restricted almost entirely to education and manpower training programs.

We recommend that sufficient funds be provided by 1976 to assure voluntary job training for every inmate of federal and state prisons in the year before his release. We estimate that such a program would cost $150 million in 1976. *In addition, the LEAA program of construction grants should be expanded to include federal loans and loan guarantees.* Outlays for this purpose will increase from the current $4.5 million to $200 million by 1976.

Treatment

A significant proportion of those arrested by the police do not belong in the court and correction systems at all. These are people with medical problems, particularly alcoholics and drug addicts.

Alcoholics represent almost one-third of all those arrested, while 23 per cent of larceny and petty theft arrests involve narcotics addicts. Many of these should, if convicted, be placed in specialized health treatment centers rather than prisons. Treatment facilities should also be available on a voluntary basis to those who are not convicted and those not yet in the criminal justice system.

In view of the striking success of many large-scale voluntary programs for drug addicts—Washington, D.C.'s methadone treatment for heroin users is a prime example—*we recommend that federal matching funds be made available to cities to operate these programs.* By 1976, treatment for 150,000 addicts should be available. Although alcoholic treatment programs have not proved as successful as some drug programs, *we recommend also that federal matching funds be made available to local governments for alcoholic treatment.*

Research into treatment techniques for both alcoholism and drug addiction (which would reduce both the recidivism rate and undesirable side effects of present drug programs) should accompany these efforts. Outlays for these two programs should reach $393 million by 1976.

The Organized Crime Problem

Although organized crime directly or indirectly affects most Americans daily, few are aware of its influence or the scope of its activities. Public unawareness contributes significantly to the ease with which organized crime is able to acquire its profits and maintain its power. The President's Commission on Law Enforcement and the Administration of Justice, in its *Task Force Report on Organized Crime* (Washington, D. C.: Government Printing Office, 1967), outlined the problem as follows:

> Organized crime is a society that seeks to operate outside the control of the American people and their governments. It involves thousands of criminals, working within structures as complex as those of any large corporation, subject to laws more rigidly enforced than those of legitimate governments. Its actions are not impulsive, but rather the result of intricate conspiracies, carried on over many years and aimed at gaining control over whole fields of activity in order to amass huge profits.

Most of organized crime's illegal revenue is raised with the cooperation of the public, which makes the task of law enforcement especially hard. Gambling, narcotics sales, and loan sharking are the major sources of revenue. The profits from these enterprises are used to infiltrate legitimate business areas (using illegal practices such as monopoly, terrorism, and extortion to achieve success).

The illegal narcotics trade has made dangerous addictive drugs easily available in our central cities. Provision of more treatment programs for narcotics addicts (see recommendations above), together with strong enforcement of the law with regard to addictive drugs, is needed to reduce organized crime's activities in this area.

The federal departments spend an estimated $68 million on investigation and prosecutions of organized crime cases. In view of the gravity of this problem, *we recommend an increase in outlays for federal activities against organized crime to $125 million in 1976.*

Crime Research and Statistics

One of the principal difficulties in evaluating present criminal justice procedures and in instituting reforms is the serious lack of research and data in this field.

We recommend that the National Institute of Law Enforcement and Criminal Justice of LEAA should continue to expand its valuable research and statistical analysis activities and should also increase research in social science areas related to criminal justice. In addition, a larger component of mental health research funds should be allocated to understanding criminal behavior.

Federal expenditure requirements to establish a central data bank, and to support the research and data collection of the National Institute of Law Enforcement and Criminal Justice, are estimated at $150 million by 1976.

Budget proposals for Law Enforcement and Criminal Justice are summarized in Table 15:1 on the following pages.

TABLE 15:1
LAW ENFORCEMENT AND CRIMINAL JUSTICE
(Outlays, in millions of current dollars)

	Administration		Urban Coalition Recommendations				
	Estimated 1971	Proposed 1972	1972	1973	1974	1975	1976
Aid to Police Departments							
Salary Supplementation	—	—	215	235	265	305	355
Block Grants for Upgrading Police Departments and Personnel[2]	84[1]	104[4]	150	200	250	300	300
Other (Primarily Equipment)	198	263	214	240	248	268	281
Subtotal	282	367	579	675	763	873	936
Treatment Programs[3]							
Drug Addicts	62	75	104	162	225	292	363
Alcoholics			7	15	30	30	30
Subtotal	62	75	111	177	255	322	393
Courts							
Assistance to States and Localities	20	27	34	82	168	216	289
Operation and Support of Federal Courts	60	73	80	100	110	115	120
Legal Assistance to Low-Income Citizens	61	61	73	87	102	116	131
Other	36	44	44	46	47	48	50
Subtotal	177	205	225	315	427	495	580
Aid to State and Local Corrections Programs[3]							
Probation and Parole Program			200	400	589	669	755
Community-Based Rehabilitation			75	90	95	100	100
Physical Rehabilitation and Construction			90	125	150	150	200
Other[4]			117	172	230	261	327
Subtotal	145	273	552	787	1,064	1,180	1,382

Federal Corrections System	118	177	122	126	129	133	137
Crime Research and Statistics	42	59	60	67	97	125	150
Federal Law Enforcement[5]							
Organized Crime	68	76	82	100	125	125	125
Narcotics	38	53	68	75	82	85	98
TOTAL	932	1,285	1,799	2,272	2,942	3,338	3,811

[1] Represents current federal spending to upgrade police departments and personnel through LEAA, Justice Department, FBI, and Veterans Administration programs. All of these programs will be replaced by a block grant in 1972.

[2] Includes intelligence and information systems, laboratory support, control of civil disorders, combat of organized crime, and general police activities.

[3] The breakdown costs were not available in official government documents.

[4] Includes prevention and control of juvenile delinquency, research grants to local corrections systems, and grants to prisons and jails for general activities and for personnel improvement and vocational training in prison.

[5] Excludes all FBI outlays, other than for organized crime and narcotics (and aid to police departments, which will be replaced by our block grant).

16

Equal Opportunity

The United States must provide all citizens an equal opportunity to participate in American society and in the shaping of governmental decisions affecting their lives.

We equate equal opportunity with the assurance of individual civil rights: in voting, health care, education, employment, and housing. One of the federal government's most fundamental responsibilities is to assure that all citizens enjoy these civil rights. But government civil rights activities—once considered a specialized, clearly identifiable set of programs—can no longer be perceived in that isolated sense. Concern for civil rights must permeate the entire federal effort to provide for the national welfare of Americans. The federal government can only be effective in this mission by constantly accenting concern for civil rights in its implementation of programs responding to hunger, poverty, unemployment, underemployment, ill health, poor housing, and inadequate education.

Discriminatory practices against racial and ethnic groups continue to deny many groups of Americans equal opportunities for self-development and enjoyment of the fruits of the American economy. Instances of discrimination range from blatant economic and social exclusion of some citizens to subtle inequities in promotion and salary practices.

While the victims of discrimination comprise many more segments of American society than most of us realize, denial of equal opportunity is most visibly and seriously a problem for many black, Mexican-American, Puerto Rican, American Indian, and some other minority citizens. The disadvantages of these minorities have been compounded by the indifference and insensitivity of many citizens to their plight.

Federal activities designed to protect the civil rights of all citizens must incorporate efforts to stem both discriminatory practices and the insensitivity that slows the elimination of these practices. In addition, federal civil rights guidelines must reflect a recognition that the traditional concept of civil rights is rapidly giving way to an expanded, more complex view of what is generally encompassed by the expression. The changing definition has resulted in part from the civil rights gains of the past decade, in part as a response to subtle and frequently more degrading forms of discrimination that have evolved to circumvent those gains, and in part from that emerging sense of pride, self-respect, and self-identity which now characterizes the feelings of many minority group citizens.

During the 1960's, enactment of new federal legislation and successful private and executive branch court initiatives opened doors of opportunity previously closed to minority groups. But the gains were fewer than the promises and expectations for three critical reasons. First, the new civil rights laws were enforced in a vacuum; they were not integrated into the major programs of the federal government. Indeed, federal civil rights enforcers were viewed by program officials as interlopers, disruptive to on-going operations. Many federal officials would not assume civil rights responsibilities in administering their programs. Second, direct enforcement efforts to support new civil rights laws and executive orders were grossly understaffed and underfunded. In almost every problem area, civil rights staffs were not even able to react to all complaints formally tendered to them—much less to actively initiate corrective proceedings. And third, since the civil rights laws contained no built-in factors to compensate for past racial and ethnic discriminatory practices, many minority citizens were unable to take advantage of new opportunities because previous wrongs had denied them the economic means and technical skills.

As a result, vast numbers of minority group citizens experienced no benefits from these civil rights advances of the past decade. Indeed, new frustrations were provoked by the unfulfilled promises of the civil rights laws of the 1960's, not only because the lack of vigorous federal enforcement of the new mandates rendered paper gains meaningless, but also because new forms of discrimination emerged.

234

These failures are in large part responsible for the belief within important segments of the various minority communities that the goal of civil rights enforcement—racial and ethnic integration with the dominant white society—is not the optimum solution to this nation's civil rights problem. Many believe that integration and equal opportunity are not synonymous and that economic, political, and social independence are the keys that unlock the doors to freedom in the United States. Such independence, rather than racial and ethnic integration, has become the civil rights goal of a growing number of minority citizens.

Federal leadership and activities in pursuit of the goal of equal opportunity must occur on four broadly defined fronts: elimination of the effects of past discriminatory practices; incorporation of civil rights goals into all federal programs and activities; an ending to discrimination in federal employment; and enforcement of existing civil rights laws and directives.

Eliminating Skill Level and Income Barriers

Without measures to eliminate barriers erected by past discriminatory practices, citizens now denied equal opportunities will never be fully able to take advantage of corrective action. A wide range of proposals promulgated in earlier chapters would, if implemented with sensitivity and awareness of civil rights concerns, have significant effect in lowering these barriers. Perhaps most critical of these are the recommendations we have set forth to improve the quality of education at all levels and increase opportunities to receive education at preschool, higher, and adult levels. Also important are our income-maintenance proposals and a broad series of employment and manpower proposals concerned with the upgrading of skills, minimum wage coverage and levels, and public-service employment. Minority citizens are expected to benefit more than proportionately from these recommendations.

In addition, we have made some recommendations relating to specialized programs—such as significantly enlarged outlays for bilingual education and adult basic education—to help citizens overcome specific handicaps like an inability to speak and write English.

We also urge that minority entrepreneurship activities of the

Commerce Department, the Office of Economic Opportunity, and the Small Business Administration be given strong support. Although such activities directly benefit only a few minority citizens, the symbolic importance of ownership participation cannot be overestimated.

INCORPORATING CIVIL RIGHTS GOALS INTO OTHER FEDERAL PROGRAMS

Perhaps the most important front for federal action will be the significant incorporation of civil rights considerations into all major federal program and policy decisions. This is the most effective means of providing economic, political, and social independence for the majority of citizens now deprived of some of their civil rights. Only .05 per cent of the federal budget directly supports civil rights enforcement; the manner in which the other 99.95 per cent of federal outlays is spent and the conditions placed on this spending are of far greater relevance to the provision of equal opportunity in American society.

Shoring up existing coordination and advocacy efforts will be a first, but limited, step toward this objective. *Prerequisites,* in our opinion, *include an expansion of the research and reporting functions of the U.S. Commission on Civil Rights, a more formalized and systematic civil rights policy leadership and coordination role for the White House and the Office of Management and Budget, and* continued *support for* such *advocacy organizations* as the Cabinet Committee on Opportunity for the Spanish-speaking and the Community Relations Service.

But *the most critical aspect of assuring equal opportunity through federal leverage lies in the institutionalization of civil rights considerations into the policy decision-making apparatus of every major federal department and agency.* This objective cannot be accomplished by a minor office in each agency assigned civil rights enforcement responsibilities. The experience of the past decade has demonstrated that such offices all too often tend to be shrugged off by program officers and senior officials as peripheral appendages and irritants.

The best guarantee of concern for civil rights considerations, of course, would be the appointment to senior policy positions of persons highly sensitive to such concerns. Surely no one insensitive to such concerns should hold high federal office. However, the subtle forms now taken by discrimination demand sophisticated countermeasures and highly specialized skills.

Accordingly, *also needed will be appointments of individuals in key policy-setting offices throughout the federal government—* including regional offices—*whose sole responsibility would be to ensure that careful consideration is given to civil rights* in all major programs and policies. If these persons are to be effective, a new formal requirement must be established, specifying that major agency programs and policies are subject to their review and advice before being promulgated.

These changes and requirements may seem only subtly different from current practice, but, properly performed, their impact could be substantial. The ways in which public services are provided have a tremendous influence on which citizens benefit socially or economically from those services.

This point is well illustrated by a simple example. Assuring that all hospitals that receive federal benefits admit patients without regard to race, color, or national origin is a civil rights enforcement matter. Deciding where in a city, town, or county to locate a new hospital is a program decision, generally made by individuals and agencies of government that have neither sensitivities to, nor responsibilities for, civil rights matters. If the program decision about where to locate the hospital results in the facility being built in an area where, because of transportation or housing problems, it is not accessible to some citizens, then assuring that the hospital is open to all without discrimination is a meaningless gesture. What would be far more important for advancement of equal opportunity, in this and similar cases, would be the establishment of a mechanism that ensured that the needs of all citizens were carefully reflected in such program decisions.

Where federal program decisions about the provision of public services have strong local dimensions—for example, the Model Cities program, elementary and secondary education aid, and highway, housing, and health facilities location decisions—an important part of the solution must be improved mechanisms for community participation in the making of those decisions. Recommendations for precisely such mechanisms have been made in specific instances in many of the preceding chapters. In every case, though, community participation needs to be bolstered by official government consideration of equal opportunity concerns when basic policies and guidelines are formulated.

This important goal of reflecting civil rights concerns in major federal policy and program decisions is not an expensive one to implement. We estimate that only $20 million more will be required annually above the $12 million currently being spent for this purpose.

ENDING FEDERAL EMPLOYMENT DISCRIMINATION

The third important area for federal involvement must be the elimination of discrimination in its own employment practices. If only because of the size and diversity of its work force, the federal government serves as the standard-bearer in the employment field for the entire country. Beyond that, it cannot fairly require practices by private employers it does not meet itself.

In terms of equal employment opportunity, the current relative position of the federal government is clearly anything but a national example of equitable job opportunity. During the past decade, the ratio of blacks to whites in the federal service has slightly exceeded the ratio of blacks to whites in the total U.S. population. (Black citizens constitute about 10 per cent of the total U.S. population.) However, year after year, most black employees consistently have been concentrated at the lower end of the salary scale within every pay plan. As of 1967, only 1.8 per cent of all federal employees earning over $12,000 were black. Spanish-speaking citizens (who constitute about 5 per cent of the U.S. population) fared even worse; they held only 2.6 per cent of federal jobs and a mere 0.6 per cent of all such jobs paying more than $8,000. Strict proportionality of representation for all groups in American society should not be a government employment goal, but opportunities for such employment must be open equally to all citizens. One can reasonably infer from such statistics as those above that that goal remains far from being achieved.

Clearly, there exist flaws in recruitment and promotion. *A restructuring of government service entrance examinations and other requirements should be made to reflect more adequately the cultural diversity of the American population. Similar changes are needed in promotion criteria.* Special training programs should be operated by the Civil Service Commission to help applicants and current low-ranking employees overcome basic educational weaknesses. Particular attention should be paid to unequal promotion practices and a general lack of cultural sensitivity pervading the military services.

ENFORCEMENT OF CIVIL RIGHTS LAWS

The final front for federal action—and one that should be emphasized only when other actions are deficient in producing desired results—is enforcement of civil rights laws and directives. For the near future, unfortunately, it appears that a dramatically more comprehensive enforcement effort will be required than exists today. For the most part, adequate civil rights laws are on the books, but they are meaningless unless accompanied by adequate enforcement.

A variety of problems common to most federal agencies with civil rights responsibilities have prevented full enforcement of the laws and have rendered the agencies incapable of achieving their goals. Without exception, all agencies with civil rights responsibilities lack sufficient staff to carry them out at an acceptable level of effectiveness. Other problems include lack of authority and decision-making responsibility among civil rights officials in various agencies; failure to define goals and priorities in civil rights efforts; failure to coordinate civil rights efforts among all government departments, agencies, and boards; undue emphasis on complaint-oriented rather than investigative programs; vague and unenforced compliance and review efforts; and failure to collect and utilize racial and ethnic data in planning and evaluating progress toward goals. Of all these flaws, inadequate staffing is the most damaging. Consider the following examples:

1. During its first year of operation, the Equal Employment Opportunity Commission anticipated receiving 2,000 charges and actually received 8,000. Since that time, the backlog has continued to grow, and the average processing time has further increased.

2. The 1968 Federal Fair Housing law mandated "affirmative

action" to further the purposes of the Act. The Department of Housing and Urban Development (HUD) has ignored taking the imaginative actions this language makes possible and has neither sought complaints nor assessed patterns and practices of discrimination. In 1969, it acted only on 979 complaints received from individuals, nearly 300 of which were immediately dismissed for lack of jurisdiction. Only once was evidence turned over to the Department of Justice to bring suit where practice of discrimination was found. Part of the problem is that funds have been provided only for 105 people to staff this function.

3. The Department of Justice acts as lawyer for all civil rights agencies, takes legal actions on its own behalf, enters cases as a friend of the court in privately initiated suits, and under specific statutes acts directly on behalf of private parties where a general public interest is demonstrated. About 100 lawyers in the Civil Rights Division—far too inadequate a number—have to handle the vast array of departmental responsibilities, including public accommodations; interference with rights; school, hospital, and employment suits; and voting actions.

There are numerous other areas of inadequacy. The 16,000 health-care facilities that must be reviewed to assure compliance with desegregation requirements are not being inspected frequently enough. Regulatory agencies have hardly begun to use their licensing and other regulatory powers to require affirmative action programs in the various transportation, communications, and power industries. Because of the educational importance of radio and television, action is particularly needed to provide opportunities for more diverse segments of the population to participate in broadcasting.

The Department of Health, Education, and Welfare (HEW) school integration activities are deficient on many counts. In the South, where such efforts have been concentrated, recent follow-through efforts have been inadequate. Far too few actions have been initiated at all in other parts of the country where segregation is even more of a problem. And in the focus on black-white integration, the equally serious problems of Spanish-speaking citizens have been slighted. A 1969 U.S. Commission on Civil Rights survey documented extensive segregation of Mexican-American students in the five Southwestern states. Although Mexican-Americans comprise 17 per cent of the student enrollment in these states, more than 65 per cent of the Mexican-American students were in schools with 50 per cent or more Mexican-American enrollment. Twenty-two per cent were found in schools with 80 to 100 per cent Mexican-American enrollment.

Altogether, *less than $80 million will be spent this year on federal civil rights enforcement. We recommend that outlays for this purpose quickly be scaled up to a level of $170 million*—still an infinitesimal fraction of the total federal budget, but one making possible dramatic improvements in effectiveness. As citizens become more conscious of the civil rights of others, and as government program decisions reflect such concerns, then the civil rights enforcement budget should level off and eventually decline.

In summary, the foundation upon which rests an increase in the exercise of fundamental civil rights by minority citizens is the reduction of barriers posed by inadequate economic means and technical skills. The implementation of economic and social measures geared to this end that we recommend is essential to developing the abilities of many minority citizens to take full advantage of their basic rights. On this foundation we can, with full effectiveness, base the other elements: elimination of discrimination in federal employment practices, more-than-doubled financial support for civil rights enforcement activities, and—most critically—the establishment of a structure and of staff positions within each of the major program divisions of the various federal departments and agencies to provide an effective and decisive civil rights element in every major program of the federal government.

These recommendations speak for a high priority for civil rights and equal opportunity concerns during the coming five years. Yet all can be accomplished with an annual expenditure level of $263 million, an increase from $122 million in 1971. This recommended sum is trivial in relation to our entire proposed federal budget, but its importance to those citizens who now lack equal opportunities for self-development can hardly be overestimated.

Budget proposals for Equal Opportunity are summarized in Table 16:1 on the following page.

TABLE 16:1
EQUAL OPPORTUNITY
(Outlays, in millions of current dollars)

	Administration		Urban Coalition Recommendations				
	Estimated 1971	Proposed 1972	1972	1973	1974	1975	1976
Coordination, Advocacy, and Policy Input							
White House and OMB	—	—	1	1	1	1	1
U.S. Commission on Civil Rights	3	4	5	7	7	8	8
Community Relations Service and Other Minority Citizen Advocacy Offices	6	7	8	8	8	8	8
Civil Rights Policy Input Mechanisms	12	14	24	32	32	32	32
Subtotal	21	25	38	48	48	49	49
Government Employment Practices							
Civil Service Commission Special Training	—	—	10	15	20	20	20
Enforcement of Laws and Directives							
Employment	30	47	50	60	70	75	78
Public School Desegregation	26	20[1]	35	40	40	35	30
Fair Housing	8	9	18	25	30	30	30
Health Facilities Desegregation	2	3	5	8	10	10	10
Federal Regulatory Agencies	—	—	1	2	2	3	3
Litigation	5	6	8	10	15	17	19
Subtotal	71	85	117	145	167	170	170
Other	19	20	20	20	22	22	24
TOTAL	111	130	185	228	257	261	263

[1]The 1972 Administration recommendation reflects an assumption that desegregation of school districts will be partially carried out by the Emergency School Assistance Program. Our recommendations regarding that program are presented in Chapter 6.

17

Consumer Protection

Protecting the American public from dangerous products, deceptive sales techniques, and rigged prices is a responsibility that the government has shouldered tardily and reluctantly. Probably the major reason for federal failures is that consumer interests, which are diffused throughout society, are not adequately represented either in Congress or in administrative departments charged with enforcing protective laws. A shift in national emphasis is needed to give consumer interests at least as great a priority as those of business, industry, labor, and other organized groups.

Our recommendations would necessitate both an increase in spending on consumer-protection programs and a significant reorganization of the machinery set up to establish and enforce standards. Congress has failed consistently to give federal agencies sufficient resources to carry out consumer-protection programs. However, merely increasing these resources will not solve the consumer's problems. Reforms are needed in the operation of federal programs and, in some areas, new legislation is required. Above all, though, the will to move aggressively to enforce strict consumer-protection standards is mandatory.

CONSUMER-PROTECTION PROGRAMS

At least thirty-nine different federal departments and agencies are responsible for protecting consumer interests. However, major responsibility is vested in the Food and Drug Administration of the Department of Health, Education, and Welfare and in the Federal Trade Commission, an independent agency.

242

The Food and Drug Administration

The Food and Drug Administration (FDA) inspects food and drug firms and tests products for safety. A report of an FDA study group submitted to Commissioner Herbert Lay, Jr., in August, 1969, declared that the agency was "unable to cope with the challenge" of guaranteeing food and drug safety in the American marketplace because of insufficient manpower and funds. Inspections of the 100,000 U.S. food processing plants and warehouses and the more than 8,000 drug manufacturers over which the FDA has jurisdiction are carried out by a staff of only 552. The entire FDA food program is operated by a total staff of fewer than 1,300, a grossly insufficient number to test and regulate all food products on the American market.

Because of its shortage of inspectors, the FDA is forced to rely heavily on voluntary compliance and self-regulation by both the food and the drug industries. Yet, in 1969,* follow-up inspections of drug firms previously cited for violations revealed that 75 per cent of them had failed to correct those violations. Such a finding suggests that voluntary compliance has not worked well in terms of protecting the public. More active regulatory efforts are needed.

Insufficient research into the effects of food additives (in part because of funding deficiencies) has resulted in the appearance of dangerous compounds, such as cyclamates, in marketed food products. A large-scale effort is under way to re-evaluate more than 600 chemicals already in foods. These chemicals were originally classified by the FDA as "Generally Recognized as Safe" without intensive investigation into their effects.

The FDA has often found it difficult to obtain the cooperation of other departments performing related work. For many years, for example, the Agriculture Department's Pesticide Registration Program** had safety standards that conflicted with FDA standards. The FDA product-safety program has also been hampered by the fact that at least ten other agencies test or set standards

---

* All references to years are to federal fiscal years unless otherwise indicated.
** This program has recently been transferred to the new Environmental Protection Agency.

for various products. Poor interagency communication and lack of official cooperation mean that new standards are often slow to be adopted.

We therefore *recommend an expansion of FDA food and drug research programs and of increased inspections designed to ensure compliance.* Sole responsibility should be given the FDA for regulation of flammable fabrics and for all mechanical and electrical household goods and appliances. Full implementation of these recommendations would require increasing the FDA budget from $79 million in 1971 to $161 million in 1976.

The Federal Trade Commission

The Federal Trade Commission (FTC) is charged with investigation and prevention of monopolistic and deceptive practices—including deceptive labeling or packaging, false advertising, and the sale of unsafe or harmful products—and with enforcement of truth-in-lending provisions. Its operations have been hindered by several factors. Principally:

- that Congress has consistently failed to appropriate sufficient funds to enable the FTC to carry out its responsibilities, particularly those new responsibilities assigned by Congress itself;
- that limited resources have all too frequently been absorbed by actions on minor violations while large-scale frauds have continued unchecked;
- that the Commission has relied too heavily on voluntary compliance with FTC regulations; and
- that staff investigations have been long and drawn out, due primarily to poor procedures.

In carrying out its over-all mission, the FTC has been hampered severely by its own misplaced priorities. Its concern with minor labeling violations is certainly laudable, but it is inappropriate to devote large numbers of staff members and considerable financial resources to these activities when the result is inadequate funding and personnel to combat serious local frauds, or to effectively police advertising in national publications, or to enforce its own voluntary compliance procedures.

The results indicate that the FTC has placed too much confidence in its voluntary compliance system (whereby a company in violation of the law agrees, at the FTC's request, to alter its practices in the future). Although voluntary compliance may be an efficient way for the FTC to protect consumers from a multitude of illegal practices, it will only be effective if supported by a real threat of strong, prompt legal action..

FTC investigations have traditionally been extremely slow. Often, action is not taken on a case for several years, and the number of cases handled has been shockingly small. In 1969, only 192 new investigations of deceptive consumer practices were opened by the FTC, although the agency received 12,000 complaints that year. If consumers are to be adequately protected, many more investigations need to be conducted, and, to do so, the FTC will need additional staff as well as improved operational procedures.

Since the appointment, in the summer of 1970, of Miles Kirkpatrick as Chairman of the FTC, the agency has stepped up its consumer actions, has improved its methods of investigation and enforcement significantly, and has taken aim at the misleading advertising and fraudulent practices of major industries and giant companies. *To allow the agency to continue to expand its activities, we recommend an increase in the budget of its Bureau of Consumer Protection from $11 million to $24 million by 1976.*

In addition, new legislation is needed to extend federal consumer protection in the areas of credit and packaging. *We recommend that:*

1. *The mailing of unsolicited credit cards be made illegal.*

2. *Consumers be permitted to review copies of their credit ratings held by any company offering credit and to submit further evidence of good credit and request removal of incorrect information.* Failure by the company to comply with such requests would leave it liable to prosecution.

3. *Unit labeling of packages be required for all appropriate goods, with price per pound, pint, or other unit of measure on the container.*

ANTITRUST ACTIVITY

The dynamics of a competitive economy normally operate to keep prices down, thereby benefiting consumers directly. The enforcement of antitrust and antimonopoly laws serves to remove any abnormal impediments to market competition and to deter unlawful exercise of market power or collusion among firms at the expense of competitors and consumers. These laws cover a variety of business practices, including mergers, but they are generally vague and permit wide latitude in judging individual cases. *We propose that the Justice Department and the FTC, which share responsibility for enforcing these laws, continue their surveillance and investigation of business activities, and that federal outlays to permit them to do so should increase from $19 million in 1971 to $22 million by 1976.*

OTHER CONSUMER-PROTECTION NEEDS

The preceding recommendations concerning the operation of the FDA and the FTC will do much to improve the effectiveness of federal consumer-protection activities. However, there are a number of other needed consumer-protection activities that do not fall comfortably within the two agencies' jurisdictions. One of them is the need for a federal consumer-advocate group.

A Consumer Protection Agency

Poor coordination among the thirty-nine different departments and agencies dealing with consumer matters, and failure of many of them to show a real commitment to consumer interests, demonstrates that consumers need to be represented as a constituency within the federal government. *We therefore recommend the establishment of a new independent Consumer Protection Agency to:*

1. *coordinate existing programs and keep federal agencies advised of all federal consumer programs;*

2. *represent consumer interests in proceedings of federal departments and agencies and in court proceedings initiated by these departments or agencies;*

3. *make recommendations on programs, regulations, and other decisions affecting consumers and require agencies to reconsider decisions deemed inimical to consumers* (the new agency would be required to make public the reasons for its objections to the decisions);

4. *prevent violations of the law or of federal regulations* (in a manner similar to that of the FTC) *in cases where other departments' actions are inadequate or in a case of extreme urgency* (it is not envisioned that this power would often be invoked);

5. *gather and disseminate information, including results of government tests, and encourage and support consumer-education programs.*

Consumer Law and Education

There are limits to what government agencies can do to protect consumers, and, when the government cannot help, the citizen must be prepared to protect himself. *We propose that a mechanism for legal recourse by individual consumers who have been victims of fraud, whether large-scale or small-scale, be established.* Currently, federal law concerning permissible legal action is inadequate. The law requires that each complaint in a federal court involve a sum over $10,000. Legislation permitting consumers to band together to sue the offending company (class action suits) would give the average consumer a legal recourse presently available only to the wealthy. *We* therefore *recommend that individuals with claims of $10 or more be permitted to join together to reach the necessary $10,000 to take a company accused of fraudulent practices to court.*

Consumers also need legal protection against contracts or agreements signed in the home as a result of high-pressure door-to-door sales techniques. *We suggest that consumers who have succumbed to such high-pressure techniques be allowed to cancel their contracts within seven days of purchase without liability for payment.*

None of these recommendations will be effective if consumers do not know what recourses are open to them. In addition, consumer-protection policing will become a losing battle if citizens do not learn how to avoid deception, to shop comparatively, and to protect their rights. For this reason, *the new Consumer Protection Agency should be charged with disseminating consumer information and conducting education campaigns. We also suggest mandatory consumer-education courses in high schools and special federal programs aimed at educating low-income consumers.*

Protecting the Poor

One group of American consumers has been disproportionately victimized and exploited—low-income consumers. Not only do they have greater problems than the affluent buyers but they are less prepared to fight back. A lack of mobility may restrict the geographical area in which they shop. Their local stores, generally small and with high overhead costs, may charge more than stores with nearly identical products in more affluent neighborhoods. This situation has, of course, created an ideal opportunity for unscrupulous merchandizers. Because many low-income consumers who attempt to deal with their problems are frustrated by a limited education or background, they are often incapable of seeking assistance or taking action, even if they realize that their legal rights are being violated. *We* therefore *recommend:*

1. *An expansion of the Office of Economic Opportunity (OEO) legal-aid program to allow service to 800,000 more consumers by 1976.* Outlays for this purpose would increase from $12 million to $30 million by 1976 (see Chapter 15).

2. *An increase in the consumer education programs of local Community Action Agencies (CAA's) and an increase in OEO grant funds for this purpose from $3.2 million to $6.4 million by 1976* (see Metropolitan Development budget, Chapter 8, for funding of CAA's).

3. *Subsidy of low-income credit unions through the National Credit Union Administration (NCUA), allowing for five-year grants to cover administrative and operating costs.* The OEO program that funds a limited number of these credit unions through local CAA's should be transferred to the NCUA.

4. *That decisions affecting the deposit of federal funds, and the use to which these funds may be put, be made consistent with the needs of financial institutions that serve lower income areas or that invest in low-income credit unions.*

Budget proposals for Consumer Protection are summarized in Table 17:1 on the following page.

TABLE 17:1
CONSUMER PROTECTION[1]
(Outlays, in millions of current dollars)

	Administration		Urban Coalition Recommendations				
	Estimated 1971	Proposed 1972	1972	1973	1974	1975	1976
Food and Drug Administration							
Food Program	33	42	44	53	70	79	86
Drugs and Devices	34	39	45	51	53	57	60
Product Safety	5	6	7	7	7	7	7
Program Direction and Administration	7	7	7	7	7	8	8
Subtotal	79	94	103	118	137	151	161
Federal Trade Commission Bureau of							
Consumer Protection	11	12	13	17	18	21	24
Antitrust Enforcement	19	21	20	20	21	22	22
Subsidies to Low-income Credit Unions							
Office of Economic Opportunity	1	1					
National Credit Union Administration			2	3	4	4	4
TOTAL[2]	110	128	138	158	180	198	211

[1] This table does not show all federal consumer-protection activities, only those mentioned in the text.
[2] Expenditures on legal assistance for low-income consumers are contained in the budget for law enforcement and criminal justice and those for local Community Action Agencies in the metropolitan development budget.

INTERNATIONAL
AFFAIRS

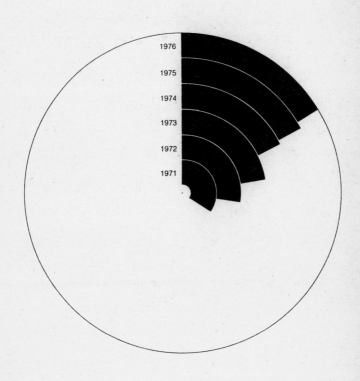

1976

1975

1974

1973

1972

1971

18

National Defense and Military Assistance

In the nuclear era, no level of military spending can guarantee a nation security against external threats. Inevitably, any level of defense spending requires acceptance of some level of risk. In deciding how much should be spent on military forces, we must keep three broad propositions in mind:

1. Military expenditures are not directly productive. They provide a protective shield that enables the United States to progress toward the achievement of national goals, but they do not directly advance us toward any of those goals. We should, therefore, spend no more on military expenditures than is sensibly needed for national security.

2. High levels of defense spending are not needed to prop up our economy. The huge backlog of other needs is more than adequate to fill any gap in aggregate demand—after appropriate conversion and retraining measures—left by reductions in defense spending.

3. Defense spending should be geared to the scope and character of predictable enemy threats, with due consideration to the relative merits of other claims on national resources. It should not, as is often argued, be pegged to the GNP.

Our assessment of defense needs for fiscal years 1972 through 1976* must begin with an examination of the capabilities and intentions of potential adversaries and of our own military commitments to allied nations. We cannot project the former with any high

---

* All references to years are to federal fiscal years unless otherwise indicated.

degree of certainty because we cannot control them. We can, however, reach some intelligent judgments based on current evidence and recent trends.

The threats to U.S. security can be readily identified. Fortunately, we are not beset upon all sides by enemies, but real potential threats do exist. Both Russia and China possess sufficient military might to cause considerable physical damage to the United States. We do not know whether either of these nations would take advantage of a future opportunity to advance its national interest by forcible use of that military might, but we cannot be certain that they would not. It is because of these Soviet and Chinese threats that we have entered into security agreements with more than forty nations. Accordingly, we must interpret the obligations entailed by these agreements in terms of the threats.

These same threats have existed for more than two decades—but they have not remained static. Indeed, in developing recommended levels of military spending, we must be sensitive to the changing nature of external threats to U.S. security. Central among recent changes are: (1) the shattering of the image of a monolithic Communist bloc, most visible in Soviet-Chinese clashes, which have kept some troops of both countries tied down along their common border; (2) a new (more conservative) estimate of objectives achievable by major American land involvement in Asia; (3) a current close balance between U.S. and U.S.S.R. nuclear destructive capabilities, but at a much higher, and therefore more dangerous level than existed a decade ago; and (4) a limited and crude Chinese nuclear capability, juxtaposed against a less imposing threat from Chinese ground troops than was previously assumed, due primarily to logistics constraints they face beyond their borders.

Taken together, these general observations strongly suggest the possibility of smaller U.S. defense forces in the 1970's than the nation provided for in the 1960's. Current defense forces are unnecessarily large in relation to the purposes they serve. This conclusion is reinforced by several additional factors: (1) the strategic and technological obsolescence of much of the surface U.S. Navy; (2) the capability of many of our allies to shoulder a fuller portion of the burden of their own defense; and (3) a tremendous backlog of high-priority, competing domestic claims on the national dollar.

With this general background, we need next to determine in greater detail what force needs will exist in the next five years and what they are likely to cost.

We can hope that the next five years will be marked by heightened international cooperation in winding down the nuclear arms race and settling conflicts through negotiations rather than resort to arms. We can hope for broadened recognition of the role, and actual use, of the United Nations as a peacekeeping agent. We can hope that significant arms limitation agreements will emerge from the Strategic Arms Limitation Talks (SALT) and any successor talks. We must work diligently, through diplomatic processes, to advance all of these ends.

But we cannot *assume* that any of these goals will be attained between now and 1976. If any are, we will have then the opportunities to cut military spending further. Today, however, we must develop defense policies without assuming that any of these improvements in international understanding will in fact be reached.

This conclusion does not mean that U.S. military forces must or should remain static. We already have cited several changes in the international climate that indicate the appropriateness of a lower U.S. military profile in the 1970's. Changes in U.S. military forces, though, must reflect those technological and political changes which *have* occurred in the world, not those we wish would occur.

To simplify the analysis, we will begin by examining the requirements for an ongoing baseline force and then turn to special additional needs in Vietnam. It is not generally realized, but even at the peak of our involvement in Vietnam only about 30 per cent of the defense budget was being spent to conduct the war. The remaining 70 per cent reflected the cost of what has come to be known as the baseline force. It is, in effect, the peacetime force that we maintain both for deterrence of enemy attack and for at least the initial stages of a conflict that might require invoking the commitments of the United States. We will examine in turn the two major components of the baseline force—strategic forces and general-purpose forces, each including required support forces.

Strategic Forces

Deterrence of nuclear attack is the fundamental purpose served by U.S. strategic forces. We deter such an attack by possessing the ability to inflict damage unacceptable to a nation that has attacked us. Thus, in order to deter an enemy's strategic nuclear attack with high confidence, we must be able to convince other nations that we have the capability to absorb a massive enemy strike, delivered with little or no warning, and still strike back with devastating power.

We now possess more than sufficient forces to perform this mission. Assuming the worst about U.S.S.R. intentions and probable capabilities, U.S. strategic forces could destroy more than 40 per cent of the Soviet Union's total population and more than 75 per cent of its industrial capacity. (The official Defense Department standard for an effective deterrent requires destruction of 20–25 per cent of an enemy's population and half its industrial capacity.)

Strategic Offensive Forces

No efforts should be stinted in pursuit of agreements on nuclear-weapon limitations at SALT or at any subsequent international forums. But even in the absence of such agreements, significant reductions in U.S. strategic forces are possible without sacrificing national security—and, perhaps, they may, in fact, increase security through a gradual winding down of the arms race. This claim rests on the assumption that recent trends in the size and composition of Russian and Chinese strategic forces continue during the coming five years.*

Part of the reason for our current surplus capability is the

---

* The Soviet Union has been vigorously improving the capabilities of its strategic submarine fleet, but has slowed and recently ceased construction of sites for additional large land-based SS-9 missiles. The Soviet intercontinental bomber force consists of less than 150 planes and is neither being enlarged nor modernized. The Chinese strategic missile force that is expected to materialize, but does not yet exist, was described by Defense Secretary Melvin R. Laird as follows: "For many years to come [it] will be far too small and will lack the accuracy to pose a threat to our strategic offensive capabilities."

maintenance of a triple deterrent—Polaris submarines, Minuteman land-based missiles, and B-52 and FB-111 bombers—with each component *by itself* sufficient to assure destruction of Russian or Chinese society on a retaliatory strike.

This redundant triple deterrent can be reduced. A marginal case might be made for maintaining a mixed strategic-offensive force as a hedge against the extremely low probability that the Soviet Union could develop some device to cripple our Polaris fleet. But Secretary of Defense Melvin R. Laird in 1970 said that increasingly vulnerable to enemy missile attack. We support cur- Polaris and Poseidon submarines at sea can be considered virtually invulnerable today." Maintaining the benefits of a mixed strategic-offensive force does not require that bomber or land-based missile forces be significantly modernized or even kept at current levels.

The strategic advantage has now shifted to sea-based deterrent systems such as Polaris; bombers and land-based missiles are increasingly vulnerable to enemy missile attack. We support current U.S. plans to convert thirty-one Polaris submarines to the Poseidon configuration (involving, essentially, the substitution of new missiles that can carry ten warheads as opposed to three on the Polaris missiles) and to expand funding for the highly promising underwater long-range missile system (ULMS), a submarine-based system proposed as an eventual successor to Poseidon. The ULMS should not, however, be rushed into production; that step should be taken *if and only if* the Soviet Union is discovered to be successfully developing a radically advanced anti-submarine warfare concept that threatens Poseidon survival.

At the same time, however, MIRVing of the land-based Minuteman missiles (that is, providing each of them with several, rather than one, nuclear warheads) should immediately cease. This program is not necessary for deterrence and would, at great expense—the total program cost is estimated to be $5.4 billion, with current year spending about $700 million—serve only to lessen security by unbalancing the arms race. Development of a new strategic bomber, the B-1, should also cease. If this program is allowed to proceed, its eventual cost is likely to be $15–20 billion. Technological trends raise doubt that we will ever again need an advanced design strategic bomber; missiles have a growing edge in accuracy, speed, and penetration. But we can retain the value of a bomber force and significantly fewer planes than are now on ready status. *We recommend phasing out by the end of 1973 two-thirds of the current twenty-seven bomber squadrons, thereby saving $1.2 billion annually.*

Strategic Defensive Forces

U.S. strategic defensive systems are less extensive and, in total, less costly to maintain than the offensive weapons just described. This is so because the fundamental purpose of our strategic arsenal is deterrence, not damage limitation.* The most important and least expensive of our strategic defensive forces is an enemy-missile warning system consisting of radars, computers, and communications devices. This network is designed to provide us with precious minutes of warning and decision-making time between the spotting of enemy missles and their striking of U.S. targets.

The contribution of other existing and proposed strategic defensive systems is highly questionable. The oldest and most expensive to maintain of these is the SAGE–Air Defense Command, a network of radar, interceptor planes, and ground-to-air missiles designed for defense against Soviet bombers. At one time, this was a critical purpose, but with a Soviet intercontinental bomber force of less than 150 planes (and no sign of plans to enlarge or modernize that force), air defense is now of much less relative importance. *We recommend phasing out a major portion of the remaining bomber air defense system, saving as a result $800 million a year—slightly over half of current costs.* We need to retain essentially a surveillance capability.

We also recommend the cessation of all attempts to operate defensive systems that would seek to intercept Russian or Chinese missiles launched toward U.S. targets. Such an approach, relying heavily on antiballistic missiles such as the Safeguard system,

---

* Damage limitation refers to a policy of attempting to curtail destruction wreaked on American cities and offensive missiles by an enemy attack. Systems employed to limit such damage generally are designed to work by intercepting and destroying enemy missiles or bombers before they reach American targets.

offers very little additional effectiveness and is extremely costly. Safeguard outlays in 1971 are expected to total $1.5 billion; the cost of the completed system is widely disputed but almost certain to be more than $10 billion. Moreover, to the extent that the United States tries to improve its strategic defensive capability, the Soviet Union and China would be likely to consider their own capability for deterrence threatened and to add enough offensive forces to nullify our defensive measures. Such a competition is expensive, fruitless, and dangerous. The economics of this competition, moreover, favor the offense. It is basically cheaper for one nation to buy additional offensive missiles than it is for its foe to buy enough defensive equipment to nullify those additional missiles. Because nuclear weapons carried today by missiles are devastatingly powerful, a defensive system guarding a city or a missile site cannot afford to permit a single enemy missile to reach that site.

Adoption of the above recommendations, supplemented by continued substantial expenditures for associated research and development and intelligence activities, would permit a reduction from $16.3 billion in current strategic outlays to $10.5 billion in 1976. These measures would leave us with an efficient early warning system and deterrent forces consisting of a large but potentially vulnerable Minuteman force, a modest-sized bomber force, and the virtually invulnerable Polaris-Poseidon fleet. This reduced strategic force would still be more than adequate in a retaliatory strike and would qualify as an effective deterrent by official Department of Defense standards.

General-Purpose Forces

The general-purpose (or conventional) force requirement relates more to the support of our commitments to more than forty other nations than to the defense of our own territory. Outlays for baseline general-purpose forces (excluding, that is, special increments for Vietnam) are estimated at $45.2 billion in 1971. This level of spending is designed to provide sufficient general-purpose forces to maintain combat capability for the initial stages of two major wars and one minor war simultaneously.* The Nixon Administration has announced, however, that future planning will be based on the capability to wage only one major war and minor war simultaneously.

The Administration has suggested that fewer men will be needed to implement this posture. They have also announced that no treaty commitments to allies will be abrogated, although some will be reinterpreted. But there remains a considerable lack of clarity concerning areas of the world where U.S. interests are considered vital, and what types and numbers of general-purpose forces are deemed necessary to protect those interests. The President did imply in his first State of the World Message that our major foreign commitments lie in Europe rather than in Asia. But he has revealed little of his thinking about the kinds and costs of military forces dictated by this new doctrine.

In order to derive an estimate of forces required to implement these broad policies, one must make some reasonable assumptions about the major considerations that dictated Administration development of a new doctrine. The experience of the past decade seems to contain three paramount lessons for the use of U.S. conventional military forces. The likelihood is that all three had some shaping influence on the new doctrine.

First, we must be strictly aware of what parts of the world are vital to U.S. interests. Conventional U.S. military forces should be committed only where those interests are affected. Treaty commitments should be invoked only when a common threat is posed to the United States and an ally—the original purpose for which all our treaty commitments were designed.

Second, we must honestly recognize the highly limited degree to

---

* It is important to understand that any such planning assumptions specifying a number of contingencies to be prepared for call only for the provision of troops to handle the initial stages of a conflict. The objective is to buy time, to make Russia or China—whichever might be an aggressor—pause and consider the nuclear catastrophe that might be unleashed as a consequence of its continuing to press an attack against conventional U.S. forces. These are sensible assumptions and objectives; the prospect of a prolonged conflict between conventional U.S. and Russian or Chinese land and/or sea forces is remote given the full spectrum of military options available to these nations.

which foreign policy objectives can be achieved by use of conventional U.S. military forces. Our involvement in Vietnam has proved, at a tragic price, how ineffective our forces can be, no matter how well they perform, in a guerrilla war in an unindustrialized nation.

Third, we must carefully evaluate the kinds and amounts of military equipment that will be useful should our forces be committed to some future war. Experience in Vietnam has illustrated the limitations of some kinds of highly sophisticated equipment— sophistication sometimes results in a loss of reliability or flexibility. In addition, continuing scrutiny is required to weed out systems made obsolete by changing technology.

Consideration of these factors makes possible translation of the Administration's announced broad planning assumptions into a statement of future general-purpose force requirement guidelines. In general, they suggest: (1) a restrictive interpretation of U.S. military commitments, with U.S. forces to be sent into action only where vital U.S. interests are threatened by China or the Soviet Union; (2) increased reliance on allies, particularly in Asia, to provide troops; (3) continued U.S. provision to allies of land-based tactical aircraft squadrons; (4) increases in the amount of weaponry supplied to all allies for their ground and air forces; (5) small reductions in airlift-sealift (although we need a modernized sealift component) and amphibious capabilities; (6) restructured and better-equipped U.S. Reserve forces; and (7) an emphasis on simply designed and reliable aircraft, ships, tactical missiles, tanks, and other weapons.

There remains wide latitude for judgment as to the prudent pace and size of force reductions. Choices must be made against the yardstick provided by competing national needs, as well as the guidelines cited above. Altogether, *we suggest that baseline general-purpose force outlays could safely be cut to $38.8 billion in 1976, a drop of $6.4 billion from present levels.* This would include a decrease of approximately $1.4 billion in the cost of Europe-oriented forces and a savings of $5 billion in Asia-oriented forces (the decrease in forces being even greater than the cost reductions due to the price increases included in cost estimates).

European Force Requirements

The United States role in European general-purpose force defense is to contribute to a NATO deterrent against a conventional attack by the Soviet Union or other Warsaw Pact nations. Symbolically, the most important part of the U.S. contribution has been the four Army divisions stationed in West Germany. These divisions represent only a small part of our total NATO contribution, which also includes three additional Army divisions, one Marine division and accompanying air wing, and seven Reserve divisions—U.S. based—plus sixteen Air Force air wings, four attack aircraft carrier groups, and a significant further complement of naval forces. All of these forces, of course, also require back-up support.

Controversy is growing over the appropriate size of the U.S. contribution to NATO, with the debate focused almost entirely on U.S. manpower levels in Europe itself. To some extent, this debate has been misdirected. We agree that our NATO allies should absorb a larger portion of troop costs in the European theatre (currently the United States allocates 7 per cent of its GNP for defense spending, versus an average of 5 per cent for our NATO allies), both because of their improved economic ability to bear such a burden and because we completely finance the strategic nuclear deterrent that protects NATO countries as well as the United States. We also agree that the number of U.S. troops oriented toward Europe can be safely reduced without lessening NATO security.

But we differ with the conclusion that the way to achieve these ends is through a reduction in the four U.S. Army combat divisions stationed in Germany. To the contrary, we feel that these divisions are among the highest priority items in our military arsenal in contributing to international stability. Their deterrent and symbolic values can hardly be overestimated. If these American forces were substantially reduced, the reaction of our NATO allies would probably be either hasty attempts to reach accommodation with the Soviet Union and other Warsaw Pact nations, or panicked efforts to augment existing military capabilities, including acquisition of nuclear weapons. Neither of these reactions would enhance European stability or U.S. security.

Instead of cutting into our Europe-based combat divisions, we recommend that the number of U.S. support troops in Europe be further reduced by 50,000 and that one Army division stationed in the United States, but oriented toward Europe, be eliminated from the force. Savings would exceed $900 million a year.

Reductions in our now redundant 22-wing Europe-oriented tactical aircraft capability should accompany these changes. The present surplus is among units assigned the deep interdiction role, the primary purpose of which is destruction of supply and communications networks (e.g. bridges, railroads, power plants). Pilots on such missions are also sometimes able to take advantage of targets of opportunity should they spot enemy tanks or airplanes caught on the ground. Prospects for success of these missions in Europe are poor because many Warsaw Pact nations' aircraft are protected by shelters and because the highly developed infrastructure in Eastern European countries offers many alternative routes while those shut down by bombing are being repaired. We already possess fully adequate numbers of planes for air-to-air combat and close air-support roles, but new aircraft of a highly maneuverable, uncluttered design are needed for both purposes.

Altogether, *we recommend that one Navy and four Air Force wings be eliminated, at an average annual savings approaching $300 million per wing.* In choosing which Air Force wings to cut, it would be wise to select U.S.-based, Europe-oriented wings in order to maximize the number of remaining wings that could be quickly flown to the Mideast and temporarily rebased there in case such a requirement emerged. We would not anticipate that U.S. forces would become directly involved in defending Israel (although the United States should continue to assist Israeli purchases of required military equipment), but it is prudent to retain the capability to do so effectively.

Asian Force Requirements

U.S. objectives and commitments in Asia are far less clearly delineated than those in Europe. Our military involvement has changed in emphasis with shifting political currents. Major U.S. military intervention since World War II has come to two bursts— Korea and Vietnam. The deployment pattern of our Asia-oriented forces as we move into 1972 reflects primarily our lingering involvement in the affairs of those two nations—with a large complement of naval general-purpose forces, and a sizable group of back-up ground troops spread over Pacific Ocean islands and the western United States.

Major adjustments in these forces are required to conform with the Administration's announced planning assumptions and the guidelines described earlier. U.S. involvement in new Southeast Asia land wars such as Vietnam can only serve to defeat further our real national purposes. We should extricate U.S. ground forces from South Korea and Thailand as expeditiously as possible, as our involvement in Vietnam is reduced. Vital U.S. interests currently exist only in Japan and Taiwan, excluding nations such as Australia and New Zealand, which provide quite adequately for their own defense. And even the threats to Japan and Taiwan are severely limited by restricted Chinese air and amphibious capability.

As President Nixon has suggested, the future U.S. general-purpose force contribution to Asian allies should consist heavily of tactical air wings. Allies will have to supply their own ground troops. U.S. military assistance funds should contribute to the cost of their weaponry.

No one knows precisely what portion of U.S. Asia-oriented forces should be eliminated as part of the implementation of this new doctrine. A strict interpretation of the shift to a one-and-a-half-war planning assumption might suggest elimination of our eight divisions and fifteen air wings now oriented to this contingency. Such a move would be highly imprudent. *Four divisions (each now costing about $800 million a year)—including the two now in Korea along with their tactical nuclear weapons—and four wings could safely be cut.* Air wings can be pruned, despite their relatively increased importance under the new doctrine, because of the net reduction in the number of allied ground divisions requiring air support. *The increased vulnerability of aircraft carriers* (described in detail below) *suggests that the major cut should be made in carrier-based wings.* The kinds of aircraft required for Asia are quite similar to those already noted for Europe.

Naval Forces

Both recommended regional force cuts include a proportionate share, larger for Asia, of recommended naval-force reductions. Naval forces require singling out because, while assignable to regional contingencies, they also serve a somewhat independent requirement for control of sea lanes.

A critical aspect of realigning general-purpose force levels should be recognition of the impact of changing technology on surface sea power requirements.

The number of missions that attack carriers can perform and the number of targets they can perform them against have been greatly reduced, mostly due to carrier vulnerability to modern tactical missiles. The number of carriers we operate ought therefore to be reduced. As already described in the regional analyses, *we recommend the operation of only seven attack carriers—four in the Pacific and three in the Atlantic, Mediterranean, and Caribbean combined*—rather than the twelve now planned by the Administration for 1972. The punch carried by carriers is the firepower of the tactical aircraft they launch. In many cases, the same mission can be performed by either a carrier-based air wing or a land-based Air Force wing. The argument for maintaining more carriers than the seven we recommend rests on the claimed loss of overseas land bases for use by Air Force wings. However, the contingency that we will be called upon to defend a nation while being denied the use of its bases must be considered highly unlikely.

Reductions in attack carriers automatically make possible similar cutbacks in destroyers and other vessels that accompany them as part of a vast flotilla, the carrier task force. Altogether, about $450 million would be saved annually for each carrier task force retired. Changing technology has also reduced to below-marginal levels the contribution of antisubmarine warfare carriers, due to increased carrier vulnerability and the development of the land-based P-3C airplane for the same mission. *The remaining antisubmarine carriers should also be scrapped.* That action would save more than $400 million in annual operating costs (including support costs), and eliminate any possible need to purchase S-3A airplanes to replace older models now stationed on those carriers.

Pay

Our estimate of outlays required to support these and other U.S. general-purpose forces depends significantly on assumptions about military pay levels and the degree of investment in new weapons systems. *We provide for future percentage pay increases for all military personnel equal to the percentage increases in the Consumer Price Index. No provision is made, however, for any special additional pay boost for noncareerists at the bottom grades of the enlisted ranks.* We favor movement toward an all-volunteer armed force, but because only 2,015,000 military personnel would be required under our recommended force levels, nearly sufficient numbers of enlistments would be forthcoming* to pre-empt the need for pay-supplement inducements. Complex questions concerning social equity and the racial, ethnic, and regional composition of the armed forces are involved in the issue of retaining the draft versus seeking an all-volunteer force. The determining factor, in our judgment, is that the $3-4 billion required annually to attract sufficient volunteers if the draft were eliminated could more equitably be invested toward further raising the level of guaranteed income support for the general population—to cite just one among several desirable social goals that could not otherwise be met in our recommended budget.

Another important reason for retaining the draft is to ensure that adequate numbers of persons will be induced to join the Reserves and National Guard. *Envisaged as part of the force levels recommended in this chapter is a restructured Reserve component of slightly reduced size, with the battalion rather than the division as the basic building block.* If these Reserve forces are to serve any useful purpose, though, they must be kept at a higher level of readiness and provided with better equipment and leadership than they currently enjoy.

---

* The members of the Gates Commission and other defense manpower experts suggest that a 2-million-man force is about the break-even point; for force sizes below that level, no extra pay would be required to create an all-volunteer force.

Modernization

Our projections for weapons procurement and modernization assume continuation of recent proportions between operating and investment costs. This mix means that considerable funding would be available to modernize forces, but that funds would not be used to pursue refinements of large systems to achieve small increments in effectiveness. This critical distinction is probably responsible for the difference of more than $5 billion in the 1972 general-purpose force outlays recommended by the Administration and the recommendations of this report. Compelling needs for modernization do exist. Notable examples include sea-lift, close-air-support aircraft, and air-combat fighters for both the Navy and the Air Force. *No sound rationale exists,* however, *for procuring wastefully expensive, oversophisticated systems like the F-14 and F-15 fighter aircraft, the MBT-70 tank, nuclear destroyers and support ships, or the S-3A carrier-based antisubmarine airplane.* In far too many such cases, the extra costs above those for more simply designed and more reliable alternative systems promise to yield little or no return in useful capability. In some instances, no new system of any type is needed.

Efficiency Measures

All the foregoing discussion has focused on force levels. Much recent public attention has been given to potential savings from elimination of waste and inefficiency in defense operations. The most thorough documentation of such weaknesses, with accompanying reform recommendations, was provided in the Fitzhugh Blue Ribbon Defense Panel report. Putting an accurate price tag on the total amount of potential savings is very difficult, but many military analysts suggest it could easily total several billion dollars a year. Our calculations assume that defense managers will be able to offset approximately $600 million of annual price increases through a yearly productivity gain of slightly more than 1 per cent, made possible by such operating improvements.

VIETNAM

A defense budget based upon our recommended changes could involve cuts totaling $11 billion in spending for baseline forces by *fiscal year 1976. These cuts are in addition to the expected decrease in outlays due solely to Vietnam,* which in 1971 totaled about $13 billion.

Continued U.S. involvement in a war in Vietnam has tragic consequences for many facets of national will, energies, and resources. *The rapid withdrawal of remaining American forces should enjoy the highest national priority.* Our projections assume 250,000 U.S. troops in Vietnam on July 1, 1971, consistent with the Administration forecast and current withdrawal rates. Even with complete withdrawal of American troops by December, 1972, outlays of $6.1 billion are estimated to be required in fiscal year 1972. Annual outlays of approximately $1 billion in 1974 and beyond reflect continuing financial support of South Vietnamese forces.

The central conclusion about national priorities to be drawn from this analysis is that a war that has consumed nearly $100 billion in federal funds during the past six years will require— based on our projections—only 10 per cent of that amount during the next five years.

SUMMARY

In summary, *major changes in the size and composition of U.S. military forces are demanded between 1971 and 1976. In several instances—notably research on a new sea-based strategic deterrent system (ULMS), sealift capacity, and modernization of Reserve forces—significant spending increases are recommended.*

These increases are more than matched by *recommended major decreases in spending stemming primarily from:*

1. *improved management and operating efficiencies;*

2. *elimination without replacement of systems rendered obsolete by changing technology, combined with careful scrutiny and pruning of new weapons system modernization;*

3. *elimination of wastefully duplicative strategic deterrent forces and a cessation of attempts to build and operate strategic defensive systems such as Safeguard;*

4. *an enlarged defense manpower and dollar burden assumed by U.S. allies in both Europe and Asia; and*

5. *an end to U.S. military involvement in Vietnam* (except for

a residual $1 billion annual military assistance contribution).

Altogether, we recommend that U.S. military spending decrease from $74.5 billion in 1971 to roughly $60 billion in 1972 and $50 billion during the following four years. Excluding Vietnam spending, the five-year decline would be only from $61 billion to $49 billion.

In constructing a defense budget, it is important to keep clear the distinction between what is minimally required to defend the United States and what additional increment we feel it prudent to bear in order to foster our interests in the world at large. Pure defense of the continental United States actually costs very little in comparison to the total size of our so-called national defense budget. Of the sums above, spending that is directly related to the national security of the United States would shift only from $30 billion in 1971 to $26 billion in 1976, primarily as a result of recommended reductions in strategic forces. The residual, which constitutes U.S. military assistance (broadly defined) to the defense of allied nations, would decline from $44 billion to $24 billion.

The term "national defense" is in fact a highly misleading description of the total purposes served by U.S. military spending. A more strictly accurate descriptive term for U.S. military spending might be "national defense and military assistance," after the two central purposes. The term "military assistance" here has a much broader connotation—representing all U.S. military forces exceeding those required to defend continental U.S. territory—than in the conventional reference to arms grants and sales to other nations.*

We think that this distinction is a useful one, which can add precision to discussion of military force requirements—but, beyond that purpose, is admittedly artificial. The United States does have

---

* The total spent by the federal government to arm foreign nations is variously estimated between $4 billion and $7 billion a year. The variance in estimates is due to different definitions about what should be included, from a mixture of cash gifts, sales for credit or cash, military advisory missions, gifts from a stockpile of "excess" weapons, and use of foreign currencies generated by other programs for weapons purchases. The only such aid considered in this chapter is the "Military Assistance Program" and "Support of Other Nations" (mostly special aid for Southeast Asia). Outlays for these programs were $2.5 billion in 1971.

TABLE 18:1
SUMMARY OF MILITARY FORCES[1]

	Actual 1964	Actual 1970	Administration Proposed 1972	Urban Coalition Recommendations 1972	Urban Coalition Recommendations 1976[2]
Military Personnel[3] (in thousands)					
Army	972	1,322	942	800	702
Navy	667	792	704	540	502
Marine Corps	190	260	206	190	190
Air Force	856	791	753	670	621
TOTAL	2,685	3,066	2,505	2,200	2,015
Strategic Forces					
Minuteman (Missiles)	600	1,000	1,000	1,000	1,000
Titan II (Missiles)	54	54	54	0	0
Polaris (Submarines/Missiles)	21/336	41/656	34/544[4]	34/544	0
Poseidon (Submarines/Missiles)	0	0	7/112[4]	7/112	31/496
Strategic Bombers[5]	1,277	516	510	380	190
Manned Fighter Intercepter Squadrons	40	14	11	7	5
Army Air Defense Firing Batteries	107	40	21	12	8
General-Purpose Forces					
Land Forces:					
Army Divisions	16⅓	17⅓	13⅓	12⅓	11⅓
Marine Corps Divisions	3	3	3	3	3
Tactical Air Forces:					
Air Force Wings	22	23	21	19	18
Navy Attack Wings	15	13	11	8	6
Marine Corps Wings	3	3	3	3	3

Naval Forces:					
Attack Carriers	15	15	12	9	7
Antisubmarine Carriers	9	4	4	0	0
Nuclear Attack Submarines	19	46	56	56	60
Escort Ships	265	231	227	150	130
Amphibious Assault Ships	139	99	76	80	80
Airlift and Sealift Forces					
Aircraft Squadrons:					
C-5A	0	1	4	4	4
C-141 and Other	32	17	13	14	14
Troopships, Cargoships, and Tankers	100	113	98	90	90

[1] All figures are as of June 30 of the cited year.
[2] With only very minor exceptions, these are the recommended force levels for the entire period from the end of 1973 through 1976.
[3] Active duty military personnel, as of the end of the fiscal year.
[4] Staff estimate of allocation between Polaris and Poseidon.
[5] B-52, B-58, and FB-111 bombers in the active aircraft inventory.

a stake in the rest of the world. We would be short-sighted to turn our backs on the international political climate, to forego our leverage in reducing tensions. In a nuclear age, every nation stands to lose from a conflagration unforestalled or unchecked.

A summary description of the U.S. defense forces that would exist during 1976 if our recommendations were implemented is provided in Table 18:1. A few comments about the capabilities of that force are in order.

If our recommendations were implemented, U.S. defense forces by 1976 would be fully adequate to deter any concerted strategic or conventional attack on the United States itself. The devastating second-strike destructive capability of the invulnerable Poseidon fleet, supplemented by bombers and Minuteman missiles, would deter any strategic attack. Even if some other nation had the transportation and logistics capability (which none now does) to launch a major conventional assault on the United States, our modest conventional forces would quickly fend them off. The United States would also continue to possess the strongest and largest military forces in the world earmarked for defense of other nations. Altogether, then, we feel confident that our recommended changes in U.S. military forces could be made without endangering the security of the United States.

Finally, we must reiterate the uncertainties about military plans and intentions of other nations. Our recommendations for U.S. military forces are dependent upon the international political and military assumptions set forth in the text. No five-year plan should ever constitute a rigid operating guideline; the United States must constantly and diligently re-examine the military threats facing it. To the extent that future projections of the behavior of other nations differ from those we have assumed, U.S. forces should be adjusted appropriately from the levels and composition we have recommended. Based on current knowledge, we consider our recommendations an appropriate set of defense policies for the five years ahead.

Budget outlays for National Defense and Military Assistance are summarized in Table 18:2 and Table 18:3 on the following pages.

TABLE 18:2

NATIONAL DEFENSE AND MILITARY ASSISTANCE:

MAJOR PURPOSES

(Outlays, in millions of current dollars)

	Administration[1]			Urban Coalition Recommendations			
	Estimated	Proposed					
	1971	1972	1972	1973	1974	1975	1976
Strategic and Related Forces	16,340	16,470	12,510	11,380	11,025	11,070	10,510
Baseline General-Purpose and Related Forces	45,160	53,630	41,830	37,255	36,525	37,915	38,815
Vietnam	13,000	5,900	5,900	1,700	1,000	1,040	1,100
TOTAL	74,500	76,000	60,240	50,355	48,550	50,025	50,425
Total, excluding Vietnam	61,500	70,100	54,340	48,635	47,550	48,985	49,325

[1] Only the totals have been made available by the Administration. Allocations are based on staff estimates.

TABLE 18:3
NATIONAL DEFENSE AND MILITARY ASSISTANCE:
BUDGET PROGRAM CATEGORIES
(Outlays, in millions of current dollars)

| | Administration[1] | | Urban Coalition Recommendations | | | | |
	Estimated 1971	Proposed 1972	1972	1973	1974	1975	1976
Strategic Forces	7,900	7,500	5,330	4,660	4,390	4,310	3,100
General-Purpose Forces	24,370	24,575	20,450	16,200	15,595	16,210	16,600
Intelligence and Communications	5,400	5,600	5,185	5,020	5,110	5,150	5,265
Airlift and Sealift	1,400	1,100	1,480	1,400	1,315	1,415	1,445
Guard and Reserve Forces	2,700	3,000	2,475	2,655	2,800	2,900	2,960
Research and Development	5,200	5,500	4,585	4,485	4,600	4,705	5,440
Central Supply and Maintenance	8,450	9,200	6,345	4,590	4,365	4,570	4,630
Training, Medical, and Other Personnel Activities	13,950	14,500	9,860	7,100	6,825	7,035	7,165
Administration and Associated Activities	1,600	1,600	1,320	1,195	1,090	1,205	1,225
Support of Other Nations	2,400	2,400	2,510	2,230	1,560	1,625	1,695
Military Assistance Program	1,130	1,025	700	800	900	900	900
TOTAL	74,500	76,000	60,240	50,335	48,550	50,025	50,425

[1] Only the totals have been made available by the Administration. Allocations are based on minor staff adjustments to translate Administration-supplied total obligational authority to outlays.

19

Foreign Economic Assistance

The substantial cuts recommended in the national defense and military assistance budget herald no return to isolationism. We strongly urge that decreases in military assistance be accompanied by well-justified increases in economic assistance to developing nations.

THE CLIMATE FOR DEVELOPMENT

The past fifteen years have witnessed a remarkable, if sometimes perplexing, era of growth and development in the less-developed nations of the world. During that time, international cooperation to encourage development has been of a nature and on a scale new to history. As might be expected, the results achieved have varied greatly from country to country. Social and economic conditions in some nations seem more desperate now than fifteen years ago. Other nations, such as Taiwan, South Korea, and Israel, have experienced remarkable growth.

The average GNP growth rate for the less-developed nations during the past decade has been 5 per cent. Population increase cut this rate to only 2.5 per cent on a per capita basis, but even this economic growth rate represents a remarkable acceleration by historical standards. Behind these statistics lie significant instances of progress in building infrastructure, large increases in school enrollment, and reductions in mortality through disease control.

Progress is now imperiled by a slackening commitment on the part of the wealthier nations, notably the United States, just at a time when the general climate for the productive use of increased capital flows to the less-developed nations is quite favorable. Many of these countries now have the experience, desire, and trained personnel to shape their own development priorities; they are also mobilizing more investment resources themselves. For these reasons, such countries now have the capacity to absorb billions more aid dollars annually.

There are additional favorable trends. Other industrial countries have steadily expanded their development assistance so that, taken together, their share now equals that of the United States. In addition, international financial organizations have grown both in experience and resources. These organizations now make more than half of all development loans. .

The nature and scope of the U.S. foreign aid program in the 1970's will determine whether these auspicious trends are nurtured or frustrated. U.S. aid still accounts for half the world contribution, and, by its extent, sets the tone and pace of the other aid-giving nations' efforts. In a framework of world economics, we should not be unmindful of the sobering fact that the United States, with but 6 per cent of the world's population, consumes 37 per cent of the earth's resources. It is in the context of all these factors, and with the same vision of domesic economic justice and social well-being shaping this entire budgetary framework, that U.S. trade and assistance policies should be shaped.

WORLD TRADE

The first requirement for rapid international development is a continuing, vigorous expansion of world trade. This will be possible only if advanced countries remove many obstacles to the growth of export earnings for less developed economies, as well as encourage the flow of private capital to these nations. Low-income countries will not be able to develop if a recent new wave of protectionist sentiment in the United States gains force. Rather, *what is needed, among other measures, is an untying* of bilateral development lending and an international agreement extending*

---

* Tying of aid is a requirement that a country receiving development grants or loans spend the money in the donor country.

*temporary tariff preferences to developing countries on a nondis-
criminatory basis.* These recommendations imply a need for fundamental revisions in international economic relations and structures.

THE U.S. ASSISTANCE PROGRAM

The existing foreign economic assistance program of the U.S.
Government is not one of which we can be proud. American economic assistance has actually been decreasing while the capacity
of developing countries to use aid has increased. Since 1963,
foreign economic assistance provided by the United States has
fallen from $3.6 billion to the $3 billion estimated for 1971.*

Purposes

This decline results from and reflects a great deal of public
confusion about the purposes of foreign economic assistance. We
have been disappointed with the accomplishments primarily because we have been misled in our expectations. The President's
Task Force on International Development (the Peterson Task
Force) in its March, 1970, report *U.S. Foreign Assistance in the
1970's: A New Approach* (Washington, D.C.: U.S. Government
Printing Office, 1970), commented:

> This country should not look for gratitude or votes, or any specific
> short-term foreign policy gains from our participation in interna-
> tional development. Nor should it expect to influence others to adopt
> U.S. cultural values or institutions. Neither can it assume that devel-
> opment will necessarily bring political stability. Development implies
> change—political and social, as well as economic—and such change,
> for a time, may be disruptive.

The compelling rationale for foreign economic assistance is a
blending of idealism and self-interest broadly construed. The moral
imperative—to do justice, to respond to needs in a humanitarian
fashion, to share—is strong and important, but insufficient by itself
to build the consensus for an effective foreign aid program. The

* Years are federal fiscal years unless otherwise indicated.

clinching argument is that aid will serve the United States' self-interest. Quoting from the Peterson report again:

> The developing countries contain two-thirds of the world's population. Their future success or failure will influence profoundly the kind of world we live in. The nations of the world are growing more interdependent—in trade, in finance, in technology, and in the critical area of political change. U.S. decision-making in such important areas as military expenditures will be influenced by the amounts of turbulence in the developing countries of the world, and U.S. prosperity will be influenced by their economic progress.

Our goal, therefore, should be to provide foreign economic assistance to help create self-reliant societies in developing countries, which, in turn, will contribute to an expanded world economy with improved prospects of world peace. In order to accomplish this goal, *we must significantly change not only our expectations, but also the structure of present economic assistance programs.*

Emphasis on Multilateral Aid

Nearly all economic assistance experts agree that a higher proportion of aid should be channeled through international—or multilateral—institutions, rather than provided bilaterally. Among the advantages of operating through multilateral institutions generally are: (1) a larger, more equal status and voice for developing nations in shaping their own development priorities; (2) a diminished presence and, consequently, less of an aura of paternalism on the part of the donor nations; and (3) improved coordination of development programs. Even with these advantages, however, expanded multilateral aid allocations will only be effective if accompanied by a strengthening of the aid-dispensing institutions; past deficiencies in the major multilateral institutions have greatly hampered potential achievements.

Currently, only 15 per cent of U.S. economic assistance is channeled through multilateral institutions; we recommend that this portion be increased by stages to 60 per cent by 1976, while bilateral aid funding is maintained at current levels in real terms.

Guidelines for Bilateral Aid

One other important way of making the U.S. aid role less political is to focus increasingly on problems and less on countries in dispensing bilateral aid.

The number one priority in U.S. bilateral aid should be family-planning programs. "No other phenomenon," reported the 1969 Commission on International Development to the World Bank (the Pearson Commission) in *Partners In Development* (New York: Praeger, 1969), "casts a darker shadow over the prospects for international development than the staggering growth of population." This priority is particularly appropriate in the context of the similar emphasis we are recommending for family-planning programs and research in the United States (see Chapter 12).

The second priority should be given to welfare and emergency relief, mostly involving provision of agricultural commodities. This would be a continuation of current programs designed to relieve human suffering and to improve nutrition in more than one hundred countries.

In selecting additional assistance projects, priority should be given to those areas in which the United States possesses distinctive competence. Particularly strong cases can be made for programs utilizing our agricultural expertise and business management skills.

The assumption by international agencies of an enlarged role would provide a desirable opportunity for the United States to become more flexible in its bilateral program. As the largest single source of development assistance, we are subjected to the constraint of responding to high numbers of demands and entreaties. Shedding our premier status as direct-aid dispenser will give us more selectivity. The choices we make will be important because the magnitude of our bilateral aid program will remain substantial.

There are three major considerations that should govern our selection of programs within problem areas. First, U.S. bilateral aid should foster innovative approaches; more heretofore untried ventures, with higher acceptable risks, should be undertaken than in the past. Second, bilateral aid should contribute meaningfully to development needs as perceived by the recipient nation. This does not imply grants without any strings. Rather, it suggests granting aid where a conjunction exists between U.S. interests and recipient nation priorities.

Finally, and most important, bilateral aid should advance U.S. interests, broadly defined. These interests are far broader than just economic growth and short-run strategic security—concerns too often in past years held to be paramount. The interests of the United States are advanced most effectively through programs that ensure broad public participation within recipient nations in the allocation and benefit sharing of U.S. aid. In the words of the Peterson Commission report:

> Development is more than economic growth. Popular participation and the dispersion of the benefits of development among all groups in society are essential to the building of dynamic and healthy nations. U.S. development policies should contribute to this end. . . . It should be a cardinal aim of U.S. foreign policy to help build an equitable political and economic order in which the world's people, their governments, and other institutions can effectively share resources and knowledge.

Under this policy prescription, *aid should be employed to further and encourage the efforts of those governments which are working toward very broad reform—in land-holding patterns, distribution of other private wealth, and reform of political institutions.*

The form of economic assistance itself should also be changed. During the Marshall Plan era, when the focus was on aiding industrial economies, more than 90 per cent of the assistance from the principal U.S. aid agency was on a grant basis. During the 1960's, when our aid went almost exclusively to less-developed, capital-deficient nations, less than 50 per cent took the form of grants. Furthermore, the trend in loans has been toward greater use of "hard" loans (the terms of which offer no special interest rate or repayment concessions).

U.S. economic assistance should continue to employ a combination of grants, hard loans, and soft loans—the appropriate approach depending on the kind of project and the financial capacity of the recipient nation in each case. We recommend that a significant proportion of grants be continued in the mix of aid, and that the impact of hard loans, when used, be made less onerous by blending them with grants and soft loans to the recipient country. To assure that long-range perspective is maintained, we should encourage the use of soft loans on the part of multilateral institutions and rely more heavily on them in our bilateral programs. Typically, such loans are for fifty years with no repayment required during the initial ten years and no interest charge (a 0.75 per cent service charge is made).

Technical assistance should increasingly be provided on a soft-loan basis rather than being provided directly by U.S. missions. The developing nations are both much more desirous and much more capable of choosing and using technical assistance experts than they were ten years ago. When they wish help in hiring U.S. technicians, our agencies should assist in recruitment. We strongly anticipate that such requests will be so numerous as to require a continuing substantial role for U.S. aid agencies. The Peace Corps has proved to be a particularly effective vehicle for certain technical assistance purposes and should continue to play an important role. Peace Corps volunteers have long served within the institutions of developing nations, working beside local technicians and under the direction of host-country supervisors. Such a pattern of employment is the probable shape of things to come in foreign technical assistance and would be fostered under the recommendations of this report.

Levels of Aid

In addition to these changes in our approach to foreign economic assistance, *we strongly recommend substantial increases in the amount of aid provided.* The Pearson Commission suggests a target level of official assistance equal to 0.7 per cent of the GNP of each industrial nation. Currently, U.S. foreign economic assistance amounts to less than 0.3 per cent of the GNP. The 0.7 per cent target clearly is not excessive in terms of needs in the less-developed nations, and its attainment should be a U.S. goal.

There is a considerable division of opinion as to whether the major multilateral lending institutions and U.S. bilateral aid agencies together can channel this much aid in the immediate future—and whether the recipient countries can absorb it. *We recommend gradually increasing U.S. economic assistance outlays until they reach 0.5 per cent of the GNP in 1976,* thus getting us slightly over halfway to the ultimate goal. Outlays for 1976 would total $7.4 billion, still less than 2.2 per cent of total federal outlays. This amount is hardly a heavy burden on the federal budget.

The conflict that many people profess to see between foreign economic assistance and unmet needs at home is highly exaggerated. We uphold the best in American traditions and values only if we respond to both. As a matter of national integrity, a country founded on the principle of human brotherhood must carry this idea beyond its own borders no less than practice it within.

Budget outlays for Foreign Economic Assistance are summarized in Table 19:1 on the following page.

TABLE 19:1
FOREIGN ECONOMIC ASSISTANCE
(Outlays, in millions of current dollars)

| | Administration | | | Urban Coalition Recommendations | | | |
	Estimated 1971	Proposed 1972	1972	1973	1974	1975	1976
Bilateral Aid	2,578	2,745	2,450	2,855	2,705	2,500	2,980
Multilateral Aid	415	495	1,050	1,905	2,705	3,745	4,465
TOTAL	2,993	3,240	3,500	4,760	5,410	6,245	7,445

EFFECTS OF THE COUNTERBUDGET

The interests of specific segments of society were carefully weighed in the development of all recommendations.
The tax changes recommended . . . would be sufficient to finance the proposed programs. The federal budget would be in balance. Part of the judgment about the achievability of the goals cited . . . depends on whether enough workers exist, or can quickly be trained.

20

Impact on Special Groups: Women; The Working Class; The Aged

Woven throughout the recommendations of this report are provisions that, if viewed from the standpoint of the effects on a specific group of citizens, could be considered the Counterbudget's package of proposed benefits for that segment of society. An example of such an analysis would be the discussion in Chapter 4 on the net effect of a variety of programs on the living conditions of the poor.

Indeed, the interests of specific segments of society were carefully weighed in the development of all recommendations. Some recommendations are addressed directly to the interests of groups requiring special assistance or protection, for example, the rights of minorities (see Chapter 16).

Although the purpose of the Counterbudget is to improve the life of all Americans, there are groups, such as the poor and the minorities mentioned above, who must first overcome considerable inequities before sharing in any general advance, and our recommendations have sought to alleviate these inequities. Other inequities currently exist for women, the working class, and the aged in relation to the whole of society. Following are summaries of how the Counterbudget's recommendations would serve to benefit these groups.

WOMEN

Opportunities for American women have traditionally been restricted both by social norms, which define their "natural roles"

287

as homemakers and childbearers, and by blatant discrimination against women in the labor market.

Although attitudes are now changing as women demand equal opportunities and the right to organize their lives as they choose, the process is slow.

Traditional views still inhibit educational opportunities for women. Long considered of secondary importance, they are encouraged to take "feminine" courses regardless of their interests or natural abilities. Admission standards to institutions of higher education are still higher for women than men. In many cases, men may more easily obtain education scholarships and loans, particularly for graduate studies.

Occupational as well as educational opportunities for women are limited (see Table 20:1). A smaller portion of high status pro-

TABLE 20:1
WOMEN IN THE WORK FORCE

| | Percentage of Selected Jobs Held by Women[1] | | | | |
Country	Lawyers	Judges	Physicians	Dentists	Total Work Force
United States	3.5	2.0	6.5	2.1	37.0
United Kingdom	3.8	*	16.0	6.9	34.4
Sweden	6.1	6.7	15.4	24.4	*
West Germany	5.5	*	20.0	*	36.7
Italy	2.8	0.5	4.9	*	28.8
Denmark	*	*	16.4	70.0	*
Poland	18.8	*	36.4	77.0	*
U.S.S.R.	36.0	30.5	75.0[2]	83.0	*

[1] An asterisk (*) indicates that the information was not available.
[2] The figure for physicians in the U.S.S.R. is not strictly comparable as it also includes some other medical personnel.
SOURCE: Cynthia F. Epstein, *Woman's Place* (Berkeley, Calif.: University of California Press, 1970).

fessional jobs are held by women in America than in most other developed countries. The cost to society of the underutilization of women due to sex discrimination in employment can be measured in billions of dollars.

Job discrimination against women occurs in several forms. Wage discrimination is apparent against women at all education levels; Department of Labor statistics show that the woman's median income is substantially lower in all major fields of employment.

For example, in 1968 the median income of full-time, year-round women clerical workers was 65 per cent that of men; for sales workers it was 40 per cent, and for operatives it was 59 per cent. Even women completing a college education can expect to be offered a lower starting salary than their male classmates. According to a Labor Department survey of 206 companies making offers to graduates, the average salary offered women was less in every field, ranging from an average difference of $20 to $100 monthly.

Women are also more likely than men to be employed in low-skilled, low-paid jobs. In the labor force as a whole, 60 per cent of women working full time the year round earn less than $5,000 annually compared to 20 per cent of the men, whereas only 3 per cent earn more than $10,000 compared to 28 per cent of the men. These figures reflect the fact that women are offered jobs below their skill levels, that in some fields women receive lower pay for performing the same jobs as men, and that women are not promoted as readily as men. The same distribution occurs in all major employment fields.

As a result of these inequities in the job market, the over-all median salary for full-time, year-round women workers is only 58 per cent of the men's. *We therefore have recommended that the equal employment laws be strongly enforced, that more equitable promotion policies be encouraged, and that action be taken in cases of clear discrimination.*

The above statistics refer only to those women presently in the labor force. Yet, the Department of Labor estimates that of 32.5 million women not working because of home responsibilities, 3.2 million would like to have jobs. Provision of preschool and child-care programs such as we recommend would enable these women to enter the labor force. In addition, *we recommend manpower training programs for women wishing to re-enter the labor force and a public-service employment program to expand the number of jobs available.* Thus, some of the barriers that might prevent women from entering the labor force will be lifted, assuming both that job discrimination can be ended and that the unemployment rate will drop as we have projected.

These work opportunities will also greatly benefit the approximately 5 million female-headed households living below the official poverty line at the present time. Although female-headed house-holds (as officially defined) represent only 20 per cent of all households, they constitute 50 per cent of those living in poverty. Primary reasons for this circumstance are the lack of adequate child-care facilities and job discrimination. For those unable to work or who have children under the age of sixteen and do not wish to work, the recommended cash-assistance grant (CAG) will provide a poverty-level income by 1976. In addition, the grant will provide a poverty-level (or above) income for all, including those who work but do not earn a living wage. Thus, by 1976, incomes of all 5 million female-headed households will be lifted to the poverty line or above.

Finally, *we have strongly recommended the goal of free family-planning assistance for all women.* This would give all women a greater freedom to organize their lives and choose the role they wish to play, as well as encourage a sensible population stabilization program.

Through all of these measures we believe it is possible to grant equal opportunities to American women, opportunities that will result in significant benefits to society as a whole.

THE WORKING CLASS*

Although it is difficult to generalize about so diverse a group as working-class Americans, nonetheless it appears that a growing number are becoming frustrated by the problems and difficulties they face.

The basic problem is economic. Many working-class Americans have been hurt badly by inflation. Since 1965, wages and salaries of blue collar Americans have increased, but inflation has increased at an even faster rate. As a result, many are worse off now than five years ago.

In addition, the working-class American carries a dispropor-tionately high burden of the costs of government, while at the

* "Working class" in this context includes families and individuals in the $5,000–$10,000 income bracket. In 1968, 68 million Americans lived in households with incomes in this range, 60 million of them white and 8 million nonwhite.

same time receiving disproportionately less of the direct benefits from government aid programs. As a result, it is hardly surprising that many working-class Americans feel that their interests are being ignored by government. Resentment of those who appear to get "something for nothing" is growing. Resentment is also growing over the ease with which wealthier citizens appear to be able to escape paying a fair share of taxes.

Working-class Americans receive some relief through the federal tax system, but this is offset by regressive state and local taxes. The impact on families at different income levels of all federal, state, and local taxes as well as transfer payments received from all levels of government can be seen in Table 20:2. Thus, working-

TABLE 20:2
Taxes and Taxes Less Transfers as Per Cent of Income, 1968

Income	Taxes	Taxes Less Transfers[1]
$ 0- 2,000	40.3	−24.7
2,000- 4,000	32.8	− 5.6
4,000- 6,000	30.8	14.9
6,000- 8,000	30.5	23.5
8,000-10,000	29.8	25.4
10,000-15,000	30.5	27.3
15,000-25,000	30.6	28.2
25,000-50,000	33.2	31.6
50,000 and over	45.3	44.9
Weighted Average	32.0	26.3

[1] Minus indicates that transfer payments from federal, state, and local governments exceeded amounts paid in taxes.
Source: Unpublished data informally presented by Dr. Herman P. Miller at a symposium of the National Manpower Council, held on February 10, 1971.

class Americans (with incomes of $4–10,000) pay approximately the same proportion of their income in taxes as do those with higher incomes ($10–25,000). At the same time, they receive less in direct benefits from the government than they pay in taxes, while those with lower incomes receive more through programs such as Old Age, Survivors, and Disability Insurance (OASDI), public assistance, unemployment compensation, and veterans' benefits than they pay in taxes.

We believe that many of the problems and resentments of working-class Americans can be reduced if the costs of public-sector spending are distributed more equitably among income groups, and if those working full time see a measurable difference between their income and the income of those who do not work.

First, *we have recommended a series of reforms in the federal income tax system* (see Chapter 23) *and OASDI payroll tax* (see Chapter 4). The result of both these recommendations would be to lower the tax burden on working-class Americans compared to higher-income groups. In addition, our proposal for federal revenue-sharing contains strong incentives for states to raise more of their own revenue through the graduated income tax, thus reducing the proportion of their revenue generated through regressive state sales and user taxes.

Second, *our cash-assistance grant (CAG) program would offer direct financial aid to many working-class Americans who receive no aid from present income-support payments.* Benefits are related to family size and are reduced gradually as earnings increase (see Chapter 4). By 1976, CAG's would be available to all working-class families of four earning less than $9,416. Incentives to work would be maintained, since our proposal would still result in a noticeable difference in income between those who work and those who do not. The effect of this CAG program on income for families of four is presented below:

Earned Income	Cash-Assistance Grant	Total Income
$ —	$4,708	$ 4,708
3,000	3,208	6,208
5,000	2,208	7,208
7,000	1,208	8,208
9,000	208	9,208
10,000	—	10,000

Third, *we propose to relieve working-class families of the burden of medical costs through institution of a universal national health insurance scheme (NHI).* We estimate that average medical costs for a family of four with an income of $7,000 yearly would be nearly $700 in 1976; the costs of NHI to this family would be $40—a 5 per cent surcharge on federal income taxes. Health-care expenditures for this family would drop more than $650.

Taken together, these three proposals would have an immediate effect on the income of working-class American families. Although our proposed tax measures would not reduce actual taxes paid (because we have recommended a 10 per cent increase in 1974), they would ensure that the burden is equitably distributed. Families in the $5–10,000 wage-earning group would receive more additional cash income through our proposals than they would pay in additional taxes. The resulting increase in disposable income is illustrated in Table 20:3.

TABLE 20:3
PROJECTED INCREASE IN DISPOSABLE INCOME
FOR A FAMILY OF FOUR IN 1976
(In current dollars)

Disposable Income Without Implementation of Counterbudget Recommendations	Disposable Income After Implementation of Recommendations	Increase
$4,092	$ 6,043	$1,951
5,107	7,102	1,995
6,054	7,522	1,468
7,784	8,454	671
8,752	9,130	378
9,909	10,061	152

We would offer working-class Americans the opportunity to increase their earning potential through manpower training and adult education programs. *We have recommended a major program to provide skill-upgrading for workers* (see Chapter 2) *and another to increase the availability of adult education* (see Chapter 6).

Our education recommendations would greatly benefit children of working-class families. *Federal funds would be provided to public secondary schools for career education programs.* These programs would provide every student with the necessary information and experience to select an occupation consistent with his abilities and aspirations. They would be coupled with a high school placement program to ensure that *every* graduating student may enter a college, a job-training program, or a full-time job immediately following commencement.

Finally, we have suggested increased federal scholarships, grants, and subsidized loans for students from families with incomes less than $8,500, and the establishment of a National Student Loan Association to purchase $9 billion in guaranteed student loans by 1976. This would quadruple the number of students able to obtain such loans.

Many of our other proposals are likely to influence the lives of the working class, notably the proposed increases in federal spending on mass-transit systems, expansion of federally assisted housing programs for low-income and moderate-income families, provision of child-care facilities for working mothers, more effective federal consumer-protection programs, expanded legal rights for the average consumer, and increased availability of federally guaranteed home mortgage loans.

THE AGED

Older Americans, frequently hit hardest by inflation, shortage of health-care facilities, and the special burdens imposed by infirmity and isolation, would have much to gain from our recommendations.

Twenty million Americans, a tenth of the population, are sixty-five or older. Nearly 25 per cent of the aged are living in poverty—among them, 5 million who were already poor and many others whose savings and fixed incomes could not withstand the strain of high property taxes and a rising cost of living. For more than 2 million of the aged, OASDI is the only source of income.

We have recommended that OASDI benefits increase automatically as the cost of living rises in order to protect the aged against inflation. In addition to cost of living increases, *we propose further substantial benefit increases, including an immediate increase of the minimum monthly benefit from $64 to $100.*

Finally, the recommended restructuring of Old Age Assistance would bring the income of all elderly households to the poverty level or above. As a result of these changes, the average income of elderly families would rise from its present level of slightly less than $5,000 yearly to $7,000 in 1976—$1,000 more than it would be in the absence of our recommended changes.

The national health insurance (NHI) plan would go far toward eliminating a nagging fear of the aged—fear of being alone, sick, and helpless. *Major changes from the present Medicare and Medicaid systems included in the NHI plan are: extension of coverage to all the aged; coverage, for the first time, of the costs of preventive health care and prescription medicines; elimination of the limits on home doctors' or nurses' visits for provision of active medical care; and creation of a network of community health service facilities, including mental health facilities.*

Increased outlays to improve urban mass transit systems will also benefit the aged, many of whom do not have access to private automobiles.

21

Economic Impact

Prepared by Dr. Otto Eckstein

Professor of Economics, Harvard University
Former member of the Council of Economic Advisers

The American economy is an extraordinary productive machine, capable of creating a real GNP of astronomical proportions. Nonetheless, the programs outlined in the preceding chapters are ambitious, and the question must be faced of whether the economy is capable of creating the necessary resources and of reallocating them to the proposed purposes. We have seen recently that the economic mechanism remains sensitive, that imperfections in the structure of markets and imbalances in fiscal and monetary policies can produce serious deviations from the balanced growth path. The inflation of the last few years and the current high rate of unemployment have created hardships for many families and have intensified social problems. In order to promote our social goals and to permit the programs in this agenda to reach full effectiveness, we must be sure that the economy can accommodate these programs without creating general instability and other distortions.

To shed light on these issues, the program outlined in earlier chapters has been converted into the standard dimensions of macroeconomic analysis and has been fed into simulation studies performed with the 330 equation Data Resources, Inc., econometric model.* This section summarizes these studies.

* The Data Resources, Inc., model of the U.S. economy is a quarterly model that forecasts over 330 economic variables, including the GNP accounts, government budgets, interest rates and other financial variables, social indicators, profits of major sectors as well as production, sales, and profits of seventeen manufacturing industries. Users can modify key assumptions to produce forecasts of expected economic behavior.

Budget Revenues

Normal growth and restoration of full employment, as described in earlier chapters, can be expected, under present federal laws, to raise federal revenues to $284 billion by 1976,* not allowing for a $4.5 billion revenue loss caused by recent Administration action liberalizing tax treatment of depreciation (an action not supported by, and therefore not reflected as part of, the Counter-budget tax recommendations). The report recommends that an additional $42 billion be obtained from new taxes to finance national health insurance plus revisions in other social insurance program taxes, that $6 billion be raised from further reforms of the personal and corporate tax structures, that $3 billion more be raised from excise taxes with sumptuary purposes and from user charges, and that $18 billion be obtained from a 10 per cent increase in corporate and personal income tax rates. Revenues for 1976 thus were estimated to total $353 billion. The simulation of these same proposals on the Data Resources model suggested that total 1976 revenues would be $355 billion, a difference so slight as not to be significant in a forecast five years ahead.

The tax changes recommended in the report would be sufficient to finance the proposed program. The federal budget would be in balance. Since the economy is projected to be in full employment by 1976 (and to have been in that state for three years), there should be no difference between the actual budget and the full-employment budget at that time. A balanced full-employment budget has long been advocated by the Committee for Economic Development and has recently become the standard doctrine of the federal government. Since the federal government does not distinguish between current and capital outlays, a balanced full-employment budget policy can safely be characterized as prudent and cautious. It should be added, however, that there is no assurance that such a policy will actually suffice to produce full employment. It is easily possible that the economy will continue to find itself in a period of somewhat below normal private

---

* References to years are to federal fiscal years unless otherwise indicated.

demand, and that deliberate full-employment deficits will be needed to achieve the job-creation goals cited in this book.

The revenue and resource projections depend upon continuation of the high growth trend of the economy's potential. Some observers have raised the spectre that our period of high growth may be over, perhaps because of changed attitudes toward work among members of the new generation as well as a less materialistic consumer attitude over all. This contingency cannot be ignored, of course. However, there are so far no signs that productivity—the driving force of growth—has slowed. Indeed, the extraordinary layoffs during the current recession make a large near-term productivity gain very likely. It is the most reasonable assumption, based on current evidence, that the high productivity trends that have characterized America's industrial development for 140 years will continue for another half-decade.

Tax Structure and Economic Performance

Even if total revenues are sufficient to finance all recommended programs, the question of whether the new tax proposals would significantly impair the performance of the economy must be considered. Would work incentives, innovation, or investment be discouraged? Would otherwise reasonable economic decisions be distorted?

The impact of taxes on behavior depends on structural specifics. Attempts to avoid taxes now lead to considerable distortions in such areas as personal investment and executive compensation. Generally, these distortions are produced not by small variations in the level of taxation, but by the discriminatory forms of taxes, which give particularly favorable treatment to one form of income over another.

The tax proposals in this report are advanced in general terms. With skilled conversion of these proposals into detailed reforms of the tax structure, the changes could improve economic performance rather than hurt it.

In terms of new revenues, the new taxes to finance national health insurance are the most important. The proposed 5 per cent surcharge on personal income taxes is similar to other recent surcharges. The 3 per cent tax on the payroll earnings base of corporations resembles present payroll taxes, except that it omits the employee contribution. In a sense, the personal surcharge is a more progressive substitute.

The over-all structure of the tax system would not be changed significantly by the proposals. Table 21:1 shows some pertinent dimensions. Only the burden of payroll taxes is raised; the rest show little change in total, even after reforms. So far, the economy has not suffered visibly from the rising payroll tax burden; other advanced economies have even higher rates. Nonetheless, it must be recognized that business usually treats such taxes as costs to be passed forward in the form of higher prices; consequently, they are regressive.

TABLE 21:1

REVENUE SOURCES AS PERCENTAGE OF THE GNP AND OF ALL TAX REVENUES

	Actual 1968	1970	Proposed 1976
Revenue Sources as Per Cent of the GNP			
Personal Taxes	8.6	9.9	9.5
Corporate Profits Taxes	4.1	3.8	4.5
Indirect Business Taxes	2.1	2.0	2.3
Contributions for Social Insurance	4.7	5.0	7.5
TOTAL	19.5	20.7	23.7
Revenue Sources as Per Cent of All Tax Revenues			
Personal Taxes	44.3	47.7	39.9
Corporate Profits Taxes	21.1	18.4	18.8
Indirect Business Taxes	10.6	9.8	9.7
Contributions for Social Insurance	24.0	24.1	31.6
TOTAL	100.0	100.0	100.0

THE EXPENDITURE PROPOSALS

Total federal spending as a per cent of the GNP under these proposals rises from 20.7 per cent in 1970 to 23.7 per cent in 1976. Most of this increase results from the proposals for national health insurance, income support, and fiscal relief for the states and localities. Savings in defense spending offset a part of these increases.

TABLE 21:2
COUNTERBUDGET PROPOSALS BY NATIONAL INCOME ACCOUNT CONCEPTS
(In billions of dollars; for calendar years)

	1970	1971	1972	1973	1974	1975	1976
Purchases of Goods and Services[1]	99.8	97.0	90.0	86.0	87.9	91.6	93.0
Transfer Payments to Persons	59.8	77.1	90.0	123.6	160.8	176.8	184.8
Transfer Payments to Foreigners	2.0	2.4	3.2	3.9	4.5	5.2	5.7
Grants to States and Localities	24.4	29.3	34.1	37.7	42.2	46.6	48.5
Net Interest Paid	14.6	15.1	15.9	16.8	17.7	19.5	20.7
Subsidies to Government Enterprises (net)	5.4	4.6	3.5	3.5	3.6	3.6	3.6
TOTAL	206.0	225.5	236.5	271.5	316.7	343.2	356.3
[1] For National Defense Purposes[2]	76.6	67.4	54.8	49.0	49.0	49.9	50.1
For Other Purposes[2]	23.3	29.7	35.1	37.0	38.9	41.7	42.9

[2] Rounded numbers do not necessarily add to total.

Because the new programs are mainly transfers to individuals and grants-in-aid, the share of the GNP absorbed by federal purchases falls very substantially, from 10.2 per cent in 1970 to 5.6 per cent in 1976. Also, since the grants-in-aid partly replace local financing and do not lead to additional local spending in the full amount of the aid, it would be incorrect to assume that the share of resources passing through budgets at all levels of government will increase by an amount equal to the federal increase. Table 21:2 shows the composition of the proposed federal budgets in the national income account concepts. It shows the large growth of transfer payments and grants, and the decline of purchases of goods and services.

With the budget as a whole in balance, the program should not give rise to general excess demand. Since grants and transfers usually have a more diffused economic impact than direct spending, the economy should be able to produce the goods demanded by the recipients of the transfers and grants.

Resource availability is questionable only where the programs greatly expand the demands for a particular industry. The extra income to be received by the poor will be spent on consumer goods that will be in ample supply. National health insurance, on the other hand, would worsen the strain in our medical care industry unless accompanied by breakthroughs on the supply side, such as those strongly recommended in the report. The specific needs for health manpower and facilities created by the present proposals are analyzed in Chapter 5.

The Economy at Full Employment

Although the budget proposals are not excessively expansionary and the economy should be able to accommodate the resource shifts, there remains the more fundamental question—whether full employment itself is possible. Without full employment, the large outlays proposed for human, social, and physical development will not produce their full social return. If there are insufficient jobs, graduates of training programs cannot be placed, or they can be placed only at the expense of another displaced worker. Even the health programs will yield a greater economic return to offset their costs if working-age beneficiaries can be returned to productive employment.

The economic projections of this report assume that full employment will be restored and maintained at an unemployment rate of 3.5 per cent. The postulated rate of price increase is 3 per cent, as measured by the GNP deflator. These assumptions are appropriate because the focus of the Counterbudget is on programs and priorities rather than on macroeconomic policy. Nonetheless, it must be pointed out that the present structure of the economy and present policies do not seem to be able to produce so favorable a combination of unemployment and price performance. Many studies have been conducted on the "trade off" question, utilizing different approaches, including econometric models. The results of our simulations are typical: We assume (1) that the federal budget follows this report's proposals (see Table 21:2); (2) that extreme bottleneck problems are solved; (3) that monetary policy raises the money supply by 6 per cent a year; and (4) that private spending patterns are sufficiently strong to achieve 3.5 per cent unemployment. Simulation then produces a rate of inflation in excess of 4 per cent in the later years.

The extra 1 to 1.5 per cent of inflation looms large in economic planning. Conceivably, a 3 per cent rate of inflation would not have the tendency to accelerate into a general price-wage spiral. But there can be little question that 4 per cent or more at a time of full employment is not a sustainable rate: the wage-price spiral would be turned loose. Thus, the general inability of the economy to hold the price level to reasonable stability at a time of full employment is the major economic obstacle to the achievement of our social goals and the execution of the proposed program. The difficulty does not lie in the scale or composition of the program.

The development of policies to improve the inherent inflationary tendency of the economy is therefore of real urgency. Manpower and other development programs will be helpful but hardly sufficient. Additional measures will need to be developed. The report recognizes this need and calls for additional measures.

22

Manpower Impact

Prepared by Dr. James Scoville

*Associate Professor of Economics and Industrial and
Labor Relations, University of Illinois*

An important dimension of any proposed new national agenda is the mix of manpower skills that will be required to implement changed social priorities. Part of the judgment about the achievability of the goals set forth in this book depends on whether enough workers exist, or can quickly be trained, in necessary skill areas. Allocating funds to new program areas is futile if skilled workers will not be available to perform the requisite tasks.

This chapter offers a preliminary assessment of the manpower impacts of the programs and priorities proposed in the Counterbudget. Comments are primarily restricted to major resource utilization issues and long-run impacts on labor and skill requirements. As the authors of the report realize, manpower and labor markets will be dominated in the short run by the problem of cyclical and conversion-related unemployment. It is unlikely that broad segments of the U.S. economy will be characterized by significant manpower shortages; the report envisions approaching near full employment (96 per cent) only by 1973.*

The report offers realistic prescriptions for these short-run conversion problems. The broad range of proposed income-maintenance programs—unemployment compensation for longer

* References to years are to federal fiscal years unless otherwise indicated.

duration, at higher rates, and for which millions more Americans would be eligible; a cash-assistance grant program (a variant of the Administration's proposed family-assistance plan); public-service employment; and supplementary assistance programs for individuals and geographic areas hit by economic conversion from defense production—constitute an appropriate and humane response to short-term adjustment problems. Although manpower training programs recommended in the report may also be desirable to develop new skills among the unemployed (particularly skilled technical workers displaced from defense work), such programs are not likely to be a major factor in reducing unemployment in the short run. These training programs should be viewed instead as a means of facilitating the long-run readjustment to a healthy, vigorous American economy in the mid-1970's.

The long-run manpower implications of the report's recommendations should be explored on at least three levels: (1) the manpower skills required to implement government program-activity recommendations; (2) the over-all direct manpower effect of federally supported employment; and (3) the total manpower impact on the economy, taking account of *all* recommended public and private expenditure reallocations. Time and resource constraints preclude any current speculation on the third issue. (A thorough examination of the impact of the report's proposal on the occupational distribution of labor demand will be made by myself and Roger H. Bezdek during 1971. We will employ an input-output model developed by Mr. Bezdek and used as the basis of the analysis in this chapter. The model is capable of translating alternate distributions of national expenditures corresponding to different priorities into detailed industrial and occupational manpower resource requirements.) *

The comments that follow address several program recommendations that raise significant manpower questions. They also offer a rough evaluation of the over-all impact of the shifts in program emphasis on certain occupational groups.

* A detailed description of the model is provided in Mr. Bezdek's paper "Manpower Implications of Alternate Patterns of Demand for Goods and Services," presented to the American Statistical Association in Detroit on December 27, 1970.

SOME SECTORAL MANPOWER QUESTIONS

Almost every section of the report involves allocation, recruitment, training, or compensation of labor resources in one fashion or another. Increasing the pay of policemen, expanding the enforcement staffs of civil rights and consumer-protection agencies, substituting cash-assistance grants and national health insurance for the present conglomeration of welfare and health programs—all these changes have significant direct and indirect manpower implications. The effects include not only the impact of staffing the programs themselves but also the broader societal impacts of more equal opportunities for minority Americans and of setting levels of labor-force participation rates. Many of the specific manpower issues related to actions recommended in a particular program area have been discussed in earlier chapters. We shall confine our attention here to two sectors where the issues are either more troublesome or require some amplification of the text.

The Military

The report proposes that armed services force levels be reduced from 2,699,000, now estimated by the Administration for the end of 1971 to 2,015,000 by the end of 1973. Training and counseling programs for the sizable number of dischargees involved are recommended. Even so, the job prospects for these new entrants to the civilian labor force look bleak indeed.

One important long-run military manpower issue not given very thorough treatment in the report is the method of recruitment of military personnel. The report recommends retaining the draft, but with diminished importance, since it should be possible to recruit a 2,015,000-man force almost completely through voluntary enlistments, even without special pay boosts for the lower enlisted ranks. The method of recruitment does, however, present social issues broader than simple feasibility. The thoughtful reader will recognize that differing techniques of recruitment will produce varying personnel distributions, perhaps most notably with regard to race. The ethnic and social structure of the military, its race relations, dependability, and effectiveness are important enough to the larger society that we must not leave them purely to chance.

Health and Medical Care

This is one of the most challenging areas tackled in this book, and one in which there is a sweeping recommendation. It is argued that provision of an adequate bundle of specific goods and services (medical care) should be a right of the American people. From a manpower point of view, such a "right in kind" differs from the cash-assistance grant (a "right in cash" income-maintenance program), whose disposition is left to the consumer's discretion. As the report recognizes, such a new "right in kind" must be, and is, accompanied by concrete proposals for the provision and financing of the goods and services involved.

In this regard, the report seems to have adopted in large part the manpower recommendations of the Carnegie Commission on Higher Education, but with a slightly stronger emphasis on the use of new types of medical personnel. I would argue that this emphasis should be even stronger; that we must get away from the tendency to conclude that the solution to an apparent shortage is simply to provide more of what we have. New thinking, new research, and new design are essential in all areas of health services—particularly in the organizational structure of delivery systems, the architectural design of facilities, and the development of new kinds of manpower inputs. The job structure of this industry has changed substantially over the past twenty years; there is reason to suspect that it could be, and should be, changed a great deal more.

THE OVER-ALL FEDERAL OCCUPATIONAL IMPACT

As a result of research recently carried out, it is possible to make some rough judgments about the impact of the Counterbudget program on the over-all pattern of occupational demand. Roger Bezdek's input-output model was of particular aid. Bezdek compared actual employment patterns in 1960 with those that would have prevailed under four reallocations of federal outlays. One of these reallocations comes fairly close, in over-all pattern, to the recommendations in this report. In his calculations, Bezdek reduced defense expenditures by 30 per cent and reallocated them to domestic social welfare programs. The fit between Bezdek's reallocation and the Counterbudget recommendations is not exact, but certainly it is close enough to use as a basis for forming some crude, interim judgments.

Reallocation of a fixed federal budget from high-cost (i.e., high outlays per job created) defense programs to lower-cost social welfare operations is sufficient to generate a modest increase in total employment. With an increased total budget, as proposed in the report, this effect should be somewhat greater.

The effects of such a shift on different occupation groups would be considerable. Engineering occupations would be, over all, the hardest hit: a balanced reallocation would reduce employment in all engineering fields by almost 2 per cent, with aeronautical engineers being nicked for about a 5 per cent loss. Only civil and mining engineers might expect increases, albeit slight, in employment.

Under the Bezdek example, medical occupations would, on the whole, experience an increase in requirements of about 1.5 per cent for all occupational groups. This is clearly an underestimate of the changes in demand that implementation of the Counterbudget would bring, since the report reallocates considerably more resources to the medical area than Bezdek's example does. Much the same can be said for the field of education, where Bezdek's reallocation points to roughly a 2 per cent increase in the demand for teachers at all levels. Nevertheless, the current loose market and projected sluggish demand for teachers would give us some confidence that manpower constraints are not likely to be encountered, even with significantly greater reallocations to this field.

Natural scientists, social scientists, and nonmedical technicians of all types might expect a modest reduction in demand from balanced reallocations in federal outlays. With but two exceptions, all other groups of occupations that require any degree of skill or training will be only minimally affected by budgetary reallocations. The exceptions are in metalworking, where the demand would be reduced by over 2 per cent due to concentration in defense sectors of the economy, and construction crafts, which might experience an increase in demand of slightly over 2 per cent. (This latter projection suggests the importance of making further attempts to de-seasonalize and otherwise rationalize the construction industry.)

It should be emphasized that all the demand shift figures given above reflect purely an aggregate reallocation of federal expenditures from defense to social welfare programs. All these figures will be altered somewhat when results of a more detailed analysis of skill requirements become available. Furthermore, all figures must be judged in the light of those increases in occupational demand which might occur between now and 1976 as a result of real expansion in the economy. The report estimates that the real GNP increase will be roughly 27.5 per cent, with employment increasing 11 per cent. Against a backdrop of employment increases for most occupations that are likely to be associated with such expansion, the inter-occupational shifts and resulting dislocations are likely to be quite small, as shown in Table 22:1. The first column shows the amount by which selected occupations are expected to grow from 1971 to 1976, based on Bureau of Labor Statistics projections of the American economy in 1980. The second column shows the further percentage-point impact on that occupation of a 30 per cent shift from defense to domestic welfare programs.

TABLE 22:1
PER CENT OF CHANGE IN THE
DEMAND FOR SELECTED OCCUPATIONS

	Expected Growth 1971–76[1,2]	Additional Impact from Changed Priorities
Engineers	13	−2
Aeronautical Engineers	*	−5
Physicians and Dentists	17	+1.5
Other Health Workers	21	+1.5
Teachers	5	+2
Natural Scientists	19	− .5
Social Scientists	*	− .5
Nonmedical Technicians	17	−1
Metal-working Craftsmen	*	−2.5
Construction Craftsmen	13	+2

[1] Figures were taken from "The United States Economy in 1980," *Monthly Labor Review,* April, 1970.
[2] An asterisk (*) indicates that the information was not available.

MANPOWER, THE PHILLIPS CURVE, AND PUBLIC OPINION

A conventional rationale for active manpower policies has been that by such activities we might shift the Phillips curve,* reducing the inflationary "price" that our economy must pay to achieve reasonably full employment. Although the authors of this report have reiterated this objective and have recommended channeling substantial resources to manpower development, they hope for something more—that is, the possibility that the American people may have to be willing, after a fairly lengthy period of full employment and larger-than-usual price increases, to live with a rate of inflation closer in magnitude to those which European countries have experienced since World War II. With slack demand and outright unemployment hitting groups outside the usual recession pattern, there is some reason to think that inflation tolerances will in fact be increased. Furthermore, this change of outlook may occur in social groups that are likely to be more influential in altering policy than are the classical unemployed.

It may be too early to pin any large hopes in this prospect. The tolerance of U.S. citizens may have increased, but thorny problems remain in the international finance field. We are not likely in the next five years to be free to use inflation as a lubricant of social progress to any significant extent. Accordingly, prompt attention to the report's call for more effective government measures to curb inflation than are currently being utilized becomes an important prerequisite for achieving the stated goals.

* A line on a graph describing the relationship between the unemployment rate and the rate of price increase.

MAKING THE
AGENDA POSSIBLE

Americans can fairly be asked to pay the
$353 billion in taxes and other charges that
will be required in 1976 . . . if that tax
burden is shared equitably and if those pro-
grams are responsive to citizen concerns.
Budget recommendations acquire full mean-
ing only in the context of the government
structures through which they are imple-
mented.
We have the economic resources to create
a better life, if we have the will to redirect
the use of these resources.

23

Revenues

The spending levels recommended in federal budgets, ours included, reflect a trade-off between how much the people of a nation wish to spend to meet their public needs and how much they are willing to deprive themselves of personally through taxation.

If we are serious about solving our problems, we must be willing to tax ourselves more to do so. Currently, governments in other Western nations command a higher proportion of their Gross National Product for taxes than does the United States. (See Table 23:1.) Only in Japan (which spends negligible sums on military defense and where the private sector carries heavy social welfare responsibilities) does a smaller proportion of the GNP accrue to the public sector (19.1 per cent, compared to 28.3 per cent for the United States). In addition, none of the major

TABLE 23:1
TAX YIELDS AND THEIR ALLOCATION FOR
BROAD USES IN NINE NATIONS, 1967
*(All figures are expressed as percentages of the GNP
of the individual countries)*

	Total Tax Yield	Tax Yield Allocated to Defense Spending	Tax Yield Available for Other Services
United States	28.3	9.5	18.8
Canada	29.9	3.2	26.7
West Germany	35.3	4.4	30.9
Italy	30.8	3.2	27.6
Japan	19.1	0.9	18.2
Sweden	40.8	4.0	36.8
United Kingdom	32.8	5.8	27.0
France	36.7	5.1	31.6

SOURCES: *The U.N. Statistical Yearbook* for 1969 and *Annual Report on Military Expenditures* for 1969 of the London Institute for Strategic Studies.

Western nations spend as large a share of their taxes supporting military forces as we do. It is not surprising that many of them provide services still not available in the United States.

Americans can fairly be asked to pay the $353 billion in taxes and other charges that will be required in 1976 to finance our recommended set of programs if that tax burden is shared equitably and if those programs are responsive to citizen concerns. In addition, we believe that, if recommended spending reductions in defense or other areas are not achieved, further tax increases should be levied. Otherwise, we would have to forego some of the recommended improvements in public services in favor of additional expenditures for consumer goods.

The aspect of forced choices in the priority-setting process cannot be avoided so long as we continue to live in a world where human wants exceed available resources. We have faced up to these choices and have recommended only those programs and funding levels for which social benefits promise to exceed social costs (as well as they can be identified), including the costs of a sacrifice of private consumption involved in raising taxes.

The amount of federal tax revenues in 1976* that would be available under present tax laws and rates is estimated to be $284.4 billion. The total of expenditures we have recommended for that year exceeds the projected revenues by $69 billion. This is the case even though our recommendations include substantial reductions in spending for defense, farm subsidies, highways, and several other programs, as well as compromises with goals we consider desirable in almost every other area of social need.

Additional tax revenues could be raised in three basic ways: (1) through tax reform; (2) by imposing new or expanded taxes or charges to finance the direct costs or indirect social costs of particular services; and/or (3) by raising the rates on existing taxes. As a matter of fairness, attention must first be directed to tax reform. Any subsequent new taxes or tax rate increases will become more politically feasible if the public is convinced that the tax system is equitable.

---

* All references to years are to federal fiscal years unless otherwise indicated.

TAX REFORM

One of the fundamental premises that underlies personal taxes in the United States is that tax incidence should vary according to an individual's ability to pay. In other words, taxes should be progressive. The reality is far different from the concept. The total burden of federal, state, and local taxes falls as heavily on the poor as on the affluent; there is virtually no difference in the proportions of their income that taxes take.*

Persons earning less than $2,000 a year pay nearly 40 per cent of their incomes in taxes. Almost everyone who earns between $2,000 and $50,000 has about 30 per cent of those earnings taken by taxes. Only for individuals earning over $50,000 does the tax bite increase to 45 per cent.

The inequities in tax incidence are particularly acute at state and local government levels, but they also afflict the federal tax system.

Federal tax reform is needed primarily in individual and corporate income taxes and in estate and gift taxes. Federal income tax rates are progressive on paper, but a variety of special exemptions and privileges in reality greatly distort the intended fairness of the graduated federal system. Elimination or modification of many of these exemptions and privileges would rightfully place a large portion of the tax burden on the more wealthy—as the tax laws were designed to do.

Special exemptions and privileges include:

1. *Preferential treatment of capital gains, the income earned from increases in the value of stocks, bonds, and other property.* Such gains are now taxed at lower rates than income from other sources.

2. *Preferential treatment available to oil, gas, and other mineral extraction industries.* The costs of exploration and development of wells are allowed to be depreciated (the equivalent term used for mineral extraction industries is "depletion") over a period of

---

* These results were concluded in an analysis published in 1969 by the Council of Economic Advisers, based on 1965 taxation and incomes. The analysis has been updated in an unpublished study based on 1968 data by Herman P. Miller, chief of the population division of the Bureau of the Census. The major conclusions of the studies are highly consistent.

years, just as are investment costs in other industries. But special privileges allowing accelerated recognition of those costs for tax purposes are extended to these mineral extraction industries.

3. *A special 100 per cent investment tax credit on commercial maritime vessels.* No other industry qualifies for any such credit.

4. *Allowance of special accounting privileges for farmers.* To ease the boookkeeping chores of farmers, income tax rules permit them to deduct from income as business expenses the amounts they paid in cash or by check during a year rather than the expenses incurred (cash instead of accrual accounting). Easing this chore remains a valid objective, but the privilege is now being manipulated by wealthy "gentlemen" farmers who use paper losses from farming sideline operations to shelter income from other sources.

5. *Exclusion from taxable income of an individual's initial $100 in dividends.*

6. *Allowance of financial institutions to shelter part of their otherwise taxable income by setting it aside as a reserve against bad debt losses.* This privilege is basically sound, but implementing rules allow the reserve amounts to be set at levels far above reasonably expected losses. The 1969 Tax Reform Act established machinery to eliminate this privilege, but only by 1987, and in phases.

7. *Allowance of deductions by homeowners for property taxes and interest on mortgages.*

8. *Allowance of deductions of interest on consumer credit.*

9. *Exclusion from taxation of interest on state and local government bonds.*

10. *Preferential income tax treatment for U.S. citizens living abroad.*

11. *Allowance of a double personal exemption, taken both by parent and dependent, in cases where a dependent works and earns income.*

12. *A network of exemptions and tax rates on gifts and estates that keeps more than 75 per cent of the wealth passed on through gifts or estates free from taxation.* Currently, federal estate taxes are imposed on the privilege of transferring property at death, rather than on the recipient of income from an estate.

If all these privileges and exemptions were completely elimi-nated, $24.8 billion above what is now expected in federal taxes in 1976 would be collected, excluding estate and gift taxes, from which the potential gains are quite open-ended. The prospects of such massive changes in tax liability being enacted *completely* are nearly nonexistent.

The reasons why these privileges and exemptions have become lodged in the tax structure—and the cases that can be marshaled for retaining all or part of them—are quite diverse. In some instances, they still make excellent sense as inducements to accomplish particular economic or social objectives. In other cases, they rest only on the raw power of special interest lobbies. In still other instances, they originally served a valid social purpose, but one that has now disappeared, or they have come to be partly misused.

In each of the examples of special tax exemptions and privileges mentioned, we believe that some reform is needed and is possible. Some currently suggested reforms of five of the relatively larger privileges follow: *

1. Treat capital gains as ordinary income for tax purposes, except in instances in which capital is supplied for new fund-raising efforts (e.g., new stock issues).

2. Eliminate completely the special privileges for oil, gas, and other mineral extraction industries.

3. Limit to $15,000 a year the amount of "phantom" farm tax loss any individual or corporation can apply against other income.

4. Continue to encourage home ownership among low- and middle-income families, but reduce the subsidy of high-income families (who would likely buy homes in any case) by setting maximum annual allowable deduction ceilings of $500 on mortgage interest and $300 on property taxes.

---

* Complete implementation of these five illustrative reform proposals would provide by 1976 an additional $13.4 billion in federal revenues as fol-lows: capital gains, $7.4 billion; mineral extraction industries, $2.2 billion; farming, $0.3 billion; home ownership, $1.5 billion; and estate and gift taxes, $2.0 billion.

5. Recoup more of the wealth being passed between generations by setting a lifetime exemption limit of $50,000 on recipients of estate and gift taxes and by taxing all appreciation of assets, realized or not, upon transfer.

Whether these particular proposals or some alternative schemes are most desirable is less important than the fact that these suggestions convey a feeling for the kind and degree of modifications that seem sensible and fair. In our judgment, a package of tax reforms should be initiated effective no later than 1974.* We estimate that reasonable reforms could produce annually at least $6 billion in additional revenues. These revenues should be considered a subsidiary social dividend. The central reason for reform must be the restoration of fairness to the federal tax system.

Many taxpayers are further aggravated by the unfair impact of state and local taxes. The main problem is heavy reliance on property taxes, which impose a particularly heavy burden on low-income and middle-income homeowners. In some states and localities, flat rate sales taxes—which do not exempt necessary items such as food, clothing, and drugs—also heavily burden those same taxpayers. *Revising state and local government tax structures to distribute their burdens more fairly is an important part of the total tax reform agenda.* It is a part that the federal government cannot directly bring about, but the federal government can and should provide incentives for states and localities to undertake such reforms as we have suggested in Chapter 7.

FINANCING PARTICULAR SERVICES

In some instances, the federal government collects revenues to be used for particular purposes. This approach harbors a potential danger—that taxes continue to be collected and earmarked for a particular purpose long after need has diminished.

There are situations when earmarked taxes are valid. Some government programs, like Old Age, Survivors, and Disability Insurance (OASDI), are primarily social insurance programs;

* As a practical political matter, Congress, having enacted a comprehensive tax reform package in December, 1969, is unlikely to consider carefully further tax reform proposals before 1972, at the earliest.

individuals contribute and later (or in an emergency) become beneficiaries. In other cases, taxes are imposed to recover social costs of particular actions (for example, taxes on alcohol to pay for the rehabilitation of alcoholics), even though the revenues may not be so earmarked directly.

We recommend a variety of increased tax rates and new taxes for the support of particular programs. In chapters 2 and 4, we have recommended increases in Unemployment Insurance, OASDI, and railroad retirement taxes to pay for expanded benefits and coverage. In a similar vein, we have recommended in Chapter 5 the imposition of a 5 per cent income tax surcharge for individuals and a 3 per cent payroll earnings base tax for corporations to indemnify part of the costs of national health insurance (NHI). The remaining costs of the NHI program, essentially contributions to pay for medical care of those who cannot themselves afford it, would come from general federal revenues. Tax receipts from these four social insurance programs are estimated to be (in billions of dollars):

	1971	1972	1973	1974	1975	1976
OASDI	34.8	37.4	47.6	53.2	60.5	69.0
Railroad Retirement	1.0	1.2	1.4	1.5	1.6	1.9
Unemployment Insurance	3.6	7.2	7.9	8.5	8.7	9.5
National Health Insurance	—	—	1.4	25.9	27.5	29.4

It is important to understand that the government role in these programs is fundamentally that of an insurance agent. Increased tax collections for these programs do *not* mean that an enlarged portion of national resources are being directed to public purposes. Rather, the government is serving as an agent to encourage saving and to spread risk so that particular individuals are not suddenly confronted with a financial crisis.

The U.S. tax system, even allowing for heavy state and local use of sales taxes, relies relatively lightly on excise taxes. We believe this light emphasis should continue. Exceptions should be made, however, as they have in the past, for sumptuary taxes on commodities or services considered socially undesirable (e.g., cigarettes), taxes imposed on those who benefit directly from particular government services (e.g., air travelers, who benefit from the Federal Aviation Administration air-traffic-control system), and regulatory taxes to assist law enforcement.

The United States has been laggard in raising sumptuary taxes to levels high enough to alter behavior. *We propose tripling the federal excise tax on cigarettes* (which would effectively increase the market price of cigarettes by one half) *to discourage their use and to help defray the public costs of cancer research and treatment.* Similarly, *we recommend raising the levy on alcohol 50 per cent to help defray added costs of treatment of alcoholism and other indirect societal costs.* In both cases, dollar tax rates have remained unchanged since 1952, but their relative bite has been considerably eroded by inflation. We have also recommended in Chapter 10 increased user charges so that generally high-income beneficiaries pay for the benefits they receive in the following areas: aviation and airways systems development; Corps of Engineers navigation projects; Coast Guard aids to commercial navigation and recreational boating; and use of the St. Lawrence Seaway.

Altogether, such increases in excise taxes and user charges would, by 1976, yield an additional $8.6 billion annually—$3.4 billion from transportation alone—even making conservative allowances for declines in the purchases of these goods and services as a result of the tax increases. As desirable as these user charges and excise tax changes are, we doubt that they can be enacted either fully or immediately. For estimating purposes, we will assume that, beginning with 1974, one-third of these potential revenue gains are achieved. This would mean additional 1976 revenues amounting to $2.8 billion.

TAX RATES

In combination, then, we foresee about $51 billion in additional revenues that should and can reasonably be expected to be produced through tax reform and increased revenues for particular purposes. (See Table 23:2.) These increases would cover only

---

* The intent is to make cigarette and alcohol users pay for part of the costs those products force upon society at large. We do *not* recommend, however, that such revenues accrue to a trust fund earmarked solely for treating persons who suffer from alcohol- or cigarette-related diseases.

TABLE 23:2
ESTIMATED 1976 TAX REVENUES AND THEIR RELATION TO PROPOSED OUTLAYS
(In billions of current dollars)

Desired Level of Outlays		353.6
Revenue Sources:		
Revenues in 1971	194.2	
Dividend from Projected Economic Growth (1971–76)	90.2	
Tax Reform	6.0	
National Health Insurance[1]	17.5	
Increase in OASDI, Railroad Retirement, and Unemployment Insurance Taxes	24.9	
Increases in Excise Taxes and User Charges	2.8	
Expected 1976 Tax Receipts at 1971 Rates	335.6	335.6
Estimated Deficit		(17.9)[2]

[1] $11.9 billion was subtracted from the $29.4 billion expected in national health insurance revenues as an allowance for hospital insurance revenues that would have been collected had that program not been supplanted.
[2] Rounded figures do not necessarily add to total.

three-fourths of the gap between the aggregate level of desired expenditures and the revenues projected before provisions for these or other changes.

Clearly, revenue increases of any substantial magnitude for general purposes must be achieved through higher income tax rates on corporations and on individuals. Present tax rates are low relative not only to other countries but also to other periods of our own history. Tax levels during the last twenty years have fallen substantially. The 1950's was a period of international peace and relative domestic tranquility, yet tax rates were a good deal higher at that time than they were in 1970, when the need for public services seemed demonstrably greater. As Arthur M. Okun in *The Political Economy of Prosperity* (Washington, D.C.: The Brookings Institution, 1970) calculated:

If the nation were willing to return to the average income tax rates that prevailed from 1954 to 1961, we could have roughly $25 billion a year more to spend on social programs than with the tax rates now in prospect for the early 1970's. If our combined federal, state and local taxes as a per cent of GNP matched the average of the major Western European countries, we would have about $40 billion to $50 billion more a year in government revenues.

TABLE 23:3
Projected Federal Revenues[1]
(Receipts, in billions of current dollars)

	Administration		Urban Coalition Recommendations				
	Estimated 1971	Proposed 1972	1972	1973	1974	1975	1976
Individual Income Taxes							
Current Laws	88.3		(93.6)	(98.6)	(105.4)	(113.0)	(120.5)
Recommended		93.7	93.6	98.6	118.0	126.3	134.5
Corporate Income Taxes[2]							
Current Laws	30.1		(33.1)	(41.0)	(48.5)	(54.7)	(58.3)
Recommended		36.7	33.1	41.0	55.5	62.3	66.3
Individual Income National Health Insurance Surtax							
Current Laws				0.3	5.9	6.3	6.7
Recommended							
Corporate National Health Insurance Taxes							
Current Laws				1.1	20.0	21.2	22.7
Recommended							
Other Social Insurance Taxes and Contributions							
Current Laws	49.0		(53.6)	(59.1)	(62.0)	(66.1)	(69.5)
Recommended		57.6	58.2	70.0	66.4	72.7	82.4
Excise Taxes							
Current Laws	16.8		(17.8)	(19.0)	(20.4)	(20.8)	(21.2)
Recommended		17.5	17.8	19.0	22.5	22.9	23.4
Estate and Gift Taxes							
Current Laws	3.7	5.3[3]	(5.3)[3]	(4.1)	(4.3)	(4.5)	(4.7)
Recommended			3.8	4.1	6.1	6.4	6.7

Other

Current Laws	6.3	(7.1)	(7.8)	(8.6)	(9.4)	(10.2)
Recommended	7.1	7.1	7.8	9.1	10.0	10.8

TOTAL

Current Laws[2]	194.2	(210.5)	(229.6)	(249.2)	(268.5)	(284.4)
Recommended	217.6	213.6	241.9	303.5	328.1	353.5

[1] These revenue estimates are based on the economic assumptions set forth in Appendix A. They also reflect consideration of projections made by the Council of Economic Advisers in the *Economic Report of the President* for 1970 and 1971 and by Charles Schultze in *Setting National Priorities: The 1971 Budget* (Washington, D.C.: The Brookings Institution, 1970).

[2] Excluding the January, 1971, Administration action allowing accelerated write-off of business depreciation costs, an action we recommend be retracted.

[3] The rapid increase is nonrecurring; it is primarily due to a recently enacted speed-up of estate tax collections. We suggest that this action be deferred and coupled with our other recommended estate and gift tax reforms.

A 10 per cent surtax on corporation and individual income*
would raise federal revenues nearly $18 billion—enough to bridge
the remaining revenue-expenditure gap. *We recommend that a
10 per cent surtax be enacted beginning in 1974 in conjunction
with the suggested tax reform measures.*

Altogether, these recommended revenue measures would produce the pattern of federal revenues described in Table 23:3. They
would support the program expenditures suggested in the Counterbudget and permit the pursuit of fiscal policy that would make
these programs possible.

* This surtax would be in addition to the 5 per cent surtax on individual
incomes earmarked for financing national health insurance.

24

Government Reform

The essence of this report is an examination of needs and program alternatives and the allocation of limited dollars to diverse public needs. Budget recommendations acquire full meaning only in the context of the government structures through which they are implemented.

We do not attempt to consider here the myriad of government reform issues. In order to keep our focus on the relative claims of various public needs, we have, for the most part, consciously avoided recommending which department or agency ought to direct a particular activity. Neither do we consider this report the proper vehicle for considering issues such as the caliber of people attracted to public service or the relationships between legislative and executive branches of government.

At the same time, we expect that the implementation of our program recommendations would have a far from neutral impact on government operations. By drawing together some of the suggestions scattered throughout earlier pages, we hope to describe here the major dimensions of the very explicit vision of responsibilities and functions of different levels of government that guided our program recommendations.

The shaping strategy has been to assign the federal government responsibility for responding to national problems, while looking to state and local jurisdictions to deal with their own unique problems and to provide everyday services.

The national government must assume responsibility for assuring that every citizen receives basic human necessities such as an adequate minimum income and quality personal health care. In both cases, we have recommended federal assumption of nearly all government costs of these functions, thereby relieving a substantial current state and local government burden. Both functions will also require an enlarged program scope—embodied in a combination of income-maintenance proposals that will assure the poorest American a sustaining income, and a national health insurance program in which nearly all Americans would participate.

We have also called for a new, but limited, federal role in public education. We have linked federal assistance to elementary and secondary schools to performance standards of students (in reading and mathematics) and in such a manner that we expect this federal assistance to affect the conduct of education nation-wide in a fundamental way. Nevertheless, central responsibility for the structure and content of elementary and secondary education would remain the province of local communities. This program is predicated on the federal responsibility to ensure that citizens leave public schools with the basic skills required for participation in the economy.

The sum thrust of these proposals is toward a federal role that concentrates on income transfer programs, rather than the delivery of services. The federal government has always done relatively well in the former role—witness its effectiveness in collecting taxes and managing such programs as OASDI and veterans' benefits. But federal performance in service delivery has often been inadequate, as measured by a lack of effectiveness in accomplishing program objectives. Despite usually excellent intentions, federal efforts to manage and deliver compensatory education, manpower training, and other services have far too often produced dismal results.

Another vital federal role is protection of the basic rights of citizens from special interests possessing far greater economic, social, or political power than does any individual. It is in the pursuit of this responsibility by the federal government that we recommend the establishment of a new Consumer Protection Agency, with far broader powers than the offices it would replace, and new mechanisms for inclusion of civil rights considerations in all major federal programs and policy decisions.

The federal government must define national priorities, making choices among the alternative possible purposes federal resources can serve, and specifying objectives to be achieved. It has a right and responsibility in dispensing financial aid to other government jurisdictions to insist that such aid be directed to those purposes. Nonetheless, differences do exist among states and localities. The prospects for achieving national objectives will be advanced by the incorporation of as much flexibility as possible into federal program guidelines.

In many instances, this purpose will be served by consolidating the present numerous, narrow categorical grants into larger-purpose block grants, which permit recipient jurisdictions to define their own local priorities within a specified area (manpower training, transportation, etc.) and to tailor their programs to specific local needs. This is the course of action that we have recommended for federal assistance in the fields of manpower training, law enforcement, and transportation. Simplification of application and reporting procedures for federal assistance should also be encouraged; the benefits of local participation in federal government programs is still far too often diminished by the expensive burden of paperwork.

It is also imperative that state and local governments sharply improve the quality and extent of services they now provide. The barrier most immediately preventing them from doing so is financial capacity. There can be no doubt that more money is an essential requirement. Cities, particularly, are going broke. Instead of improving the quality of services they provide, they are reducing the number and reach of those services. But money alone will not be sufficient. New dollars must be accompanied by reform of state and local government structures. An essential part of a strategy for increasing federal aid to states and localities must be provisions that tie such aid to guidelines and requirements for reform.

Diverse kinds of reform are called for, including:

- requiring states and localities to prepare and implement their own comprehensive development plans as prerequisites for receiving any federal assistance;
- greater metropolitan-wide and state-wide cooperation; and
- reform of archaic local government structures.

By far the most important reform required is in state and local government tax structures. We recommend increased federal financial contributions to states and localities; national purposes will be well served by improving the capacity of local governments to respond to the needs of their citizens. But the major increase in financial resources will have to be provided by states and localities through their own taxes. Federal aid should incorporate incentives for, and in some cases be premised on, additional state and local tax effort. The incentives should be designed to ensure that, as the burden of state and local taxes grows, it also becomes more equitably distributed. This latter concern is essential; failure to respond to it would, among other things, frustrate federal income maintenance objectives and increase the expense of fulfilling them.

Finally, attention needs to be focused on the need for improved evaluation of programs at all levels of government. Far too many government programs have been initiated hastily in recent years, rather than being based on sound social data. An even more inadequate job has been done in evaluating program results to determine whether they conform to objectives, and thus to provide a knowledgeable basis for renewing, revising, or scrapping them. Government reviews have generally been confined to financial inspection to protect against fraud. That sort of review is important, but must be supplemented by performance reviews by trained social scientists whose assignment is to assess program effectiveness and impact. Much of present citizen unease about government has a valid basis in the perpetuation of public programs that provide poor returns on investments of tax dollars. Improved evaluation is required to ferret out these ineffective activities and to make government officials more accountable.

Our Counterbudget itself is designed to contribute to accountability on a somewhat broader plane. By showing in disciplined analytical terms what social objectives could potentially be accomplished by the federal government, we have attempted to provide a mark against which the performance of the Administration, the Congress, and the American people can be tested.

25

The Will to Act

A principal reason why we Americans have not accomplished our goals in the past has been our unwillingness to provide sufficient monies to the public sector. Whenever there has been the prospect of a budget surplus, Americans have traditionally chosen to enjoy the sweet but illusory fruits of tax reductions rather than to support needed public-service programs.

With good reasons—even beyond the inappropriate effect such an action would have on our deflated economy—Americans would vigorously oppose an *immediate* increase in taxes. To increase income taxes now without previous tax reform would be intolerably unjust. Nor can American citizens be expected to support tax increases when the current pattern of uses for tax receipts—including a residual $3 billion allocation for a war in Southeast Asia—is so distorted.

If, however, our nation's priorities are reordered in the directions we propose, Americans can fairly be asked to support higher taxes in 1974—the year when we suggest that an increase take effect. People must be willing to pay larger tax bills in return for tangible improvements in public employment, health, education, law enforcement, and other services that rank high on their personal lists of priority needs.

In this document, we have made a serious effort to show very clearly what the real social needs of the United States are and how much it is likely to cost to address various portions of those needs. The case must now to put squarely to all Americans: Are we at last ready to support the priority shifts and make the tax effort necessary to achieve reasonable and rational goals?

That the proposals of our Counterbudget provide all the answers

329

we need, or even necessarily the best answers, is not our claim. Our study was an attempt to measure the extent of the nation's problems and to offer one interconnected set of solutions. We argue strongly only that the basic direction of priority shifts we recommend and the accompanying levels of public revenue we estimate will have to be raised make sense.

As a nation, we can accomplish what we must. We can provide for the basic needs of all our citizens, while preserving the free enterprise system that has fueled the development of the most powerful economy in the world. We can provide the quality of health care, education, housing—indeed, of life—that its citizens have a right to expect from the richest country in the world. We have the economic resources to create a better life, if we have the will to redirect the use of these resources.

But national priorities will not be reordered to reflect the needs of the nation without the stimulus of an informed, broadly reaching national debate. The immediate objective to which we have bent our efforts is to stimulate Americans of many different persuasions to respond to the task of making budget choices. The measure of our success will lie in the degree to which we provoke responsible, benevolent, and practical argument and thought.

APPENDIXES

Appendix A: Economic Assumptions

The basic economic assumptions that guided the development of our estimates of outlays and revenues and of the impact of government activities on the economy are listed in Table A:1. In general, these are staff estimates based upon official projections, such as those issued by the Council of Economic Advisers, the Bureau of Labor Statistics, the Bureau of the Census, and other accepted economic experts. All projections are for fiscal years, unless otherwise noted.

TABLE A:1
ECONOMIC ASSUMPTIONS

	1971	1972	1973	1974	1975	1976
Gross National Product, in billions	1,004	1,094	1,190	1,288	1,388	1,489
GNP Price Deflator	100.0	103.3	106.5	109.7	113.0	116.4
GNP Real Growth Rate	5.6%	5.5%	5.0%	4.7%	4.3%	
Personal Income, Excluding Transfers, in billions	737	801	870	940	1,012	1,085
Corporate Profits, Before Taxes, in billions	80	88	107	129	146	156
Number Employed, in millions[1]	86.5	88.6	91.1	93.3	94.7	96.3
Number Unemployed, in millions	4.3	3.8	3.5	3.3	3.3	3.4
Unemployment Rate[2]	5.6%	5.0%	4.0%	3.5%	3.5%	3.5%
Consumer Price Index	100.0	104.1	108.2	112.3	116.6	121.0
Wholesale Price Index	100.0	102.3	104.3	106.2	108.1	110.1
Population, in millions, as of July 1	207	209	211	213	215	218

[1] Excluding members of the armed forces.
[2] The unemployment projections take into consideration the impact of our recommended public-service employment program described in Chapter 2.

Appendix B: Glossary of Terms

Fiscal Year (FY)—July 1 through June 30.

FY Expenditures—Payments for operations and activities of the federal government during a fiscal year. These payments add directly to the incomes of the recipients.

FY Net Lending—Loans disbursed by the federal government in a fiscal year minus repayments made on the principal of outstanding loans during that year.

FY Outlays—Expenditures plus net outlays in a fiscal year. If federal budget outlays equal federal revenues, the budget is balanced.

Budget Authority—The amount of money federal agencies are allowed by Congress to obligate.

Obligations—Federal government commitments to acquire materials or services or to make payments. These commitments will eventually result in outlays.

Appropriations—Budget authority granted to federal agencies by Congress permitting obligations to be incurred *and* payments to be made when due (Appropriations also include contract authority, which permits obligations to be made, but requires an additional appropriation "to liquidate" in order to permit payment of the obligations.) Appropriations made in the current year often do not result in outlays until future years. For example, most federal programs providing construction grants or loans have two- to three-year lags between obligation and outlay. There may also be a lag between appropriation and obligation.

Budget Receipts—Federal revenues, not including loan repayments.

General Fund—Federal funds into which all receipts not earmarked for a specific purpose by law are placed and from which .all payments not otherwise specified from another fund are made.

Trust Funds—Funds established to account for receipts held in a fiduciary capacity by the federal government for use in carrying out specific purposes or programs, such as Old Age, Survivors, and Disability Insurance.

Appendix C: Description and Critique of the Budget Process

Since the federal budget is the primary mechanism through which national priorities are determined, the process of budget-making ought to be of major interest and concern to American citizens. In fact, few Americans realize the purpose and importance of the budget, much less understand how it is put together. In this appendix, we present a "layman's guide" to the budget process. This guide describes the basic chronology of budget-making and summarizes the major deficiencies in present procedures.

THE PROCESS OF BUDGET-MAKING

The President's annual Budget Message is usually presented to Congress in January, but this public event marks only one step in a process that takes more than a year. Although there are variations in the schedule the budget follows from year to year, the steps involved are usually as follows. We have used the budget preparation for fiscal year 1972 as an example.

Executive Consideration

Late spring, 1970: The Office of Management and Budget (OMB), in cooperation with the Council of Economic Advisers (CEA) and the Departments of the Treasury and Commerce, sets forth economic assumptions on which an estimate of federal revenues can be based and develops economic projections and forecasts for FY 1972.

Summer, 1970: The OMB, the CEA, and the Treasury review the economic outlook for FY 1972 and recommend tax and expenditure policies to the President.

Late summer, 1970: The President and his top economic advisers make tentative judgments about the total size of the prospective budget and about major allocations to various areas within it. The Office of Management and Budget then sends to all federal agencies* general guidelines concerning the amount and nature of their budgets.

September and October, 1970: The agencies prepare budget and new program recommendations for FY 1972 and submit them to the Office of Management and Budget.

October and November, 1970: The OMB reviews the submitted budgets and holds hearings with representatives from the agencies and departments. At such hearings, the representatives are challenged to justify their departments' budget requests.

November, 1970: The OMB makes recommendations to the President for trimming the total budget and the various agency budgets within it to the targeted size and informs the agencies of these recommendations. The agencies, if dissatisfied, may appeal the recommendations to the President.

December, 1970: The President, in conjunction with his top advisers and the director of the Office of Management and Budget, makes final decisions on the composition of programs and on the allocation of resources within the budget.

January, 1971: The President and his staff write the Budget Message, which, along with the budget for FY 1972, is transmitted to Congress.

February, 1971: Appropriations bills, which contain the amount of obligational authority the President has proposed for each federal agency for FY 1972, are introduced in Congress. Appropriations are the authority granted by Congress to federal agencies to permit them to make obligations (commitments to spend federal funds). Outlays occur when these funds are finally spent—in some cases, more than a year after funds are appropriated. Budget authority granted in appropriation legislation for a program cannot exceed the amount authorized by Congress in the "substantive" legislation creating that program.

---

* "Agencies," as used here, refers to both federal departments and agencies.

Congressional Consideration

It is important to understand that congressional consideration of federal programs consists of two parts: (1) legislation creating or continuing the existence of a program and authorizing a specific amount of funds for it, and (2) appropriations legislation providing budget authority allowing these funds, or some portion of them, to be obligated and spent. Usually, public attention focuses on the former process, although the latter is of equal importance.

Appropriations bills for the various federal agencies (in some cases, several agencies' appropriations are included in a single bill) are sent to the Appropriations Committee of the House of Representatives, where each bill is considered by a separate subcomittee.

Each House appropriations subcommittee then holds hearings, traditionally closed to the public, on the appropriations bill it is considering. The subcommittee (or, more accurately, the subcommittee chairman and ranking minority member) examines each program administered by the agency as well as agency administrative and overhead costs. Finally, sometime between March and December, the subcommittee "marks up" and "reports out" a revised version of the President's original submission. The revision is likely to be, in most instances, only marginally different from the original submission. The changes usually consist of cuts from the President's original proposal. Almost invariably, the full Appropriations Committee simply accepts *in toto* the recommendations of its subcommittees, and the House as a body also acquiesces.

After House passage, the appropriations bill goes to the Senate. As in the House, subcommittees of the Senate Appropriations Committee consider the separate parts of the bill. The Senate Appropriations Committee subcommittees serve primarily as "courts of appeal." A dissatisfied agency can submit a written appeal to the subcommittee dealing with its budget asking for reconsideration of various items cut by the House. In many cases, the Senate subcommittee restores the cut, or a part of it. Occasionally, the subcommittee will recommend more funds than the amount originally sought in the President's bill. As in the House, subcommittee decisions are in most cases merely ratified by the full Appropriations Committee and then by the entire Senate.

Differences in the House and Senate appropriations bills are settled at a conference committee meeting attended by members of the relevant appropriations subcommittees from each body. Often, differences are settled by the simple expedient of "splitting the difference," that is, of settling on an appropriation figure for an item at a dollar level halfway between those specified in the House and Senate bills. At other times, one item is traded off for another. Although appropriations bills are supposed to deal only with the allocation of money to agencies (obligational authority) rather than the content of agency programs, this rule is quite often violated. The agreed-upon bill is then reported out of the conference committee in a Conference Committee Report.

After both houses have given approval (usually pro-forma) to the Conference Committee Report, the President signs the appropriations bill into law. Only rarely does a President veto an appropriations bill, since he cannot veto specific items within it but must veto it in its entirety.

DEFICIENCIES IN THE PROCESS

If the budget's importance were understood, Americans would have good reason to question the adequacy of the present budget-making process.

Neither the public nor its elected representatives in Congress have a significant impact on the budget's final shape. The President and his Administration dominate the process. Their decisions, arrived at in a process nearly invisible to the public and the press, are usually changed only incrementally by congressional conderation.

Secrecy

The secrecy surrounding the entire budget process is one of its major deficiencies. Although the budget is the vehicle through which the nation's priorities are determined, the great public debate that ought to accompany these decisions is absent. The public receives only the final outcome; the alternatives that were considered and rejected are never made public. There may be good reasons, as many argue, why budget conferences and meetings inside the executive branch should not be open to the public. There are no good reasons, however, why the public should not be informed about the nature of the debate, the alternatives being considered, and the arguments for and against their adoption. Indeed, the quality of the final decisions might well be enhanced by public hearings held simultaneously on national priorities and the budget.

Both the public and Congress suffer from the secrecy shrouding budgetary decisions in the executive branch. The public fares no better when the budget goes before Congress. The most important hearings on the budget are conducted by subcommittees of the House Appropriations Committee in sessions that have, in the past, been closed to the public. Senate Appropriations Subcommittee hearings, of less importance in the shaping of the budget, are public, but the conference committee session at which the final decisions are made is not.

Lack of Comprehensive Review

Since the budget is the major instrument through which national priorities are set, the process of putting it together ought to permit the government and the public to review comprehensively the nation's needs, the available resources, and the possible allocations of those resources among the needs. Unfortunately, this comprehensive approach prevails rarely even within the executive branch. In reality, the most significant basis for determining budgetary allocations is not the relative importance of competing needs but the allocation pattern in the previous year's budget. This "let's-see-what-we-gave-them-last-year-and-give-them-a-little-more-this-year" approach limits greatly our ability to reorder priorities as needs change. It may be true, as such political scientists as Aaron Wildavsky have pointed out, that a truly comprehensive yearly review would be humanly impossible—but surely we should move in that direction.

Congress, even more than the executive, reviews the budget in a fragmented fashion. The congressional apparatus for dealing with the budget is so poorly structured that efforts to review it comprehensively seem impossible. Indeed, the lack of an appropriate congressional structure for considering the budget is a major reason for congressional impotence and Presidential dominance in shaping priorities.

For one thing, Congress never considers the budget as a whole. The House Ways and Means Committee and the Senate Finance Committee deal with tax and revenue legislation, and the appropriations committees in each body deal with expenditures, but at no time does any one committee consider revenues and expenditures together. The appropriations Committees that deal with the budget must, in effect, accept tax policy and the amount of available revenue as given.

In addition, the appropriations committees themselves violate the most basic rule of resource allocation: They do not make decisions by comparing the desirability of expenditures for different purposes. Each subcommittee (Agriculture, Defense, Labor-HEW, Transportation, etc.) deals only with the budget for its specific department, and the full appropriations committee merely ratifies the separate and unrelated decisions of its subcommittees. The purposes for which scarce dollars should be spent, the fundamental questions of budgeting, are never explicitly considered.

Inadequate Decision Criteria

Both the executive branch and Congress (and particularly Congress) often lack an adequate conception of how to make priority decisions in the budget. There is a tendency to focus solely on dollars spent rather than on what can be accomplished for dollars spent.

In an effort to remedy this flaw, the executive branch has recently adopted the Planning-Programing-Budgeting System (PPBS) as a conceptual device to aid the process of budgetary decision-making. PPBS logically requires the following process:

- defining broad goals;
- estimating needs (the distance from the goals);
- suggesting alternative means (programs) for meeting various portions of needs;

- estimating the costs and the benefits of each alternative;
- ranking alternatives in order of priority by listing the programs with the most benefit for the least cost (benefit:cost ratio) in descending order;
- allocating funds to those programs which have the highest ratio of benefits to costs; and
- continuing this process until all available resources have been allocated.

PPBS has been regarded by many people as a mysterious and magical device that produces "the correct decisions." PPBS cannot guarantee correct decisions; it is merely a device to help decision-makers think logically about the *process* of making decisions.

"Correct" decisions would be possible only if we were able to measure accurately the costs and the benefits of the various alternatives. In some cases, this is possible, but, in most, it is not. We lack a scale of measurement on which all forms of costs and benefits can be placed. Dollar costs and benefits are most often used, but not all costs and benefits to individuals or society are measurable in dollars. Even those which can be are often excluded from benefit-cost analysis because the costs or the benefits are viewed as by-products (externalities) instead of as part of the price of a good or a service.

Budget-making and priority-setting will undoubtedly remain more an art than a science, more a matter of judgment than precise formula. The changes that we have cited as necessary in the process of budget-making will help improve the quality of the budget decisions, but they will not ensure that the resulting decisions are "correct." Priorities, as expressed through the budget, rest, in the end, on basic value judgments about the kind of society we want. Since there are as many value judgments as individuals, no one "correct" set of budgetary allocations will ever be possible without total agreement on social goals.

Index

343